Enhancing
Evaluation
Use

Enhancing **Evaluation Use**

Insights from
Internal
Evaluation Units

Marlène Läubli Loud
John Mayne

Editors

Los Angeles | London | New Delhi
Singapore | Washington DC

Los Angeles | London | New Delhi
Singapore | Washington DC

FOR INFORMATION:

SAGE Publications, Inc.
2455 Teller Road
Thousand Oaks, California 91320
E-mail: order@sagepub.com

SAGE Publications Ltd.
1 Oliver's Yard
55 City Road
London EC1Y 1SP
United Kingdom

SAGE Publications India Pvt. Ltd.
B 1/I 1 Mohan Cooperative Industrial Area
Mathura Road, New Delhi 110 044
India

SAGE Publications Asia-Pacific Pte. Ltd.
3 Church Street
#10-04 Samsung Hub
Singapore 049483

Printed in the United States of America

A catalog record of this book is available from the Library of Congress.

978-1-4522-0547-2

This book is printed on acid-free paper.

Acquisitions Editor: Helen Salmon
Editorial Assistant: Kaitlin Perry
Production Editor: Jane Haenel
Copy Editor: Patrice Sutton
Typesetter: C&M Digitals (P) Ltd.
Proofreader: Jeff Bryant
Cover Designer: Edgar Abarca
Permissions Editor: Jennifer Barron
Marketing Manager: Nicole Elliott

13 14 15 16 17 10 9 8 7 6 5 4 3 2 1

CONTENTS

PREFACE

Evaluation symposia and conferences are great hubs for evaluation academics, practitioners, and commissioners alike to hear about new ideas, new trends, and past experiences; they are also an important setting for getting a feel for who's doing what and where. But on such occasions, I noticed that there was a great void; for whatever reason, the voice of those working inside the commissioning bodies was often silent.

This book aims to fill that gap; it provides a wealth of information for a range of audiences interested in program and policy evaluation, particularly in the public sector. Graduate students, academics, practicing evaluators, commissioners, public administrators, and evaluation and program managers alike will learn about the challenges, solutions, and lessons drawn from the experience of those working on the "inside" to enhance the use and usefulness of evaluation. The issues being dealt with and the strategies and measures being adopted to deal with them should be sufficiently generic so as to make the lessons drawn relevant and useful to a wide range of situations. The book is written from the multiple perspectives of those working in national, supranational, and international agencies. Their accounts demonstrate their initiative and innovative thinking in rising to the challenges they face in sometimes quite complex settings. You may find yourself nodding in agreement when reading through some of their experiences, but maybe not. Whatever the case, there is certainly something of interest here for everyone whose work deals either directly or indirectly with evaluation.

SAGE and the editors wish to thank the following reviewers: Samuel L. Brown, College of Public Affairs, School of Public and International Affairs, University of Baltimore; Diane D. Chapman, North Carolina State University; Kay Davis, Graduate School of Education and Psychology and academic chair for doctoral program in Organization Change, Pepperdine University; Donna Haig Freedman, Department of Public Policy and Public Affairs and Center for Social Policy, University of Massachusetts, Boston; Sheldon Gen, San Francisco State University; Danica G. Hays, Old Dominion University; Wendy L. Hicks, Loyola University, New Orleans; John B. Nash, University of Kentucky; Kathryn E. Newcomer, The George Washington University; Kathleen Norris, Plymouth State University; John Clayton Thomas, Andrew Young School of Policy Studies, Georgia State University; and Mike Trevisan, Washington State University.

Marlène Läubli Loud
September 2012

CHAPTER 1

ISSUES IN ENHANCING EVALUATION USE

John Mayne

Underutilization of evaluation in organizations is much lamented in the evaluation literature (e.g., Mayne, 2009; Pollitt, 2006; Stame, 2004). The literature is full of advice on how to address this shortcoming, which ranges from producing better evaluations (e.g., Patton, 2012; Preskill & Jones, 2009; Russ-Eft & Preskill, 2009) to getting closer to decision making (e.g., Vanlandingham, 2011) to building up an evaluation culture (e.g., Botcheva, Shih, & Huffman, 2009; Hernandez & Visher, 2001; Mayne, 2009; Perrin, 2006) to communicating better (e.g., Ramalingam, 2011). Johnson et al. (2009) provide an overview of the literature on evaluation use. And much of this advice is well founded and useful.

There is also a large body of literature on organizational learning with significant discussion and debate on how organizations learn (e.g., Easterby-Smith, Crossman, & Nicolint, 2000; Garvin, Edmondson, & Gino, 2008). There is also a literature on how evaluation relates to organizational learning (e.g., Torres & Preskill, 2001; Cousins, 2007; Russ-Eft & Preskill, 2009). Cousins, Goh, Clark, and Lee (2004) review much of this literature and make suggestions for enhancing evaluation utilization in organizations.

But a great deal of this and related literature has been written by outside observers, experts, and academics and, as a result, may have to some extent a built-in bias—a bias in favor of focusing on "bad news," on the problems and shortcomings faced by evaluation in an organization which can then be discussed and analyzed. This perspective is perhaps seen as more interesting reading. Articles on successful evaluation in organizations are much harder to find. Further, those who might be inclined to write these articles such as consultants working for organizations or evaluators inside an organization may see little incentive for writing up "good news" stories—which might have a harder time getting published.

This book's editors try to counter this phenomenon by getting "insiders" to write up their experiences with evaluation in organizations. The aim is not to have good news stories written, per se, but to explore the actual challenges faced in organizations that are trying to make evaluation useful and used and to discuss, in light of the related literature, what strategies have been used in practice to address these challenges and enhance the utilization of evaluation.

These insiders are those involved in commissioning, managing, and/or carrying out evaluations in organizations. These individuals and units want the evaluations they are involved with to be useful: to be used to inform decision making at different levels in the organization and lead to improved performance of the organization and its activities. Organizations are not interested in supporting activities that are not adding value to the organization.

The chapters in this book address a variety of issues:

- The different ways evaluation is set up—institutionalized—in government sectors and in public organizations and with what results
- Why it is so hard to make evaluation a regular aspect of good management
- Building organizational cultures that support effective evaluation
- Strategies that are being used to ensure better value for money and enhance utilization of evaluation findings in organizations
- How evaluations can be strengthened to make them more effective

While many of these issues have been addressed in the literature, what this book offers is discussion based on well-grounded experience on implementing evaluations in organizations. The chapters in this book cover a range of institutionalized evaluation, from evaluation being done in and by government agencies (in Canada, New Zealand, Scotland, and Switzerland) to evaluations being done in and by a supranational government (the European Commission), to evaluations being done in and by international organizations (World Health Organization [WHO] and the International Labour Organization [ILO]).

In this introductory chapter, the stage is set for these discussions by setting out some of the underlying issues:

- What is meant by "use" of evaluation?
- Who uses evaluation?
- What are the challenges to making evaluation useful?
- What are the key issues in designing and carrying out evaluations?
- Why are evaluations done, for what purpose?
- How is evaluation structured and organized in an organization?
- What is the context within which evaluation operates in an organization?

The Organisation for Economic Co-operation and Development, Development Assistance Committee (OECD-DAC, 2002) defines (*ex post*) evaluation as "the systematic and objective assessment of an on-going or completed project, pro-gramme or policy, its design, implementation and results" (p. 21). This book adopts a similar broad perspective in that what is being evaluated—the evaluand—can be any grouping of activities aimed at achieving some end in an organiza-tion. Thus, evaluation often involves an assessment of some aspect of an organization's or several organizations' performance.

Evaluation can also be *ex ante*, an assessment undertaken of a planned project, program, or policy to determine if it is reasonable to expect that the interven-tion will achieve its intended aims.

DIFFERENT TYPES OF UTILIZATION

Using evaluation can have a range of meanings, all well discussed in the litera-ture (Kirkhart, 2000; Mark & Henry, 2004; Moynihan, 2009; Patton, 2012; Preskill & Torres, 1999, 2000; Weiss, 1998). The following types of use can be identified:

- *Instrumental use*—use made of evaluation findings to directly improve the programming (Caracelli & Preskill, 2000; Nutley, Walter, & Davies, 2007)
- *Enlightenment use*—both long and short term
    - o *Conceptual use*—use made of evaluation findings to enhance knowledge about the type of intervention under study, "to influence thinking about issues in a general way" (Rossi, Lipsey, & Freemen, 2004, p. 411)
    - o *Reflective use*—use made of the evaluation findings about the program, its operations, and about future strategies, for example, Jacobson, Carter, Hockings, and Kelman's (2011) discussion on use of workshops to encourage and support reflection on the results of a major conservation evaluation in Australia
- *Persuasive use*—use made to legitimize or criticize an intervention (Rossi et al., 2004, p. 411) or to build support to scale up or out a pilot intervention
- *Process use*—use made of engagement in the process of carrying out an evaluation to better understand both the program and the evaluation process (Cousins et al., 2004; Forss, Rebien, & Carlson, 2002; Patton, 2007, 2008)
- *Symbolic use*—use made of an evaluation to fulfill a requirement to do evaluation or to show support for an intervention area; token use (Patton, 2008, p. 112)

Instrumental use is the kind of use that most people probably imagine for evaluation, especially in organizations that support evaluation. But studies often suggest that most use is in fact various forms of enlightenment use (e.g., Peck & Gorzalski, 2009). Is this what organizations expect when they fund evaluation activity? Or are they expecting a shorter term return on their investment?

Chapters in this book explore these issues.

USE BY WHOM?

When talking about use, besides being clear about the kind of use or uses that we are discussing, as advisers or evaluators of public sector performance, we also need to be clear about just whom we are referring to. There are many potential users of evaluative information, both inside and outside an organization, such as the following:

- Insiders
  - Program managers
  - Policy analysts
  - Senior managers

- Outsiders
  - Politicians
  - Control bodies
  - Stakeholders
  - Academics
  - Critics
  - Beneficiaries

These different users will have different

- perspectives on what is being evaluated in terms of knowledge about and experience with the program and its history, views on its relevance and importance, and so on;
- perspectives on evaluation, from seeing evaluation as a tool for enhanced understanding of the program and how it is operating to a tool to provide critical evidence on the program;
- vested interests in the program and its future from unquestionable support to outright hostility or skepticism;
- information needs about the *what* that is being evaluated that the evaluation could address (Mayne, Divorski, & Lemaire, 1999, pp. 28–29).

This simple delineation of different types of uses and different potential users of evaluation begins to illuminate the complex nature and meaning of the seemingly simple issue of "enhanced use of evaluation."

WHY EVALUATIONS MAY NOT BE USED

Authors discuss many reasons in the literature about why evaluations may not get used in organizations (Nutley et al., 2007; Torres & Preskill, 2001):

Poor product quality (Schwartz & Mayne, 2005)

- *Not timely*—evaluations that do not produce findings when they are needed for decision making
- *Not relevant*—evaluation findings not related to the decisions being made
- *Not credible*—evaluation findings, conclusions, and recommendations not seen as credible enough to be used in decision making (weak data and/or analysis, biased)
- *Not clear*—evaluation findings not well communicated, with no communication strategy and no recognition of different stakeholders' interests

Poor evaluation process (Johnson et al., 2009)

- *Not inclusive*—evaluation considered the purview of the "experts" only

Limited evaluation culture

- *Not accepted*—evaluation findings not given much weight in comparison to experience and wisdom, unless perhaps they support the experience

Unclear evaluator role

- Evaluator seen more as an outsider, as an auditor, and hence seen as a burden, not seen as useful

Uncomfortable findings

- Program managers, senior management, and/or politicians who may not like or agree with the findings of the evaluation, which may challenge their beliefs or agendas

Most of these "challenges" can be a death knell to utilization, or at least some types of utilization. That is, any one could well result in limited use. It is evident that a lot can go wrong. Many diverse factors have to come together to make evaluation work well, that is, get used in organizations. This might explain why it is so difficult to have good utilization of evaluation in an organization; many factors have to line up. The chapters in this book discuss these kinds of issues.

EVALUATION FOR WHAT PURPOSE?

Another important aspect to consider is the intended purpose of the evaluation. A useful distinction can be made between evaluation done for learning and that done for accountability. Immediately, one can see the implication for use and by whom.

Much evaluation seems to be done or is seen as being done for accountability purposes (Mayne, 2007). That is, it is done for someone outside the organization (or outside the evaluand) to check on how well things are going, typically to assess if the program should continue to be funded. Most international aid donors, for example, require evaluations as a condition of continued funding. As a result, use by the evaluand, or organization, for improving design or delivery is much less likely, with attention focused more on defending the program than learning what is working and what is not. Evaluation with a clear goal of learning about programs and how they are working will have a much greater chance of being used by the evaluand.

But need there be such a dichotomy between evaluation for learning and evaluation for accountability? Some have argued (Auditor General of Canada, 2002; Mayne, 2007; Perrin, 2007; Zapico-Goni, 2007) that in the age of accountability for results—which programs do not have complete control over—and especially in the context of increasingly complex interventions, accountability should in large part be focused on accountability for learning rather than for results per se. This could be a way of reducing the accountability versus learning tension.

In any event, how organizations see their evaluation efforts is clearly quite important.

KEY EVALUATION DECISIONS

The quality of an evaluation product and process is largely determined by how the evaluation is designed and carried out. An organization undertaking an evaluation needs to make quite a few important decisions. Mayne (2011) provides a list:

- Which program to evaluate?
- What evaluation process to follow? Whom to involve in the evaluation?

- Which issues about the performance of the program to address?
- How credible does the evidence have to be?
- How much time and resources to spend on the evaluation?
- How to make decisions on the methodology (evaluation design, data gathering, and analysis)?
- Which evaluators to use to carry out the evaluation?
- How evaluation findings, conclusions, and recommendations receive agreement or approval?
- What gets reported to whom and when, during and at the end of the evaluation?
- How to determine the terms of reference for the evaluation?

The last issue on terms of reference—what the evaluation will comprise—is where many of these decisions are manifest. Who decides the terms of reference can decide most of the key issues in an evaluation, although it clearly depends on how comprehensive the terms of reference are.

How and by whom these decisions get made will affect the quality of the evaluation product and process. All are potential sources of bias in an evaluation. How such questions get decided determines how an evaluation study or the evaluation function in an organization is structured and organized.

These decisions could be made by any or all of the following:

- Those calling for—commissioning—the evaluation
- Those funding the evaluation
- Those managing the evaluation
- Those managing the program being evaluated
- Stakeholders associated with the evaluation
- Those carrying out the evaluation—the evaluators
- The policy under which evaluation operates

EVALUATION STRUCTURES IN ORGANIZATION

Wide variation exists on how evaluation is structured in organizations, as is made clear in the various chapters in this volume. This is not unexpected given the wide variation among organizations in how they are set up and managed:

- Significantly sized internal Evaluation Units that conduct much of the evaluation activity of the organization, as well as minimally sized internal organization units, which rely on externally hired evaluators to do most of the evaluation effort

- Evaluations commissioned within the organization and evaluations commissioned from outside the organization by, for example, governing bodies
- Organizations with a formal evaluation policy and structured practices and those with a more informal approach to evaluation
- Organizations with well-established performance-monitoring practices and those with limited monitoring efforts
- Organizations with Evaluation Units organizationally quite separate from programming and organizations with evaluation embedded in programming with no central Evaluation Unit per se
- Organizations with Evaluation Units strongly supported by senior management and organizations with Evaluation Units with a less strategic support

Given such wide variation, it is clear that the challenges faced by evaluation in organizations and responses to those challenges will also vary considerably, providing a wealth of potential discussion, as the chapters in this book demonstrate.

In particular, the second introductory chapter in this book, "Evaluator, Evaluand, Evaluation Commissioner: A Tricky Triangle," discusses the issues of who decides what in relation to the different possible structures between the evaluators, the program being evaluated, and those commissioning the evaluation.

THE ORGANIZATIONAL CONTEXT

The history, nature, and values of the organization in question also clearly will have an impact on the extent to which it uses evaluation. Some organizations have a long history of evaluation activities, others, a much more limited experience.

More fundamentally, the organizational culture matters greatly, in particular the extent to which they have an evaluative culture. I have described a strong evaluative culture in an organization (Mayne, 2009, p. 4):

- Engages in self-reflection and self-examination (i.e., self-evaluation)
  - ○ Deliberately seeks evidence on what it is achieving, such as through monitoring and evaluation
  - ○ Uses results information to challenge and support what it is doing
  - ○ Values candor, challenge, and genuine dialogue

- Engages in evidence-based learning
  - o Makes time to learn
  - o Learns from mistakes and weak performance
  - o Encourages knowledge transfer

- Encourages experimentation and change
  - o Supports deliberate risk taking
  - o Seeks out new ways of doing business

Implied in these characteristics of a strong evaluative culture, although not explicit, is a willingness to demonstrate publicly what the organization is accomplishing and a willingness to report on its performance and tell its performance story. Thus, added to this list describing a strong evaluative culture should be the following:

- Encourages public reporting on its performance
  - o Makes evaluation reports public
  - o Reports regularly on the performance of its activities

Authors of many chapters in this book recognize the importance of building and strengthening the evaluative culture in an organization and discuss their experiences in doing so.

Overall, we see a wide variety of issues and contexts that can influence evaluation utilization in an organization. This perhaps should not be unexpected given the complex nature of organizations and how they work and make decisions. Evaluation is one tool for trying to bring evidence to inform such decision making.

CHAPTERS IN THIS BOOK

The authors of the chapters in this book offer insights gained from hands-on experience in the challenges faced in making use of evaluation in an organization. They in general address the following questions:

- What is the context in the organization?
- What specific challenges were faced?
- What does the literature say?
- What actual strategies were used in addressing the challenges?
- How well did the strategies work?

The chapters are written by people closely involved with evaluation in the relevant organizations who share their experiences and lessons learned in the ongoing effort to make evaluation useful to the organization.

The book brings attention to those who call for and commission evaluation. In the second chapter of the book, in addition to the need to consider those being evaluated and those doing the evaluation, Bastiaan de Laat argues for the need to focus on evaluation commissioners, a focus that has received considerably less attention in the literature. He then proceeds to discuss the relationships among these three parties: the evaluand, the evaluator, and the commissioner in different evaluation situations, de Laat's "tricky triangle."

The next five chapters are discussions on a variety of cases of evaluation being done for a government department, agency, or ministry. Penny Hawkins leads off with a discussion on two key aspects of commissioning evaluations: the need to be able to manage the evaluation process and the need to be able to intelligently take account of context. She discusses a number of challenges and good practices in managing evaluations, based on her long experience in the New Zealand Ministry of Foreign Affairs and Trade and the Ministry of Social Development and her more recent experience with the Rockefeller Foundation. She then discusses in particular the importance of culture and context in evaluation, based on experiences in conducting evaluations with the Māori of New Zealand, emphasizing the need to diligently take into account the indigenous people's own culture and social practices, some of which do not immediately fit with "standard" evaluation practice.

Marlène Läubli's chapter on the ups and downs over several decades of building an Evaluation Unit in the Swiss Federal Office of Public Health illustrates the constant need to build and maintain evaluation in an organization. The need to be able to adapt to changing organizational contexts and realities and the challenges of building an evaluation culture in the agency are highlighted. She asks whether institutionalization of evaluation helps or hinders the development of an evaluation culture. Numerous lessons for evaluation commissioners and evaluators are discussed, such as the need for good communication, deliberate planning at the outset for use of findings, and the need to educate programs and commissioners about evaluation.

In her chapter, Erica Wimbush discusses efforts in the public health field in Scotland to bring evaluation evidence to bear on decisions about public health issues. She discusses first the literature on knowledge utilization and the emergence of "knowledge to action strategies" as ways of bridging the gap between the evaluator-researcher and the policy decision maker. Wimbush introduces the context within which Scotland's public health agency operates and describes several strategies the agency has been working with to enhance the use of evidence. A number of lessons learned are highlighted, such as the need to create reflective space for the consideration of available evidence, the usefulness of identifying champions, and the need for collaboration and networking.

Nancy Porteous and Steve Montague discuss the evolution of internal evaluation in the Canadian Public Health Agency, shifting from the traditional focus on one-off evaluation studies of individual programs to taking a more holistic, organizational approach to evaluative work in the agency. The chapter indicates four strategies they used for this transformation: keeping well informed about the organization, creating an organizational-level logic model, developing a multiyear evaluation plan for the organization, and focusing on cumulative evaluative learning across the organization. The result, they argue was not only improved quality and use of evaluation but also an enhanced ability of the organization to learn and adapt.

The chapter by de Laat and Williams on evaluation at the European Commission (EC) presents a case of a supra-level government organization and reports on the findings from two large empirical studies undertaken on evaluation at the EC. Five types of use were identified and a large number of evaluations reviewed to see what use had been made of them. Based on those findings, the implications for commissioning evaluations are drawn out. The chapter concludes with a discussion of a number of factors that are seen as affecting use, such as the timing of the evaluation, senior management support, involving potential users, and following up on recommendations.

The next two chapters of the book show evaluation in international organizations, namely, the UN system. The World Health Organization (WHO) is a well recognized UN body and a typical UN organization with both a "centralized" corporate Evaluation Unit and a considerable body of "decentralized" evaluation being conducted around the world in its regional and country offices. After describing this complex evaluation environment, Maria J. Santamaria Hergueta, Alan Schnur, and Deepak Thapa discuss the evolution of evaluation in WHO over the past several decades that involve first being located in planning, then with the oversight services, and now facing financial pressures. Challenges to developing and building an evaluation culture within WHO and an outline of a new evaluation policy to address these issues are presented. Also discussed are the pros and cons of locating the evaluation within the Internal Oversight Services, which undertakes audits and investigations.

The second UN case is evaluation at the International Labour Organization (ILO). Janet Neubecker, Matthew Ripley, and Craig Russon argue the need to measure the extent and nature of the use of evaluation findings and present a five-level utilization maturity model, which they developed at ILO. They discuss how specific strategies can be developed to enhance utilization at each level at each stage of the programming model and by each of the partners in the evaluation process. To build a culture of inquiry, they discuss the importance of establishing and maintaining an active evaluation network of evaluators and managers. Criteria for quality evaluation reports, recommendations, management responses, and dissemination of reports are outlined. When and how each partner in the evaluation process can enhance utilization is discussed.

The concluding chapter looks across the specific cases discussed and draws out themes and lessons that have been identified. Collectively, a wealth of experience is presented in the chapters and considerable practical advice offered on how to enhance use of evaluation in organizations.

REFERENCES

Auditor General of Canada. (2002). Modernizing accountability in the public sector. In *December 2002 Report of the auditor general of Canada to the House of Commons* (Chapter 9). Retrieved from http://www.oag-bvg.gc.ca/internet/English/parl_oag_200212_09_e_12403.html

Botcheva, L., Shih, J., & Huffman, L. C. (2009). Emphasizing cultural competence in evaluation: A process oriented approach. *American Journal of Evaluation, 30*(2), 176–188.

Caracelli, V. J., & Preskill, H. (Eds.). (2000). *The expanding scope of evaluation use: No. 88. New directions for evaluation.* San Francisco, CA: Jossey-Bass.

Cousins, B., Goh, S. Clark, S. & Lee, L. (2004). Integrating evaluative inquiry into the organizational culture: A review and synthesis of the knowledge base. *Canadian Journal of Program Evaluation, 19*(2), 99–141.

Cousins, J. B. (Ed.). (2007). *Process use in theory, research, and practice: No. 116. New directions for evaluation.* San Francisco, CA: Jossey-Bass and American Evaluation Association.

Easterby-Smith, M., Crossman, M., & Nicolint, D. (2000). Organizational learning: Debates past, present and future. *Journal of Management Studies, 37*(6), 783–796.

Forss, K., Rebien, C. C., & Carlson, J. (2002). Process use of evaluations. *Evaluation, 8*(1), 29–45.

Garvin, D. A., Edmondson, A. C., & Gino, F. (2008, March). Is yours a learning organization? *Harvard Business Review,* 109–116.

Hernandez, G., & Visher, M. (2001). *Creating a culture of inquiry: Changing methods—and minds—on the use of evaluation in nonprofit organizations.* James Irving Foundation. Retrieved from http://www.irvine.org/assets/pdf/pubs/evaluation/Creating_Culture.pdf

Jacobson, C., Carter, R. W., Hockings, M., & Kelman, J. (2011). Maximizing conservation evaluation utilization. *Evaluation, 17*(1), 53–71.

Johnson, K., Greenseid, L. O., Toal, S. A., King, J. A., Lawrenz, F., & Volkov, B. (2009). Research on evaluation use: A review of the empirical literature from 1986 to 2005. *American Journal of Evaluation, 30*(3), 377–410.

Kirkhart, K. E. (2000). Reconceptualizing evaluation use: An integrated theory of influence. *New Directions for Evaluation, 88,* 5–23.

Mark, M., & Henry, G. (2004). The mechanisms and outcomes of evaluation influence. *Evaluation, 10*(1), 35–57.

Mayne, J. (2007). Evaluation for accountability: Reality or myth? In M.-L. Bemelmans-Videc, J. Lonsdale, & B. Perrin (Eds.), *Making accountability work: Dilemmas for evaluation and for audit* (pp. 63–84). New Brunswick, NJ: Transaction.

Mayne, J. (2009). Building an evaluative culture in organizations: The key to effective evaluation and results management. *Canadian Journal of Program Evaluation, 24*(2), 1–30.

Mayne, J. (2011). Independence in evaluation and the role of culture [Abstract notes from a chapter]. *Evaluation Notes, No. 1: INTEVAL.* Retrieved from http://www.inteval-group.org/IMG/ckfinder/files/Inteval%20Notes%202011-1.PDF

Mayne, J., Divorski, S., & Lemaire, D. (1999). Locating evaluation: Anchoring evaluation in the executive or the legislature, or both or elsewhere? In R. Boyle & D. Lemaire (Eds.), *Building evaluation capacity: Lessons from practice* (pp. 23–52). New Brunswick, NJ: Transaction.

Moynihan, D. P. (2009). Through a glass, darkly: Understanding the effects of performance regimes. *Public Performance & Management Review, 32*(4), 592–603.

Nutley, S. M., Walter, I., & Davies, H. T. O. (2007). *Using evidence: How research can inform public services.* Bristol, UK: Policy Press.

Organisation for Economic Co-operation and Development, Development Assistance Committee (OECD-DAC). (2002). *Glossary of key terms in evaluation and results based management.* Paris, France: Author. Retrieved March 8, 2008, from http://www.oecd.org/dataoecd/29/21/2754804.pdf

Patton, M. Q. (2007, Winter). Process use as a usefulism. *New Directions for Evaluation, 2007*(116), 99–112.

Patton, M. Q. (2008). *Utilization-focused evaluation* (4th ed.). Thousand Oaks, CA: Sage.

Patton, M. Q. (2012). *Essentials of utilization-focused evaluation.* Thousand Oaks, CA: Sage.

Peck, L. R., & Gorzalski, L. M. (2009). An evaluation use framework and empirical assessment. *Journal of MultiDisciplinary Evaluation, 6*(12), 139–156.

Perrin, B. (2006). *Moving from outputs to outcomes: Practical advice from governments around the world.* Washington, DC: IBM Centre for The Business of Government and World Bank. Retrieved from http://www.businessofgovernment.org/report/moving-outputs-outcomes-practical-advice-governments-around-world

Perrin, B. (2007). A new view of accountability. In M.-L. Bemelmans-Videc, J. Lonsdale, & B. Perrin (Eds.), *Making accountability work: Dilemmas for evaluation and for audit* (pp. 63–84). New Brunswick, NJ: Transaction.

Pollitt, C. (2006). Performance information for democracy: The missing link? *Evaluation, 12*(1), 38–55.

Preskill, H., & Jones, N. (2009). *A practical guide for engaging stakeholders in developing evaluation questions.* Princeton, NJ: Robert Wood Johnson Foundation Evaluation Series. Retrieved from http://www.rwjf.org

Preskill, H., & Torres, R. T. (1999). *Evaluative inquiry for learning in organizations.* Thousand Oaks, CA: Sage.

Preskill, H., & Torres, R. T. (2000). The learning dimension of evaluation use. *New Directions for Evaluation, 2000*(88), 25–37.

Ramalingam, B. (2011). *Learning how to learn: Eight lessons for impact evaluations that make a difference.* London, UK: Overseas Development Institute. Retrieved from http://www.odi.org.uk/resources/download/5716.pdf

Rossi, P. H., Lipsey, M. W., & Freemen, H. E. (2004). *Evaluation: A systematic approach* (7th ed.). Thousand Oaks, CA: Sage.

Russ-Eft, D., & Preskill, J. (2009). *Evaluation in organizations: A systematic approach to enhancing learning, performance, and change.* New York, NY: Basic Books.

Schwartz, R., & Mayne, J. (2005). Assuring the quality of evaluation: Theory and practice. *Evaluation and Program Planning, 28*(1), 1–14.

Stame, N. (2004). Theory-based evaluation and varieties of complexity. *Evaluation, 10*(1), 58–76.

Torres, R. T., & Preskill, H. (2001). Evaluation and organizational learning: Past, present and future. *American Journal of Evaluation, 22*(3), 387–395.

Vanlandingham, G. (2011). Escaping the dusty shelf: Legislative evaluation offices' efforts to promote utilization. *American Journal of Evaluation, 32*(1), 85–97.

Weiss, C. H. (1998). Have we learned anything new about the use of evaluation? *American Journal of Evaluation, 19*(1), 21–33.

Zapico-Goni, E. (2007). Matching public management, accountability and evaluation in uncertain contexts. *Evaluation, 13*(4), 421–438.

CHAPTER 2

EVALUATOR, EVALUAND, EVALUATION COMMISSIONER

A Tricky Triangle

Bastiaan de Laat

CHAPTER TOPICS

- Internal versus external debate and the role of the evaluation commissioner
- Different configurations of commissioning and managing evaluations
- Issues of control and independence in relation to these different configurations

PRELUDE

Let's start with a personal story. A couple of years ago, I was, as an external consultant, in charge of the evaluation of a series of programs of a well-known and important multilateral organization. My client was the unit within this organization responsible for those programs. More precisely, the evaluation was commissioned by the people personally involved in the implementation of the programs.

While preparing the beneficiary questionnaire, my client was hesitant to include an item on what was seen as a competing program. Initially, not realizing how serious the

---

Note: A rudimentary version of this chapter was presented at the Biennial Conference of the European Evaluation Society in Lisbon, 2008.

Disclaimer: Any views and opinions expressed by the author do not necessarily reflect the views and opinions of the European Investment Bank.

resistance was going to be, I presented subsequent versions of the questionnaire with variants of the question in it, until my client clearly stated that I was kindly advised to simply take all reference to the other programs out. The question would be "irrelevant" as this other program "had very different objectives and therefore could not show any overlap." I argued that, precisely, the evaluation would be a good opportunity to find out more about the coherence and consistency between the two programs. But my client did not want to know, and the answer remained no. Moreover, the client threatened to stop the contract were I not to give in to his desire to influence the evaluation methodology, whose design I thus far had thought to be mostly the realm of the evaluator. Of course, this was not the argument he used: In fact, the excuse would have been that the evaluator would not have delivered the final questionnaire in time thus missing a deadline, which could contractually constitute a reason to stop the contract.

At that time, I was running a small consultancy company and had, so to speak, several mouths to feed; after two weeks of fighting with this client over the questionnaire item, I had to give in and gave up, choosing to not lose the, substantial, contract. What had happened, however, for me was unfair; I felt bitter and somewhat helpless, having only colleagues and friends—not even an "evaluation ombudsman"—to turn to. Eventually, this event for me was one of the reasons to leave the consultancy business to see whether "on the other side," that is, the side of the evaluation commissioner, things were indeed so laden with politics that one had no choice. I continued thinking about this event (and several other, similar, but fortunately less successful, attempts by clients), and this led to more general theorizing about the relationships between evaluator, evaluand, and evaluation commissioner. The "tricky triangle" concept is the fruit of these reflections.

INTRODUCTION

The evaluation literature generally makes a distinction between two roles that are involved in the evaluation process, namely, the *evaluator* who performs the evaluation and the *evaluand*, that is, the evaluated entity (a project, program, policy, institute, etc.). The evaluator can relate to the evaluand in two different ways: The evaluator can be internal to the organization that implemented the evaluand or external to it. Correspondingly, one speaks of "internal evaluation" versus "external evaluation." Although many organizations use external evaluators explicitly because (they claim) this would safeguard independence—internal evaluators would be more biased—the literature shows that external evaluation and independence are not identical at all (Conley-Tyler, 2005; Kaiser & Brass, 2010; Mathison, 2005).

This chapter proposes a fresh way of looking at external-internal debates by taking into account the role of the *evaluation commissioner*, which seems overlooked in the literature. This omission is surprising since in reality an evaluation commissioner is *always* present: Whether it is implicit or explicit, someone will always *ask* for an evaluation to be performed, propose terms of reference (ToR), and pay—that is, evaluators do not initiate evaluations on their own behalf, just for the sake of it. However, much of the literature implicitly seems to consider that the evaluation commissioner simply coincides with program management, that is, the entity being evaluated. In reality, many situations exist where these roles do not coincide and where the evaluation commissioner may well be positioned *outside* the organization of the evaluand—for instance, a ministry which is commissioning an evaluation of a national agency or a budget office calling for an evaluation in a department. The way in which the evaluation commissioner relates to the evaluator and to the evaluand is crucial in shaping the relations between two parties and may have a great impact on the way in which evaluation procedures and processes are established and unfold. It is surprising that this role has not been studied much. The present book started from this observation and aims to fill the gap in the literature, through discussions on different facets of the commissioner's role.

The aim for this chapter is to propose a simple analytical framework to analyze the evaluation commissioner *role* alongside the roles of evaluator and the evaluand. Depending on the situation, the evaluation commissioner can be positioned in various places. In this chapter, the proposed concept of the tricky triangle is shown to capture the three roles and their relationships in an evaluation process. It is a *tricky* triangle because of the, sometimes sensitive, relationships between the three entities. However, it is also a tricky triangle because of the supposed roles the three have—especially with regard to independence and external evaluation—which in reality may turn out to be quite different from what is generally supposed, as argued in the next section. The chapter will describe the five typical organizational configurations under which the three roles can relate to each other, refer these back, if applicable, to the classic distinction between internal and external evaluation, and analyze the consequences for independence of the evaluation.

The remainder of this chapter is organized as follows. After a brief review of the issue of independence in evaluation—because this was the underlying reason for this chapter, that is, to focus explicitly on the evaluation commissioner's role and to propose the triangle concept as an analytical framework—this chapter will describe the five different organizational configurations in which the three roles can relate to each other. The final section of this chapter provides a brief conclusion.

INDEPENDENCE AND INTERNAL AND EXTERNAL EVALUATION

Discussions on relationships between evaluator and evaluand, which are more often than not closely related to issues of independence, bias, and control, are not new to the evaluation community; they are inherent to the political nature of evaluation and have been the subject of debate since the advent of "modern" evaluation as it has been slowly institutionalizing since the 1960s. Most prominently, Scriven (1975) reviewed the wide range of sources of bias in evaluation and proposed preventive measures; his seminal paper since its publication nearly 40 years ago has lost nothing of its sharpness and relevance. Unbiased evaluators do not exist, "but there are arrangements which discourage them from bringing [. . .] biases to bear, or where their biases are (at least partially) balanced off" (p. 22). Relations between the different parties in evaluation remain sometimes in conflict as testified by a recent discussion in the LinkedIn Group of the American Evaluation Association (AEA), which holds great similarities to the story presented at the beginning of this chapter. This discussion started with the question about fellow evaluators' experiences with clients who complained about the methodology of the evaluation report when annoyed by the results of the evaluation. The long series of replies would provide perfect real-life examples for the points made in Scriven's paper. I will come back to it later.

Traditionally, the evaluation literature—but also different political institutions, such as the European Commission in Europe—has a tendency to equate external evaluation with "independent" evaluation, as opposed to evaluation performed by staff members internal to the institution which implement the evaluated program. An internal staff member, it is argued, would be more easily biased. The distinction of internal versus external, and especially whether the latter is by definition preferential over the former, is, however, not so clear-cut. Even what independence exactly means is not always very clear (Kaiser & Brass, 2010). The general argument is that whereas the external evaluator would identify with the professional "evaluation community," the internal evaluator would be more likely to identify with his or her own workplace and would therefore be more easily biased or put under pressure from "inside" to conform to internal bias.

Now Scriven (1975) already suggested that "the quest for objectivity via the criterion of independence often leads to the use of 'external' evaluators in both the formative and summative situations [but] of course, externality is always relative" (p. 11). Indeed, the external evaluator may at some point give in to pressures from a client if winning the next bid is at stake, and this may harm independent judgment (Mathison, 1999). In this respect, building long-term relationships between external evaluators and program managers would be particularly harmful as it would lead to the evaluator identifying increasingly with the organization she or he works for, therewith, increasingly behaving as a "biased" internal evaluator or being exchanged for another long-term relationship (Ray, 2006).

Inversely, an internal evaluator, even if there is a risk that she or he is sanctioned upon delivering critical evaluation results, may as a matter of fact be far less easy "to get rid of" than an external evaluator, on condition that the organization has the necessary safeguards in place to protect his position. Internal evaluation then may well be more independent than external evaluation. This is confirmed by a recent study for U.S. Congress on the independence of evaluators of federal programs (Kaiser & Brass, 2010). This paper in the end chooses to refer to independent evaluation, not as external evaluation but as being the review and assessment of how well programs and projects are working when conducted by a unit *outside* the program office itself. Also, Michaelova and Borrmann (2006, p. 321) suggest that under certain institutional safeguard provisions, it may well be that the internal evaluator is actually more independent than an external evaluator. They argue that an Evaluation Unit can be in the same institution or agency and still remain independent. An example is the Independent Evaluation Group at the World Bank, which is part of the bank but quite independent from the management and operations of the bank, reporting to the Executive Board.

In my view, the confusion in the literature is caused by two shortcomings. First, mirroring Kaiser and Brass's (2010) statement that there is no common understanding of what *independent* evaluation is, there does not seem to be a sufficiently precise definition of *internal* evaluation either. Is it internal to the evaluand (i.e., the project, program, policy, or institution evaluated) or only internal to the agency that implements the program—but outside the program unit itself? The literature calls both types internal evaluation—the first being viewed as less independent than the second. Inversely, the term *external evaluation* is used to mean evaluation performed by evaluators positioned *outside of the agency* who are responsible for program implementation. Under this definition, in Europe, national governmental ministries or the European Commission—as examples—have mostly external evaluations performed. Most multilateral financial institutions on the other hand would perform internal evaluation, as their evaluators are staff of the same organization as those who implement the programs to be evaluated. Starting from this definition, the literature equates internal-external with dependent-independent, and the authors generally conclude that these are not identical distinctions; Conley-Tyler (2005), Mathison (2005), and Kaiser and Brass (2010) all finish by stating that the internal-external distinction is not the determining factor for the debate on independence. To oppose internal versus external evaluation in order to explain the level of independence of evaluation therefore is to create a false dichotomy. Independence depends on other factors.

However, there is a second shortcoming in the literature. Coming back to the LinkedIn discussion cited above, all contributors (who, interestingly enough, were all evaluators) referred only to the evaluator and their client—the latter being the evaluated party. Although some contributors were internal evaluators, the relationship between evaluator and evaluand was systematically described as being direct or binary. With one exception (Michaelova & Bormann, 2006), this corresponds exactly to the situations described by the literature: By focusing on the evaluator and the evaluand, there seems to be no role for the client or commissioner of the evaluation. One of the peer reviewers of this chapter even suggested that "in the US there is no evaluation commissioner role"! But who then is it that requests an evaluation be carried out and often sets key aspects of the ToR? Obviously, the commissioner of an evaluation has a crucial role. In some settings, the roles of evaluation commissioner and evaluand may coincide more often than in others. But the role of evaluation commissioner necessarily exists in most if not all evaluation settings, and this needs to be acknowledged in order to better understand how evaluations are organized and unfold, especially, though not exclusively, with regard to independence versus internal-external debates.

That is, depending on *whom*—which client, which evaluation commissioner—the evaluator works for, the power relationships between evaluator and the program being evaluated may well change. Interposing an explicit evaluation commissioner between evaluand and evaluator may provide a buffer between the two. However, the evaluator may subsequently become more dependent, not on the evaluand but on the evaluation commissioner—who may have her own agenda.

THE TRICKY TRIANGLE: CONCEPT AND DEFINITIONS

How do practitioners come to grips with the three different roles? Although different terms have been mentioned loosely above, they have not really been defined yet. I will first summarize the roles of evaluand, evaluator, and evaluation commissioner and subsequently describe the relationships they have.

- The *evaluand* is the object of the evaluation. It can be a program, a project, a policy, an institution, or another entity. It refers simultaneously to what is implemented and those responsible for implementation (e.g., program managers).
- The *evaluator* performs the evaluation.
- The *evaluation commissioner* is the body,[1] which calls for[2] the evaluation to be conducted and pays for the evaluation service that is delivered. The evaluation commissioner is responsible for establishing terms of reference, monitors progress of the evaluation work, and is generally the prime addressee of the evaluation even if a wider audience is generally targeted. Some organizations such as the United Nations Evaluation Group (UNEG), the network of UN Evaluation Units, define explicit duties and obligations for evaluation commissioners (see Box 2.1).

BOX 2.1
DUTIES AND OBLIGATIONS OF EVALUATION
COMMISSIONERS ACCORDING TO UNEG

- Consult with all parties to the evaluation to support the development of a relevant, realistic, and viable specification.
- Make clear from the outset how the evaluation report will be used and disseminated.
- Operate a tendering procedure that is transparent and fair and [in] accordance with agency procedure, making explicit the criteria upon which a tender decision will be made.
- Ensure that the ideas or intellectual property provided within proposals submitted by potential evaluators is not exploited or otherwise misused.
- Preserve the integrity of the evaluation findings, for example, by not quoting selectively from the evaluation findings or publicising them out of context.
- Disseminate interim findings and evaluation reports to intended users, so they can be used in a timely fashion.
- Provide the results of evaluations to stakeholders (of the entities) they cover, including government ministries and other partners.

Source: United Nations Evaluation Group (UNEG), 2007, p. 10.

The relationships between the three roles are as follows:

- *Evaluand and evaluator.* The evaluator examines the evaluand, through different means with the help of different evaluation tools (i.e., desk research, interviews, surveys, expert opinion, etc.). In the opposite direction, the evaluand is expected to provide information about itself to the evaluator. The evaluator provides an evidence-based assessment of the evaluand, including, notably, a *judgment*—the latter explains in part why there may be friction between evaluator and evaluand.

- *Evaluation commissioner and evaluator.* The evaluation commissioner establishes or warrants the ToR, or "specifications," which the evaluator is expected to follow. The evaluation commissioner has a contractual relationship with the evaluator and *remunerates* the evaluator for his or her work. The evaluator produces a variety of products,[3] but generally, evaluation results come in the form of one or several evaluation *reports*, the prime addressee of which is the evaluation commissioner even though eventually a wider audience is typically targeted. The commissioner furthermore defines (through the contract) whether there is an editorial role for the commissioner, or whether the evaluator remains the sole author,[4] and how evaluation reports are published and released (public, confidential, anonymous, etc.).

- *Evaluation commissioner and evaluand.* The evaluation commissioner has the power to initiate or request evaluation of the evaluand. This is because it has either been given the explicit role of doing so or because the evaluand operates under the auspices of the evaluation commissioner, for example, when the latter is responsible for setting the evaluand's strategic directions (a research institute working under the auspices of a research ministry, for instance). The evaluation commissioner also has the (potential) power (through evaluation or through other types of policy activities) to guide the evaluand. Inversely, from evaluand to evaluation commissioner, there can also be an *accountability flow* about achievements and efficiency. This influence may not be direct but mediated.

What makes the triangle particularly tricky is that the different actors involved in the evaluation process anticipate *publication* of evaluation results in some form. Evaluations contain a *judgment* on the evaluand by the evaluator as well as *recommendations*, meaning that results should be acted upon in some way. Having control over the evaluation means having control over the publication of evaluation results, and this means in turn having possible control over the judgment that is made on the evaluand—which can be critical (Oliver, 2007)—as well as over possible recommendations and follow-up efforts to be made. Participating in and acting upon the results of an evaluation

Figure 2.1 A Tricky Triangle

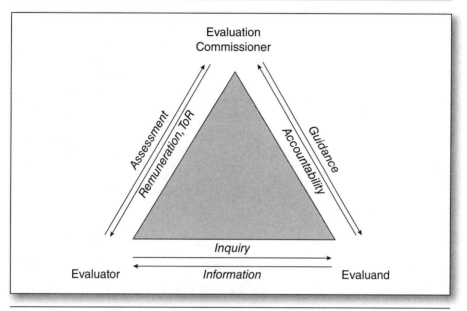

Note: Summarizes the triangular relationship between the three roles.

are first of all a lot of work, and this work may become particularly unpleasant to carry out if an evaluation is critical.

CONFIGURATIONS AND EXAMPLES

The three different roles can be taken on by actors belonging to one (A), two (A & B), or three different organizations (A, B, & C). Following simple arithmetic, this leads to five possible configurations (Table 2.1). It needs to be noted, however, that these five configurations are stylized and do not exhaust the possible arrangements in organizations for evaluation. For example, for the sake of the argument, the evaluation commissioner will be assumed to be a single organization and not, for example, a mix of organizations referred to earlier. Further, as will be noted, one can find variations within and among most of these five configurations. They are used here to illustrate the issues that can arise in the tricky triangle rather than to represent all possible arrangements.

The following sections will discuss each of these five configurations, provide examples of typical situations where they apply, and discuss the degrees and modalities of control by the different parties over the evaluation.

Table 2.1   Different Types of Configurations

N	Label	Evaluation Commissioner	Evaluand	Evaluator	Verbal Description
I	Threefold Separation	A	B	C	An evaluation body independent from the evaluand contracting out its evaluation externally.
II	Self-Evaluation	A	B	B	An entity evaluating its own action.
III	External Evaluand	A	B	A	An organization evaluating programs implemented by third parties using its own internal evaluator.
IV	Internal Evaluation	A	A	A	All three belong to the same *formal* entity (but can be in distinct departments).
V	External Evaluation	A	A	B	An entity hiring an external evaluator to evaluate its own programs, projects, and policies.

I. Threefold Separation: The Supposed Ideal for Independence

The first situation is the one whereby the three roles are institutionally separated: Evaluation commissioner, evaluator, and evaluand belong to three distinct organizations.

A typical example of this configuration is when a national ministry commissions an external consultancy firm to evaluate the programs it is financing which are implemented by a separate agency. This can be found at the national level in areas such as research and development, health, education, and so on. The Australian Health Ministers Advisory Council (AHMAC) example given in Box 2.2 is one; the various evaluations of national or regional research and technology organizations (RTOs), technology programs, or related initiatives conducted by independent consultancy firms and commissioned by the respective national or regional governments are other examples whereby the three parties belong to three different organizations. This type of evaluation is very common practice in many northern EU countries, such as Scandinavia or the Netherlands, where much policy implementation is traditionally performed by implementing agencies independent from—though steered by—national ministries.

Whereas the relationship between a ministry and the implementing agency is still quite direct, the distance, or level of intermediation, between evaluation commissioner and evaluand is variable depending on the situation. Highly

Figure 2.2 Configuration I: Threefold Separation

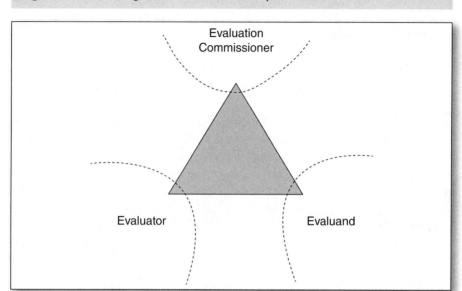

intermediated relationships exist in the case of advisory councils, whose role is to provide (evaluative) advice to national ministries, for example, in areas such as research and innovation policy, health, or education. Those inter alia work on the basis of evaluations or other studies on which they base their advice.

BOX 2.2
AN EXAMPLE OF INTERMEDIATIONS: AHMAC

An example of the intermediated setup described in Figure 2.2, in the health area, is the evaluation of the National Mental Health Strategy (evaluand) conducted in 1997 for the Australian Health Ministers Advisory Council (AHMAC, the commissioner), by the National Mental Health Strategy Evaluation Steering Committee (evaluator)—which also commissioned further research studies as input to its evaluation. The AHMAC's purpose is to provide effective and efficient support to the Australian Health Ministers' Conference, whose members are all Australian government, state, and territory ministers and New Zealand ministers with direct responsibility for health matters, and who are therefore the "sponsors" of the health policy.

Source: Australian Health Ministers Advisory Council (AHMAC), 1997.

The configuration whereby the three roles are hosted by three different organizations is often considered ideal, because the roles of evaluation commissioner is separated from that of the evaluand—providing a higher chance of the two being independent—and the evaluand has no direct control over the evaluator. Having the General Accounting Office (GAO, today known as General Accountability Office) evaluate an agency program commissioned by Congress was also advocated in Scriven's original paper as an act leading to more independent evaluation than having an agency itself commission its evaluations. It was not dismissed for reasons of principle but on the basis of Scriven's own limited faith in the ability of the GAO to conduct evaluations.

Although this configuration is often presented as warranting the most independence, there certainly are pitfalls. Even though most organizations (cf. UNEG guidelines cited in Box 2.1) will expect the evaluation commissioner to be neutral, the evaluation commissioner may adapt the ToR to its own agenda and influence the evaluation questions to be asked or the methodology to be adopted. It should be noted that this is not necessarily on purpose but could simply be the outcome of the—often collective, that is, involving a variety of stakeholders with different interests and opinions—process of defining the ToR. The evaluator may well be less vigilant in this configuration, working with an independent commissioner, than in the case of working directly for the evaluand, and the evaluator should be aware of this.

The evaluand in turn may want to influence the ToR to its advantage. The possibilities for doing so will depend on how influential it is with regard to the evaluation commissioner. Again, when the evaluand is not represented by one single party (program management, an institution) but more of a collective entity (e.g., policy evaluation), such an influence becomes difficult as it may be difficult for the evaluand to speak as one voice. Furthermore, during the evaluation process, the evaluand may withhold information or more generally be uncooperative. The latter two items concern behavior that is not specific to this configuration alone: It is also likely in several other configurations. It is true, however, that in the present configuration, the evaluator may only have intermediated access to evaluand information (i.e., through the evaluation commissioner), which makes it more difficult to obtain information.

II. Evaluator = Evaluand: Self-Evaluation

The second configuration is when evaluator and evaluand overlap, that is, when the same *persons* who are operationally responsible for program implementation perform the evaluation of the program themselves. This is the central idea of *self-evaluation*, whereby the evaluand reports to a third party (e.g., the organization's board, the hierarchy). Generally, there is no discrete evaluation commissioner for every self-evaluation, but self-evaluation practice is ruled by the internal or external procedures that the organization obeys, which substitute for the commissioner and provide the guidance for the self-evaluation to take place.

Self-evaluation—in the form of individual self-assessment forms, project completion reports, or monitoring reports—is widespread practice, traditionally often used in the education sector, in operations units of multilateral development organizations, and today, increasingly within public sector management and performance measurement of public programs.[5]

In self-evaluation, the control of the evaluator by the evaluand is total as the two roles coincide. The validity and use of self-evaluation greatly depends on the extent to which the self-evaluators play the game seriously and honestly. It is based on the idea that people want to learn and progress from the analysis of their achievements against set objectives. Therefore, it is mainly used for formative or developmental (Patton, 2011) evaluation rather than for accountability as the risk of bias for the latter type of application is, by the very nature of self-evaluation, probably deemed too high (Wenar, 2006, p. 19). Often, self-evaluation may also be part of a wider evaluation approach in the process of triangulation with other data sources, or, as practiced in several multilateral development banks (MDBs), as one input in a broader evaluation process, which would aggregate a series of self-evaluations, combined with other sources, to form an overall judgment on a given sector or theme.[6]

Figure 2.3 Self-Evaluation: Evaluator = Evaluand

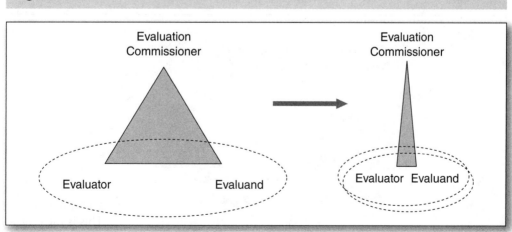

III. The External Evaluand: Evaluation Commissioner = Evaluator

The third configuration occurs when the roles of evaluation commissioner and evaluator coincide and the evaluand is separate (Figure 2.4).

Now, how can an evaluator at the same time be an evaluation commissioner? At first sight, this may indeed be a counterintuitive configuration but, as a matter of fact, it is not so uncommon. One may encounter it in bilateral, and some multilateral, development agencies, which provide aid and financing programs to developing countries. In such a case, the evaluand is the program or project in country X to which the agency has contributed alongside several other donors. Equally, it could be where the implementation of a federal program has been delegated to third parties or where national authorities delegate implementation to district authorities. In such cases, these externally implemented programs may well be evaluated by the evaluation department *within the funding agency*.

This configuration leads easily to hybrids within the triangle. First, boundaries may be blurred as, often, part of the responsibility for the implementation of a project or program lies in house. In other words, it is not always clear how external the evaluand really is to the organization, especially when the agency has a strong stake in the program that is evaluated. The degree of ownership and direct involvement of the program or project by the agency will determine how external the evaluand is, for example, whether those implementing the project or program are independent. In this configuration, as Scriven, and more recently

Figure 2.4 External Evaluand

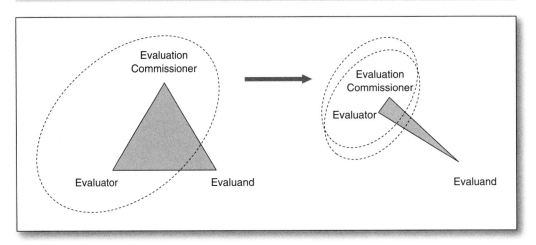

Michaelowa and Borrmann (2006), suggested, the agency may be biased because it is in a *parental* role. Depending on the level of involvement, this configuration would in such a case hybridize with, or even completely transform into, the type of configuration discussed in the next Configuration, type IV.

The second form of hybridization in Configuration III occurs as soon as external evaluators are brought in by the agencies' Evaluation Units, when this situation reverts back to *Configuration I*, that is, when the agency becomes the evaluation commissioner of an external evaluation of the programs it has funded.

Third, even if work is contracted out to external consultants, there may still be a substantial role for the internal evaluator. An example is the International Fund for Agricultural Development (IFAD), which actually hires external consultants to perform evaluation fieldwork; however, the so-called lead evaluator—who is internal—is responsible for the terms of reference, accompanies the external evaluator on fieldwork, reviews the draft evaluation and finalizes the document, and makes sure it meets the Evaluation Units requirements.[7] The lead evaluator also manages the communication with the program management department. In such a case, the external evaluator seems mobilized mainly for reasons of internal resources, the intellectual lead remaining clearly within the internal evaluation department.[8] Therefore, this hybrid configuration is considered closer to the present configuration than to either the Threefold Separation discussed under the first configuration or Configuration IV discussed in the next section.

IV. Internal Evaluation: All Within the Walls of One Organization

When evaluation commissioner, evaluator, and evaluand are located within the same organization, the situation, as described in the literature, usually refers to internal evaluation (Figure 2.5).

Internal evaluation is generally organized within multilateral development banks (MDBs) and other multilateral financial institutions (MFIs) as well as in different multilateral organizations (e.g., UN bodies). Even though they are within one organization, the three roles are generally separated with evaluation under the responsibility of dedicated Evaluation Units or *offices* reporting to executive boards, not the management of the organization, and financing or implementation of programs under the responsibility of operations services. Evaluation Units can either perform evaluations with their own staff or hire external consultants for specific evaluations or evaluation tasks (e.g., a survey).

MFIs and MDBs often *combine* the two modes and use both fully fledged internal evaluators, while sometimes seeking support of external evaluators,

Figure 2.5 Internal Evaluation: All Within the Walls of One Institution

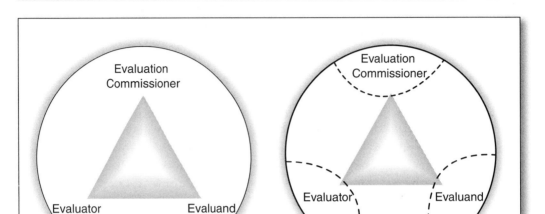

even within the same evaluation assignment. Reasons for hiring external evaluators include need for specific sector expertise or lack of in-house capacity to perform the evaluation. Other multilateral organizations (UN bodies) more systematically externalize evaluations to external evaluators *through* their evaluation departments, which then have a supervisory role.

In the *Encyclopedia of Evaluation* (Mathison, 2005), it is suggested that this configuration is more likely to cause the experience of role pressure for evaluators who are internal and thus members of the setting they are evaluating. Also, Wenar (2006, pp. 19–20), in discussing accountability of development aid, sees this as a configuration with a potentially strong tendency toward positive bias: "Evaluators are currently employed by those who fund the projects that they evaluate. These funding organizations have strong interests in receiving positive evaluations of their projects' effectiveness" (p. 20). It can be argued, however, that possible positive bias does not depend on the fact that the Evaluation Unit is internal to the organization per se but on the safeguards that guarantee independence. The Evaluation Cooperation Group (ECG, 2010)—the peer group of MDB's and MFIs' evaluation departments—proposes a set of "good practice standards" that should be followed in order to make internal Evaluation Units as independent as possible. These good practices reflect, in particular, the body the internal Evaluation Unit reports to, how its head and staff should be recruited and their career paths within the organization, and how reports are published and cleared (see African Development Bank [ADB], 2005, for a specific assessment of the independence of an MDB's evaluation department). That the ECG experienced the need to establish those good practice guidelines suggests that independence of internal Evaluation Units, indeed, is not a given and has to be protected if not reinstated regularly.

Interestingly, the ECG good practice standards referred to above do not refer to an evaluation commissioner as such but to "evaluation stakeholders." This is not totally surprising because when the Evaluation Unit is internal to the organization no client relationship exists as in the case of an external evaluator—when a one-off transaction for each individual evaluation assignment can be identified. The Evaluation Unit can of course be the commissioner of external evaluations or other studies. However, the Evaluation Unit's own work is also commissioned, albeit indirectly. That is, Evaluation Units generally work on the basis of multiannual work plans approved by the management and the governing board of the organization. Even though the Evaluation Unit can be very proactive in establishing its work plan, its endorsement by the governing bodies of the organization makes the group's members de facto commissioners of the evaluations; the Evaluation Unit engages in a *contract* with the board in order for the planned evaluations to be carried out within the planned time and resources.

V. The Evaluand as Commissioner

The fifth configuration exists when the evaluation commissioner and the evaluand are part of the same organization and the evaluator is external. A further subdivision can be made. First, the evaluation commissioner is the evaluand. Traditional internal-external debates implicitly seem to refer to this situation when they discuss external evaluation. The second case occurs within the organization when a clear distinction is made between the evaluand (e.g., program officers) and the evaluation commissioner (e.g., an Evaluation Unit). In the latter situation, the evaluation commissioner, although internal to the organization is not involved in implementation and thus can be deemed relatively external to the evaluand.

Although one might expect it a rarity that the evaluand directly contracts with the external evaluator, the situation still exists. As a former external consultant, I was confronted in several settings (both in work for national governments and for multilateral organizations) where there was a direct contractual relationship

Figure 2.6 The Client Is in the Same Organization or Overlaps With the Evaluand

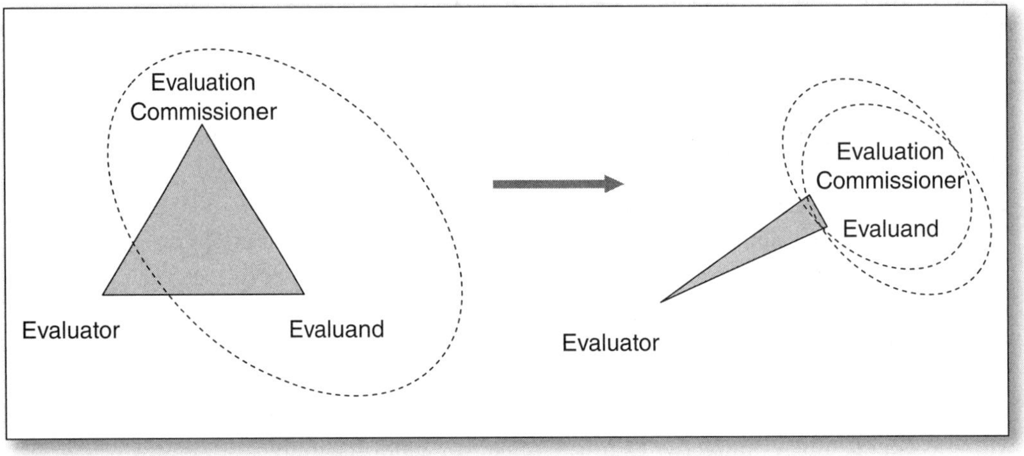

between external evaluator and the evaluand, which, at least in two cases (see one instance at the beginning of this chapter), led to conflicts; in the other cases, it led at least to some tensions. Unless purely for learning purposes—which can be a good reason to conduct an evaluation—this situation is the least desirable from the point of view of evaluator independence and accountability: Criticism of the program is difficult for the evaluand to accept and, in this configuration, the influence on the evaluator to bend the evaluation results (or, alternatively, abandon) too strong.

Many organizations that use external evaluation increasingly have these evaluations commissioned and managed by *internal Evaluation Units*, which belong to the same organization but are not directly involved with the programs that are evaluated. These may act as a buffer between the external evaluator and program management. Such a setup typically exists within the European Commission, where most of the larger departments of directorates-general each has an internal Evaluation Unit (de Laat, 2005). It also exists, as part of the Office of Internal Oversight Services (OIOS, which also covers internal audit), within the different bodies of the UN system. Contrary to the action of internal Evaluation Units in the MDBs and MFIs discussed in the previous configuration, these internal Evaluation Units generally do *not* perform evaluations themselves and do not finalize evaluation reports as in the IFAD example. They do, however, establish ToRs for the evaluations that they subsequently contract out externally, and they have ongoing relationships with the external evaluators, during the work. They can play a role in the accompaniment of evaluations within the organization when these are managed directly by the operations units.

CONCLUSION

This chapter showed analyses of the five different conceptual configurations under which evaluation commissioner, evaluand, and evaluator can relate. All five configurations correspond to different real-life situations, but they do not exhaust the possible real-life arrangements that may be more complex. The tricky triangle should therefore be interpreted as a model, allowing us to further explore those real-life situations. Table 2.2 summarizes, for each configuration, the possible risks in view of independence, the preferred uses of the different configurations, and possible measures that can be taken in order to strengthen the independence of the evaluator.

Evaluator independence does not depend on the internal/external distinction, agreeing with the general opinion expressed in relevant literature. Whatever the configuration is, tensions in the tricky triangle will depend on anticipated evaluation outcomes and (mis)use of the evaluation by each of the three parties, combined with the possibility and desire to actually influence the evaluation in a certain direction. In some cases, the temptation to do so may be bigger than in others; in some of the configurations discussed, the possibilities to do so may also be easier than in others.

Table 2.2 Different Types of Configurations

N	Label	Organizational Setups Under Types Used (Examples)	Potential Risks for Biased Evaluation	Preferred Use	Measures to Ensure Independence of Evaluator Should Aim to . . .
I	Threefold Separation	National evaluation councils; national ministry evaluating implementing agency.	"Ideal type" for independent evaluation; however, the independent evaluation commissioner may have own agenda; evaluand may be noncooperative.	Accountability-geared evaluations. Strategic evaluations of programs, policies, or organizations.	. . . explicitly ensure full cooperation of evaluand in information provision and lower influence of the evaluand over the evaluation commissioner.

(Continued)

Table 2.2 (Continued)

N	Label	Organizational Setups Under Types Used (Examples)	Potential Risks for Biased Evaluation	Preferred Use	Measures to Ensure Independence of Evaluator Should Aim to . . .
II	Self-Evaluation	Great variety of organizations.	De facto no independence. Evaluator and evaluand coincide.	Learning. Input to broader evaluation exercises.	. . . make sure that objective, verifiable indicators are used.
III	External Evaluand	Not frequent. Sometimes in bilateral aid agencies and multilateral institutions.	Blurred boundaries between internal versus external implementation responsibilities; hybridization between internal and external evaluator roles.	Equally for learning and accountability—on the condition that the organization is not involved in program implementation.	. . . clarify the distinction between the parts of the programs implemented and hence evaluated in house in order to prevent de facto self-evaluation.
IV	Internal Evaluation	MFIs and MDBs; some multilateral organizations.	Too strong identification of internal evaluator with the organization (cf. traditional internal evaluation).	Depending on the particular arrangements, it can be suitable for accountability or for learning purposes.	. . . warrant the independence of internal Evaluation Units from operations services and hierarchy. Good practice standards for this exist.
V	External Evaluation	Public administrations; multilateral organizations.	Strong control of evaluand over the external evaluator.	Relatively better suited for learning than for accountability, unless conditions in the right hand column are well fulfilled.	. . . mitigate the effect of a too great control of the evaluation-commissioner-alias-evaluand over the evaluator. Warrant independence of Evaluation Units from operations services.

In the end, further analysis is desired—in at least two directions. First, as suggested in the previous section, some configurations may be better adapted to specific situations than others (e.g., accountability vs. learning), but a stronger empirical basis is needed to confirm the optimal situation in different cases. Second, for each individual configuration, the probably wide variety of different arrangements (organizational, contractual, reporting flows, etc.) put in place by the organizations involved to make evaluation work deserves a closer look.

DISCUSSION QUESTIONS

1. Can you describe what, according to the evaluation literature, are the relationships between independent and external evaluation?

2. Why is it useful to distinguish the five organizational configurations described in this chapter?

3. Is there one configuration in which independence of the evaluator is generally accepted as most guaranteed and why? What, nevertheless, are the potential pitfalls for this configuration with regard to evaluation bias?

4. In Configuration IV, which corresponds to what the literature would call *internal evaluation*, what is the type of practices that organizations can take in order to protect evaluations from bias?

NOTES

1. It is convenient for the discussion here to see the commissioner as a single body. However, this may not always be the case. For example, a budget office might call for an evaluation to be done by a certain time and require certain issues to be addressed. The internal evaluation in the organization may set up the ToR perhaps with additional issues to address, manage the evaluation, and perhaps pay for the evaluator. Here, the commissioner is the budget office plus the Evaluation Unit. Further, the evaluation commissioner may be a formal policy, requiring evaluation to be undertaken with the evaluator and/or evaluand setting the ToR. In other words, in reality, the commissioner (as well as any of the other roles discussed below) will often be hybrids.

2. This is opposed to the *formal* requirement, that is, a legal obligation to conduct an evaluation at a certain point in the program's lifetime.

3. For "process use" in evaluation, see Cousins (2008).

4. Part of the LinkedIn discussion referred to above indeed discusses with which party the copyright lies or ought to lie.

5. Such are the guidelines for self-evaluation of state operators as developed in France within the framework of the General Revision of Public Policies; see http://www.performance-publique.budget.gouv.fr/fileadmin/medias/documents/budget/approfondir/GuideAutoEvaluation_mars2011.pdf

6. At multilateral developments banks, this is the case, for example, the XSR/Expanded Supervision Report (AfDB), the XMR/Expanded Monitoring Report (EBRD), the XPSR/Expanded

Project Supervision Report (IADB), the ICR/Implementation Completion Report (World Bank), and "Self-assessment" (International Fund for Agricultural Development [IFAD]).

7. IFAD, 2009, p. 27.

8. This is contrary to EC practice (Configuration V) where Evaluation Units as a general rule never directly seem to intervene in drafting evaluation reports.

REFERENCES

African Development Bank (ADB). (2005). *Rapport sur l'indépendance du département de l'évaluation des operations (OPEV) de la Banque Africaine de Developpement.* Tunis, Tunisia: African Development Bank.

American Evaluation Association (AEA). LinkedIn Group. (2011). Retrieved September 23, 2011, from http://www.linkedin.com/groupItem?view=&gid=1021707&type=member&item=697803 37&qid=9967a144-9de5-44f2-8168-02e26d209201&trk=group_most_popular-0-b-ttl&goback=%2Egmp_1021707

Australian Health Ministers Advisory Council (AHMAC). (1997). *Evaluation of the National Mental Health Strategy.* Canberra, Australia: Author.

Conley-Tyler, M. (2005). A fundamental choice: Internal or external evaluation? *Evaluation Journal of Australasia, 4*(1–2), 3–11.

Cousins, J. B. (2008). *Process use in theory, research, and practice: No. 116. New directions for evaluation.* San Francisco, CA: Jossey-Bass and American Evaluation Association.

de Laat, B. (Ed.). (2005). *Study on the use of evaluation in the European Commission, dossier 1: Main report, dossier 2: Case studies.* Brussels, UK: European Commission.

Evaluation Cooperation Group. (2010). *Good practice standards on independence of international financial institutions' central evaluation departments.* Retrieved September 25, 2011, from www.ecgnet.org

International Fund for Agricultural Development (IFAD). (2009). *Evaluation manual: Methodology and processes.* Rome, Italy: Author.

Kaiser, F. M., & Brass, C. T. (2010). *Independent evaluators of federal programs: Approaches, devices, and examples.* Washington, DC: Congressional Research Service.

Mathison, S. (1999). Rights, responsibilities and duties: A comparison of ethics for internal and external evaluation [Special issue]. *New Directions for Evaluation, 1999*(82), 25–34.

Mathison, S. (Ed.). (2005). *Encyclopedia of evaluation.* Thousand Oaks, CA: Sage.

Michaelova, K., & Borrmann, A. (2006). Evaluation bias and incentive structures in bi- and multilateral aid agencies. *Review of Development Economics, 10*(2), 313–329.

Oliver, P. (2007, July). *Would you like the good news first or . . . ? Communicating critical evaluation findings effectively.* Paper presented at the Inaugural Anzea Conference, Masterton, New Zealand.

Patton, M. Q. (2011). *Developmental evaluation: Applying complexity concepts to enhance innovation and use.* New York, NY: Guilford Press.

Scriven, M. (1975). *Evaluation bias and its control.* Berkeley: University of California.

Ray, M. (2006). Choosing a truly external evaluator. *American Journal of Evaluation, 27*(3), 372–377.

United Nations Evaluation Group (UNEG). (2007). *Ethical guidelines for evaluation.* New York, NY: United Nations.

Wenar, L. (2006). Accountability in international development aid. *Ethics and International Affairs, 20*(1), 1–23.

CHAPTER 3

EVALUATION MANAGEMENT

Lessons From New Zealand and International Development Evaluation

Penny Hawkins

CHAPTER TOPICS

- Challenges and good practices in managing evaluations
- The importance of culture and context in evaluation design
- Balancing independence and participation

This chapter presents some of the issues to be addressed in managing evaluations in the public sector and examines a variety of ways this function is structured in the context of government organizations. A range of tensions facing evaluation commissioners and managers will be presented with discussion of the ways in which the role of the evaluation manager and the processes followed are critical for ensuring good quality and useful evaluations. Examples will be used from the New Zealand public sector and the field of international development aid.

Public sector organizations operate within political, organizational, and cultural contexts. This chapter discusses some of the challenges that confront the practice of evaluation, including those related to the location of the function, independence and the resources allocated to evaluation, and issues arising over its management. The question of values comes sharply into focus when evaluation and culture intersect. Intercultural dialogue becomes an important concern for evaluation managers and evaluators in the development of their professional practice. The next section of this chapter focuses attention on some considerations and understandings from evaluation practice in different cultural settings. In the final section, the issues raised are discussed and some final conclusions drawn.

CHALLENGES CONFRONTING THE PRACTICE OF EVALUATION

Locating an Evaluation Function

The question of where to place the evaluation function in an organization arises whenever an organization pauses to assess, and inevitably change, its structure in an effort to be more efficient and effective. A range of forces, including political ideology or even transient managerial fads, may drive these assessments and changes. In the New Zealand public sector, this happens with almost alarming regularity with changes occurring in most central government organizations every few years, most often following a change of government. In the context of a three-year electoral cycle, this allows little time to fully establish any new arrangements before the next change cycle begins.

The location of an organization's evaluation function varies from fully independent and separate from policy and operations to being implanted within the daily work of a program or operations unit. In the New Zealand public sector, the evaluation function is often placed within a policy or strategy division that reports to senior management. The manager of an Evaluation Unit does not usually report directly to the head of the organization and is more often placed in a subordinate position, reporting to a second-tier manager. This tends to be at odds with the more widely accepted good practice principle (at least in bilateral and multilateral international development agencies) of evaluation, which needs to be set up as an independent function within organizations for it to effectively carry out its purpose. In the public sector, this issue extends beyond organizations to the wider governmental system with the potential for evaluation functions to be positioned outside specific government agencies, departments, or ministries yet remain within the public sector as a whole. Although there are examples of this kind of setup in Europe, when the idea was discussed several years ago in the New Zealand government's social sector, there appeared to be insufficient political will for it to happen. Hence, in this context, without a degree of autonomy and separation from policy and operations, the independence of evaluation cannot be assured.

Independence in this setting refers to the ability of evaluators to "speak truth to power" without being compromised by the competing demands of policy and operation managers oriented toward meeting the demands of their executive team members, who in turn are focused on directives from their political leaders.

In the official development assistance setting, the Organisation for Economic Co-operation and Development's (OECD's) Development Assistance Committee's Expert Group on Aid Evaluation (now called the Network on Development Evaluation) developed a set of principles (Organisation for Economic Co-operation and Development [OECD], 1991). One of these principles is that the Evaluation Unit should be completely independent of the processes of policy making and the delivery and management of development assistance (Cracknell, 2000). While this principle has been generally accepted as good practice internationally, apart from recent changes in the United Kingdom, it has not been sufficiently influential for ensuring the location or independence of an Evaluation Unit in most bilateral development agencies. Indeed, other factors and criteria influence decisions on the location of the evaluation function. Operations managers need evaluation findings that are both relevant and useful. The common argument is that if an Evaluation Unit is too remote from the day-to-day operations of the organization, then the evaluations carried out may not be closely enough aligned with managers' information needs. They may also be less able to transmit and reflect the implications of evaluation findings and to translate these into useful and operationally relevant recommendations for change.

The decision about where to locate an Evaluation Unit needs to include a consideration of the balance between independence and other factors relevant to the organization. One of these will be the relative importance placed by the organization on the *purposes* of evaluation. If *accountability* is paramount, then this will predicate a more independent evaluation unit. If ongoing and continuous *learning* is the prime purpose, then a case can be made for an Evaluation Unit located closer to policy or operations units with an emphasis on monitoring and a quick turnaround of reviews and evaluations. Even without structural independence of the evaluation function, it is still important that evaluations are managed in a way that supports them in being as impartial as possible and of sufficient quality. Much will depend on the prevailing practice within an organization and its culture and values and also, through its actions and its collegial relationships, the Evaluation Unit's ability to influence the development of an "evaluation culture" within the organization as a whole. However, we must not forget that decisions are made by the people who have the power to make them in an organization and this can all too often manifest in decisions that result from internal personality politics and vested interests rather than a rational decision-making process. Within an organization, there are networks of people with diverse interests, including technical experts, administrators, and managers (Cracknell, 2000). Some have the power to make decisions, for example, about the allocation of resources, and others do not. This has implications for the evaluation function as it affects not only the administrative arrangements and resources that relate to the commissioning and management of evaluation but also the use of evaluative information. The commissioning and management of an evaluation and the associated decisions can have a significant effect on its independence and integrity.

The Issue of Independence

In recent years, the principle of independence has become more prominent in both the evaluation literature and in discussion forums. Although contested by some, it is often one of the key criteria in assessing the quality and credibility of an evaluation. For example, the OECD guide, *DAC Quality Standards for Development Evaluation* (OECD, 2010a), includes independence as one of the overarching considerations: "The evaluation process is transparent and independent from programme management and policy-making, to enhance credibility" (Sec 1, item 6).

When an internal Evaluation Unit is set up to be directly accountable to the head of an organization, such a central position helps to facilitate equal and arms' length relationships with all groups in the organization; it also provides for an appropriate level of independence, at least from the managers responsible for implementing the policies and programs being evaluated.

The credibility of evaluation will often be at least partly dependent on the level of independence accorded to the evaluation function. In this regard, evaluation is similar to the audit function. When this is not the case, greater efforts need to be made to ensure the independence and management of evaluation processes. This can be done through the development of evaluation policy and practice guidelines as well as by establishing formal protocols for decision making and follow-up. However, even when these efforts are made in order to increase the quality of evaluation work, Robert Picciotto, a former director of the World Bank's Independent Evaluation Group, has argued that particularly for external parties, independence may remain an issue that can affect an evaluation's credibility (2003). Credibility of evaluation is essential, both to internal and external stakeholders and audiences, and it is a key factor that can affect the use of findings and recommendations. Lack of perceived independence is sometimes used as a reason to dismiss the evaluation findings in favor of other types of information or simply a strongly held opinion expressed by an influential decision maker. Strengthening the independence of the evaluation function also signals an organization's recognition of evaluation's importance to its work and signals its serious commitment to, rather than being ambivalent about, enhancing corporate accountability. In commenting on international trends in evaluation, Picciotto (2003) stated:

> The credibility of evaluation hinges in large part on its governance, that is, on the set up of independent evaluation units that report to country legislatures or governing bodies—or other independent verification mechanisms. The prerequisite of credibility is missing in the evaluation

systems used by most governments, companies and development agencies. The frequent option of resorting to consultants does not guarantee independence. (p. 233)

In the international development assistance sector in recent years, almost all official development aid agencies have made efforts to increase the institutional independence of their Evaluation Units. The heads of evaluation functions in most of these now report directly to the head of the organization, or to a second-tier director responsible for strategy. However, according to Picciotto, this still falls short of the bar and threatens credibility. A recent report compiled by the secretariat of the OECD DAC Network on Development Evaluation (OECD, 2010b) states that only two official development aid agencies have implemented institutional arrangements where their Evaluation Units report their evaluations directly to their parliament. The multilateral development banks all have autonomous evaluation functions that report directly to their boards. These institutional arrangements are put in place to increase the independence and credibility of accountability evaluations and are designed to prevent the blocking or changing of reports with negative findings by program managers or other nonevaluation staff (OECD, 2010b).

Sustaining full independence without becoming too remote from policy and practice realities—as well as remaining relevant and useful—is a significant challenge. There are a number of ways to ensure evaluation remains relevant and useful to an organization:

- Ensure that evaluation staff members are well connected to the rest of the organization through involvement in internal cross-organization groups and processes and are thus well informed about current issues
- Optimize physical location and proximity to other groups
- Create good communication mechanisms and practices in order to enhance information sharing between different groups across the organization

The issue of independence of the evaluation function comes into sharp focus with the commissioning of internal evaluations of the organization's capability and effectiveness. It has been my experience that in most organizations, it becomes possible to undertake these types of evaluations only if the evaluation function is independent of other groups and has a clear mandate and policy that covers internally focused evaluation. Even when this is the case, there may still be limits on what can be achieved. I have found that commissioning and managing evaluations with this internal focus is where the most resistance and defensiveness from operations managers is encountered. The use of external evaluation teams can increase the likelihood of acceptance of evaluation findings and recommendations, providing the evaluator(s) adheres to standards of good practice. Evaluation is also likely to be valued and used well where there is good tolerance of risk taking and where learning from mistakes is supported and accepted. Sadly, despite espoused values along these lines, there appear to be very few organizations where it consistently happens in practice.

The role and positioning of the evaluation function in organizations comes under pressure at times of change. (See more on this, for example, in Marlène Läubli's chapter in this book.) This can be particularly acute in times of austerity when evaluation can be viewed as a nonessential or "back room" function rather than an essential element of an organization that wants to continue to improve its efficiency and effectiveness. When this happens, resources for evaluation can be reduced or, in extreme cases, completely wound down. These times offer opportunities for the rationale for Evaluation Units to be restated and evidence for their usefulness presented to decision makers.

Evaluation Resources

The allocation and management of evaluation resources is also an issue that influences the relative independence of evaluation. Some organizations approach the resourcing of the evaluation function by allocating a proportion of program budgets. A recent survey of evaluation functions by the OECD DAC Evaluation Network secretariat found that for DAC bilateral aid donor agencies, central Evaluation Units have an average budget of US$3.3 million, representing the equivalent of 0.1% of the development and cooperation budget. For the multilateral aid institutions, the average evaluation budget is US$10 million, or approximately 1.4% of the overall administrative budgets of these institutions. Just over half of the development agencies reported concerns over the adequacy of their evaluation budgets (OECD, 2010b).

The adequacy of an internal Evaluation Unit's resources can be problematic. Even though evaluation work may be contracted out, it is important not to underestimate the internal capacity (and capability) that is required to manage evaluation contracts. Getting the right balance between internal human resources and external consultants and the range of competencies needed for good quality evaluation can be a significant challenge. On the one hand, expertise in a wide range of evaluation approaches is desirable along with sector and context knowledge, and on the other, an "insider's" insight and understanding of the organization is useful, particularly when it comes to interpreting findings and formulating useful recommendations. It has therefore become more common to see mixed teams of internal and external evaluators who undertake evaluations. Aside from the competencies needed for the evaluation team that is undertaking the evaluation, the competencies for managing evaluations extend into the more relational dimensions of social interaction. This aspect often comes into sharp focus with evaluations that cross cultural boundaries, which will be discussed later in the chapter.

Promoting Quality and Use

Ensuring the quality and use of evaluations is a central focus of an evaluation function that requires careful management and goes beyond the issues of the location, independence, and resourcing of the Evaluation Unit. Acceptance and use of evaluation findings and recommendations is also dependent to some degree on the quality of an evaluation; and the quality of the end products of an evaluation is largely dependent on a good quality process. Evaluation managers and practitioners have a range of quality standards to reach for to assist with this. Different sets of standards will be more or less relevant and appropriate in ways that are dependent on geographical location and sector focus. For example, in the international development arena, the OECD's Development Assistance Committee (DAC) evaluation standards (OECD, 2010a) are used by aid agencies and their partners as well as other players (e.g., nongovernmental organizations). These evaluation standards cover the different stages of an evaluation from planning to follow up and use. They can therefore be used to guide the process from start to finish and can be particularly useful when issues arise and tensions need to be resolved.

Tensions surrounding the evaluation process can include differences of opinion between an external evaluator and an evaluation manager in the commissioning organization (see de Laat's chapter in this book for more discussion on tensions between the evaluator, the *evaluand,* and the commissioner). Significant tensions can arise when a policy or program manager challenges the findings of an evaluation. When this happens, the Evaluation Unit staff member responsible for managing the evaluation will often assume the role of mediator between the external evaluator and her or his internal staff colleagues. This may well test her or his skills in managing these relationships and resolving conflicts. Both an ability to defend the technical quality of the evaluation, if challenged, and an awareness of, and insight into, the political dimensions and power play within the organization are needed.

Evaluation Contract Management

For the past two decades or so, the contracting out of evaluation has been the prevailing practice in the public sectors of New Zealand, in other OECD countries, and worldwide in the field of international development evaluation.

Like most projects, successful evaluations will occur because of the combination of procedures (the rules and protocols), process (the formal and informal patterns of interactions throughout the evaluation), and people (their competencies, attitudes, and flexibility).

One important prerequisite of a good process that produces a successful evaluation is the establishment of a positive working relationship between the contract manager and the evaluator. If this does not happen, there is a risk that, through either lack of awareness or simply neglect, different and contrasting expectations are held by the two parties, resulting in conflict when the process deviates from what they thought had been agreed at the outset (Hawkins, 2012).

Elsewhere, I have stated (Hawkins, 2012) that it is often at the reporting stage that perverse, or improper, incentives lead evaluation managers to change their behavior and become critical of the evaluator. This is a particular risk when an evaluation contract manager is also the person responsible for managing the program being evaluated, a situation that typically occurs in organizations that have not created an independent Evaluation Unit that commissions and manages their program evaluations. Whether conscious, or unconscious, a resistance to negative findings is not uncommon in this situation. As human beings, it is common for us to feel discomfort when others judge our own performance; complex psychological defense mechanisms come to the fore that can be conscious or unconscious. These can manifest in rebuttal of findings and requests to change the content of the evaluation report and/or harsh criticism of the quality of the report and the evaluator's performance. Murray, cited in Morra-Imas and Rist (2009), describes the basis of these disagreements and conflict as "inherent problems with technical elements of evaluation methods and very common frailties in many human beings" (p. 500). Therefore, a focus on only the technical aspects of an evaluation can overlook the specific issues involved in its relational aspects. Experienced evaluators would generally agree that inept management can turn a technically sound evaluation into a waste of scarce resources.

The scenario in Box 3.1 illustrates a case in which the evaluation contract manager pursued the technical aspects that related to evaluation quality, at the same time ignoring the process management and relational dimension. This led to a breakdown in the relationship and an impasse in the process, resulting in an incomplete evaluation report. It is clear in such a situation that there are losses by both parties, and the effects of this can go beyond the immediate players if the evaluation is never properly completed.

To manage these challenges well and enhance the potential for a successful evaluation, it is worthwhile making explicit the responsibilities of both the evaluation contract manager and the evaluator. In a previous publication (Hawkins, 2003), the responsibilities of the evaluation contract manager were outlined:

- Keeping the goals and objectives clear
- Maintaining ownership of the study
- Making prompt decisions
- Being open to negotiation if changes are needed
- Delivering the findings to the relevant audiences

Cumulative practice experience points to a few more items to add to this list along with others identified in some of the guidance documents recently produced by several international organizations, such as the OECD (2010a), UN Population Fund (UNFPA, 2007), and UN Development Programme (UNDP, 2006):

- Discuss and agree on communication protocols before the evaluation starts
- Ensure that evaluators have full access to all relevant documents and other information as early as possible
- Follow the progress of the evaluation and provide feedback and guidance to evaluators, during all phases of implementation
- Arrange for a meeting with evaluators and key stakeholders to discuss and comment on the draft report and agree on any changes or revisions
- Approve the final report and arrange a presentation of the evaluation findings

The evaluator's responsibilities are different but complementary to those of the evaluation contract manager:

- Ensure that the contract, terms of reference (ToR), and the client's business processes are well understood
- Design and, once the client approves the evaluation plan, conduct the evaluation within the allotted time frame and budget
- Provide regular progress reports to the evaluation contract manager
- Participate in discussions about the draft evaluation report and correct any factual errors or misinterpretations

- Respond to reviewers' comments and finalize the evaluation report on time
- Defend the evaluation findings if challenges occur

If a principle of partnership underpins the relationship between the evaluation manager and the evaluation contractor, it can provide a good basis for dealing with difficult issues as they arise during the course of an evaluation. The discussion before the evaluation commences will consist of a question, such as, How will we work together? followed by a negotiation concerning the management of the various stages of the process, as well as a clarification of the products to be delivered and expectations regarding their quality.

BOX 3.1
AN EVALUATION MANAGEMENT SCENARIO

An evaluation contract was set up with terms of reference that set out the purpose and scope of the work as well as the key questions to be answered and a description of the initiative to be evaluated. The timeline, milestones, and payments were detailed in the usual way in a contract for services. The evaluation team selected had done previous evaluation work successfully and had a good track record with the organization.

The evaluation team delivered the draft report on the date agreed along with an invoice as this was earmarked as a milestone payment. Several weeks passed, and they had received neither an acknowledgment, nor any other response from the contract manager. During this time, the deadline for submission of the final version of the report passed as did the invoice payment date. After trying several times to contact the evaluation manager's office via telephone calls and e-mails, the contractor was eventually informed that the original contract manager was on extended leave and that another contract manager had taken over who would be out of the office for the next two weeks. Shortly after receiving this e-mail, the evaluation contractor was advised that the draft report was being reviewed, followed by a formal letter that advised the contractor that payment of the invoice was being withheld as the quality of the draft report was considered unacceptable. This was a complete surprise to the evaluation contractor, and concerns were raised with the contract management about the process and, more specifically, why they were not informed of this within the agreed time frame. Later that same week, a letter was sent to the evaluator from the client, demanding a revised report within two weeks or the contract would be cancelled.

In the above scenario, the evaluators were unaware there would be a change of contract manager partway through the process. The responsibilities of the contract manager weren't made explicit at the outset, and there were no clearly agreed on expectations about communication, decision making, dispute resolution, or opportunities for renegotiation should problems occur. In their previous dealings with the organization, the evaluators had experienced shared understanding and flexibility with other evaluation managers in dealing with unexpected obstacles. However, the new evaluation contract manager appeared to take the view that any negotiation ceased as soon as the written contract was signed. A situation of this type can easily precipitate conflict and turn what could have been a potentially successful relationship and evaluation process into a situation of conflict, potentially resulting in significant losses to both parties, both in terms of the relationship and the final evaluation product.

CONTEXT, CULTURE, AND THE VALUE OF EVALUATION

Evaluation has become a common feature in the context of public policy and program management globally, and yet the use of evaluative information for decision making is still not fully developed. One of the challenges that faces evaluation is aligning the time frames for an evaluation with decision-making processes. Rist and Stame (2006) have argued that the debate about use has been only among evaluators and has therefore been disconnected from the significant changes in thinking across the fields of public management, organizational theory, and information and communications technology and knowledge management. They present a challenge to evaluation practitioners to forge a different approach to evaluation if it is to remain useful and used, requiring a shift from discrete studies to streams of information.

With the advent of information technology and real-time data flows, it's not hard to see a future where traditional evaluation reports that use large amounts of paper are replaced by electronic media—in other words, a transformation from paper reams to electronic information streams. Does this, then, imply a shift in emphasis from evaluation to monitoring, where information collection and analysis is continuous and managers can tap into evaluative information whenever they need it for decision making? Stame (Rist & Stame, 2006) makes the salient point that a move to results-based management creates a requirement for a continuous flow of data and evaluative information for use in making course corrections to policy implementation and programs. If we, as evaluation practitioners, accept this change as likely, if not inevitable, then it has implications for the role of the commissioner and evaluation manager as well as the forms of reporting. Whether or not the types of evaluation reports currently produced are replaced by shorter, more frequent reports remains to be seen. If so, there are likely to be implications, regarding the scope and quality of such reports.

As information systems become more sophisticated and able to supply multiple types of information from different sources, evaluation managers and practitioners have to become highly skilled in selecting from and pulling together data and information that can be used in an evaluative way for the purposes of accountability, learning, and improvement. This implies a need for new approaches and a wider set of skills for evaluators and evaluation managers— it also means a move away from approaches based on 19th-century determinism toward 21st-century systems approaches. Evaluators will need to be able to design and implement evaluations that are better able to make sense of complexity and deal with multiple and dynamic data flows. The end users of the information will increasingly need evaluation professionals to provide time sensitive and relevant evaluative information that can usefully inform decisions. The implication for evaluation practitioners and managers is that, over time, competence in the use of information technology will become indispensable as an adjunct to, but not replacing, good analysis and rigorous, critical thinking.

Cultures of Evaluation and Cultural Contexts

Whatever forms evaluation takes, the underlying values of stakeholders will often emerge during the process, even if not made explicit from the start. The evaluation literature includes references to values (e.g., Greene, Boyce, & Ahn, 2011; House & Howe, 1999) and also culture as mediating factors in evaluation, a discussion that has become a more prominent feature of analysis and debate in recent years (Thompson-Robinson, Hopson, & SenGupta, 2004). This latter topic includes the culture of organizations or institutions, as well as national cultures and local or indigenous cultures. The factors involved tend to be subtle and difficult to determine through evaluation but nevertheless important enough to consider in order to gain a sound understanding of what works, for whom, and under what conditions.

At an organizational level, Mayne (2012) refers to evaluation culture as "the norms, values, attitudes and general practices in the organization that relate to evaluative practices" (p. 105). These attitudinal factors influence evaluation and the degree of support for evaluation. They go hand-in-hand with processes that are clearly guided by explicit policy and related practice guidelines, and, when evaluation is promoted and supported by senior management.

However, even when an organization has established an evaluation culture, is open to critical evaluation reports, and has a system in place that ensures the use of the evaluative information for learning and improvement, other external influences affect how the organization behaves and makes decisions. In not-for-profit and philanthropic organizations, these influences may include the board, peer organizations, working partners, and grantees. In public sector organizations, it also includes politicians, central government agencies (e.g., treasuries and auditors general), and the media. In the midst of all these competing demands and pressures, the enduring challenge for the evaluation function is to produce relevant, credible, and useful information that aims to meet the needs of particular targeted decision makers and audiences. In public sector organizations, the ability to create and maintain an evaluation culture will depend upon the organization's ability to remain open to critical reflection and challenge within a sometimes turbulent and anxiety-creating political context. Managing and balancing these various pressures so that the organization can stay on track in terms of maintaining a culture where evaluation is valued and used can be a continuous struggle with no clear-cut solutions.

With the emergence of a growing literature on evaluation and culture along with an increasing realization of the need for sensitivity to cultural factors, many in the professional evaluation community would now agree that the cultural context of evaluation is a critically important factor that influences whether evaluations are used, by whom, and for what. In considering the different ways evaluation is used or, alternatively, not used by decision makers, it is interesting to look not only at organizations but also at the national cultures in which they are operating. Several examples of national cultures are explored in the book *Evaluation Cultures: Sense-Making in Complex Times* (Barbier & Hawkins, 2012).

So how then can an evaluation's sensitivity to culture be enhanced to ensure use and best value from investments in evaluation?

EVALUATION IN CROSS-CULTURAL CONTEXTS

Given the existing literature on evaluation and organizational culture and evaluation capacity development (e.g., Boyle & Lemaire, 1999), these topics will not be dwelt on here. However, as yet, there is only a small body of literature with regard to national and local culture and evaluation. Indigenous evaluators and their peers would argue that this is a significant issue, and it is thus important to look at some of the challenges and what these mean for evaluation commissioners.

In New Zealand, there is a growing cadre of indigenous evaluators who have been working on the development of indigenous approaches in evaluation that are responsive to cultural factors and, going a step further, incorporating cultural norms and values as essential determinants of an evaluation approach. Some evaluation approaches, such as participatory evaluation and, more recently, realist approaches and developmental evaluation, are consistent with a sensitivity to cultural contexts. The fundamental principle of realist evaluation is that without a thorough understanding of the context, gaining a good understanding of the outcomes of a policy or program is simply not possible (Pawson & Tilley, 1997). Also, more recent additions to evaluation approaches, such as developmental evaluation and the use of complexity theory and systems thinking, are potentially useful in helping to understand the patterns of effects of an intervention. These recent additions to the evaluation field offer more promise for capturing the larger array of factors and considerations that are needed to understand cultural settings and how they interact with the formulation and implementation of policies and programs. In particular, they can be useful in evaluations where the unit of analysis is the social group rather than the individual (Patton, 2011). These newer approaches and methods have a bearing on the evaluation process from commissioning through to follow up and use, as more thought has to be given to who is involved and when and how they are involved. More divergent thinking is therefore required to be able to encompass the richness of a context and an openness to factoring-in rather than factoring-out particular variables, including cultural factors.

In New Zealand, the principles of partnership and self-determination are central to cultural integrity in evaluation. The Treaty of Waitangi[1] enshrines these principles and shapes the relationship between the government and the indigenous Māori people. The ways in which the business of government is carried out, including evaluations commissioned by government departments, are therefore influenced by these principles. Much work has been carried out in recent years by both Māori and non-Māori evaluators, working separately and together, to develop evaluation approaches that are compatible with these principles and which are also culturally relevant in a more general sense. A key issue is the extent to which evaluation approaches and methodologies are based on, or incorporate, indigenous cultural values and frameworks. For example, an important consideration is whether, on the one hand, the evaluation has been predetermined by "outsiders" or, on the other, determined by the cultural group itself with no outside involvement. Typically, with evaluations commissioned by a New Zealand government department, the evaluation space (protocols and processes) is often negotiated by insiders and outsiders working together, ideally in a spirit of partnership rather than one that is competitive or hierarchical. However, what this actually requires in practice is often contested. The issue of independence can often emerge during such a negotiation process and requires discussion and agreement. Such discussions take time for successful resolution and consequently a longer time frame, particularly in the initial stages of an evaluation.

So what are some of the practice implications when commissioning and undertaking evaluations in this context? One example is the use of evaluation advisory groups, which are now quite common in the wider evaluation field and have become essential for evaluations across most of the New Zealand public sector where there are multiple stakeholders, including different cultural groups. Their purpose is to guide the evaluation through what can be a cross-cultural minefield. The fundamental aim is to support and produce evaluations that reflect the realities of indigenous people's lives and values in a way that is meaningful to all stakeholders (Wehipeihana, Davidson, McKegg, & Shanker, 2010). In so doing, this helps policymakers and program managers gain a better understanding of the effects of interventions on different cultural groups and develop more effective initiatives.

If an advisory group is used, it should be set up at the very beginning, even before the evaluation is commissioned. It then has the potential to guide the process from start to finish and fully benefit from the experience and expertise of the group at all stages. For example, for an evaluation to be culturally relevant and responsive, a dialogue with the relevant communities will need to be achieved before an evaluation is designed or carried out. In a partnership framework, agreement on the evaluation is reached before it is commissioned, so that the processes of engagement are equally discussed and agreed on beforehand. Advisory groups therefore should comprise members who bring cultural perspectives to the table as well as technical and subject area experts.

Evaluation teams also need to comprise either indigenous evaluators alone or a mix of indigenous and nonindigenous evaluators with experience and understanding of indigenous evaluation frameworks and practices and competence in their use. Smith (1999) in her book *Decolonizing Methodologies* emphasizes the importance of developing designs based on indigenous knowledge and values to ensure valid and reliable studies that have credibility and value with the communities to which they aim to contribute. Taking this a step further, the cultural dimension of evaluation reaches beyond design to what Nan Wehipeihana, a prominent Māori evaluator in New Zealand, has emphasized as critically important—the "how to" of engagement and the sense-making process of the analysis and formulation of findings. In a recent journal article (Wehipeihana et al., 2010), she makes the case that "there are some things that can't be learnt, known or explored except from within the culture" (p. 188) and that "evaluation in Māori communities should be led by Māori" (p. 187).

For the principle of self-determination to be upheld, indigenous people must be able to take charge of the whole evaluation process from deciding what gets evaluated to managing the entire process, using evaluation frameworks and methodologies that are compatible with the place, the people, and their values and cultural norms. Clearly, this goes far beyond participation in an evaluation that has been determined by outsiders. It places the evaluation completely within the control of the cultural group and allows it to be carried out on their terms. This can be challenging for some government officials charged with responsibility for delivering evaluations of programs delivered to indigenous communities. Misunderstandings and tensions can arise even with goodwill on both sides; they can "talk past each other" (Metge & Kinloch, 1978). For example, negotiating an evaluation by using a culturally compatible process can take a long time and typically much longer than is planned for by a government agency that runs on a different timeline. It is also challenging for evaluation contractors responsible for delivering within the specific deadlines in a contract. However, when the time and effort is put into following a process that has cultural integrity, there are lasting benefits in terms of delivering an evaluation that meets the needs of both the commissioning agency and the groups whose needs the policy or program is intended to serve.

Commissioners of evaluations in the government's sector have responsibility for ensuring that evaluations provide good value for money and produce the best information possible within the constraints of the available resources. This value needs to apply to all stakeholders and taxpaying citizens, and culturally relevant evaluations are therefore essential rather than optional if all groups of people are to be valued and treated equitably. Fortunately, in recent years in New Zealand, there has been a growing interest and, with an increasing number of evaluators, an eagerness to learn more about cultures other than their own and how these can shape evaluation approaches.

DISCUSSION AND CONCLUSION

This chapter has focused on several elements of the evaluation function as it is created and placed in organizations and considered a number of issues that can arise in commissioning and contracting evaluations. The importance of cultural context and the ways in which this can affect evaluation practice has also been discussed with reference to New Zealand.

One of the threads running through these areas is the need for evaluation commissioners and practitioners to effectively navigate and facilitate evaluation processes through the various challenges discussed in this chapter, with the aim of making the products as credible and useful as possible. Some emphasis has been on the relational factors involved as well as those that involve resourcing and decision making. Evaluation is a social as much as a technical exercise, and the quality of the relationships between those people must be recognized and sustained.

This chapter has discussed a range of issues and considerations in relation to the management of evaluation and some of the strategies that can be used in addressing them; one of which is illustrated with a case example.

Some challenges relate to the location of the evaluation function within an organization and the resources allocated, others relate more to the purpose and processes followed in an evaluation. The culture and values within an organization also come to the fore in evaluation and affect the ways in which it is perceived and used. This can include the issues of independence and credibility, as well as the quality assessment of evaluations.

The role of the evaluation manager in the facilitation of evaluation processes and in dealing with the many issues that can arise is critical to the success of an evaluation. Awareness of common pitfalls and an understanding of good practice standards assist a manager in dealing with problems effectively. Where evaluation spans different cultural settings, an awareness of the importance of culture and how this can influence the choice of evaluation approach as well as its relevance and usefulness to key stakeholders has also been emphasized. The fundamental concern is to assure them that evaluations are both meaningful and useful, not only to the commissioners but also to those whose lives are likely to be most affected by decisions informed by the evaluation.

DISCUSSION QUESTIONS

1. To what extent do you think the credibility of evaluations relates to the independence of the evaluation function and why?

2. The chapter suggests several steps that an evaluation manager can take to ensure a successful evaluation. What else can be added to ensure optimal utilization of the findings?

3. What role do you see for evaluation standards in contracting evaluations and why?

4. How can an evaluation's sensitivity to cultural context(s) be enhanced in your country to thus reassure a meaningful and useful evaluation for all stakeholders?

NOTE

1. The Treaty of Waitangi was signed in 1840 between the British Crown and Māori Chiefs and is the founding document of New Zealand as a nation-state.

REFERENCES

Barbier, J. C., & Hawkins, P. (Eds.). (2012). *Evaluation cultures: Sense-making in complex times*. New Brunswick, NJ: Transaction.

Boyle, R., & Lemaire, D. (Eds.). (1999). *Building effective evaluation capacity: Lessons from practice*. New Brunswick, NJ: Transaction.

Cracknell, B. (2000). *Evaluating development aid: Issues, problems and solutions*. London, UK: Sage.

Greene, J. C., Boyce, A., & Ahn, J. (2011). *A values-engaged, educative approach for evaluating educational programs: A guidebook for practice*. Champaign: University of Illinois.

Hawkins, P. (2003). Contracting evaluation: A tender topic. In N. Lunt, C. Davidson, & K. McKegg (Eds.), *Evaluating policy and practice: A New Zealand reader*. Auckland, New Zealand: Pearson Education New Zealand.

Hawkins, P. (2012). Successful evaluation management: Engaging mind and spirit. *Canadian Journal of Program Evaluation, 25*(3), 27–36.

House, E., & Howe, K. (1999). *Values in evaluation and social research*. Thousand Oaks, CA: Sage.

Mayne, J. (2012). Independence in evaluation and the role of culture. In J. C. Barbier & P. Hawkins (Eds.), *Evaluation cultures: Sense-making in complex times* (pp. 105–138). New Brunswick, NJ: Transaction.

Metge, J., & Kinloch, P. (1978). *Talking past each other: Problems of cross-cultural communication*. Wellington, New Zealand: Victoria University Press.

Morra-Imas, L., & Rist, R. (2009). *The road to results: Designing and conducting effective development evaluations*. Washington, DC: World Bank. Retrieved from http://www.worldbank.org/r2r

Organisation for Economic Co-operation and Development (OECD). (1991). *Principles for the evaluation of development assistance*. Paris, France: Author.

Organisation for Economic Co-operation and Development (OECD). (2010a). *DAC quality standards for development evaluation*. Paris, France: Development Assistance Committee. Retrieved February 18, 2011, from http://www.oecd.org/dataoecd/55/0/44798177.pdf

Organisation for Economic Co-operation and Development (OECD). (2010b). *Evaluation in development agencies, better aid*. Paris, France: Author. Retrieved February 18, 2011, from http://dx.doi.org/10.1787/9789284094857-en

Patton, M. Q. (2011). *Developmental evaluation: Applying complexity concepts to enhance innovation and use*. New York, NY: Guilford Press.

Pawson, R., & Tilley, N. (1997). *Realistic evaluation*. London, UK: Sage.

Picciotto, R. (2003). International trends and development evaluation: The need for ideas. *American Journal of Evaluation, 24*(2), 227–234.

Rist, R. C., & Stame, N. (Eds.). (2006). *From studies to streams: Managing evaluation systems*. New Brunswick, NJ: Transaction.

Smith, L. T. *Decolonizing methodologies: Research and indigenous peoples*. (1999). London, UK: Zed Books.

Thompson-Robinson, M., Hopson, R., & SenGupta, S. (Eds.). (2004). *In search of cultural competence in evaluation: Toward principles and practices: No. 102. New directions in evaluation*. San Francisco, CA: Jossey-Bass.

UN Development Programme (UNDP). (2006). *Planning and managing an evaluation*. New York, NY: Author. Retrieved July 10, 2011, from http://web.undp.org/evaluation/handbook

UN Population Fund (UNFPA). (2007). *Tool no. 5: Planning and managing an evaluation: Program managers planning, monitoring and evaluation toolkit*. New York, NY: Author. Retrieved February 20, 2011, from http://www.unfpa.org/monitoring/toolkit/5managing.pdf

Wehipeihana, N., Davidson, J., McKegg, K., & Shanker, V. (2010). What does it take to do evaluation in communities and cultural contexts other than our own? *Journal of Multi-Disciplinary Evaluation, 6*(13), 182–192.

CHAPTER 4

INSTITUTIONALIZATION AND EVALUATION CULTURE—INTERPLAY BETWEEN THE ONE AND THE OTHER

Lessons From the Swiss Federal Office of Public Health (FOPH)

Marlène Läubli Loud

CHAPTER TOPICS

- Interrelations between evaluation institutionalization, evaluation capacity, and evaluation culture
- The case of institutionalization and cultural development of evaluation in a public administration agency
- The role of an internal evaluation service in establishing the framework and building capacity and developing evaluation culture at an organizational level

---

There has been much effort over the last 20 years or so to institutionalize evaluation so that it becomes a sustainable process for analyzing and reporting on the effectiveness of public actions. Indeed, the evaluation of public policies and actions is becoming very much an "institutionalized" practice in many developed countries and in a growing number of developing countries as well. It would appear that evaluation (and monitoring) is being

---

Disclaimer: Any views and opinions expressed by the author do not necessarily reflect the views and opinions of the Swiss Federal Office of Public Health.

integrated as part and parcel of "good management," "results-based management," and "new public management." Program donors, funders, and politicians alike expect to be informed about the effective and efficient use of public and private funds.

But does institutionalizing evaluation guarantee its effective use? What can help optimize organizational use of evaluation? Developing an evaluation culture within an organization is arguably necessary for optimizing evaluation's use; it signifies commitment and an understanding of the benefits evaluation can offer. So does institutionalization help or hinder the development of an evaluation culture and in what ways? What is the interplay between institutionalization and culture? This chapter explores the interrelationship between these two notions and examines the value of both for providing favorable conditions for enhancing evaluation practice and use.

First, the notions of "institutionalization" and "culture" are briefly examined before embarking on a brief review of evaluation's development in the Swiss federal administration. Some of the challenges and strategies adopted for introducing evaluation into a federal agency will then be examined in order to compare and contrast achievements with the relevant indicators. The chapter concludes with some reflections about partnering institutionalization and culture and the contributing role of an internal Evaluation Unit in bringing this about.

EVALUATION INSTITUTIONALIZATION AND CULTURE: WHAT DO THEY MEAN?

The institutionalization of evaluation as a theme is not new; Guba and Stufflebeam discussed the concept within the framework of the U.S. educational system more than 40 years ago (Guba & Stufflebeam, 1970, and revised it later, Stufflebeam, 1997). Today, the term is associated in the literature with evaluation in a broader range of domains. Consequently, the number of relevant publications is on the increase, particularly in relation to cooperation and development (e.g., Balthasar, 2006, 2007; Jacob, 2005a, 2005b, 2005c; The World Bank, 2009; Varone & Jacob, 2002; and Widmer & Neuenschwander, 2004).

According to Hartz (1999), institutionalizing evaluation means its integration "into an organizational system whose behavior it is capable of influencing" (p. 2). Similarly, Mayne (1992) suggests that institutionalization requires a minimum set of policy guidelines, especially with regard to *structures* (setting out the purpose and objectives of evaluation for the organization and resources attributed to its practice); *practice* or types of evaluation (e.g., formative, summative, etc.)

methods, approaches, and quality standards; and *utilization* (establishing responsibilities for managing results). In other words, evaluation has to be integrated into an organizational framework or foundation that provides all the rules, resources, and communication mechanisms to support its application (e.g., an evaluation system).

Bussmann (2008), however, suggests that for evaluation to be institutionalized, it needs to be legitimized and therefore provided with a legal basis. In Switzerland, he says, "Parliament plays an important role in evaluation, which corresponds to its law-making function. Around 90 legal acts (laws, ordinances, etc.) carry evaluation clauses (i.e. obligations to carry out an evaluation)" (p. 499). Switzerland also has a constitutional article for ensuring that the effectiveness of federal measures is assessed (Article 170 of Federal Constitution).

Similarly, Furubo, Rist, and Sandahl (2002) used nine indicators in their comparative analysis of 21 countries and three international organizations with regard to levels of evaluation "maturity" and "cultural" development. Of these, three refer specifically to having institutional arrangements and procedures in place in government, parliament, and the supreme audit institutions to ensure that evaluation findings are put to (policy) use. Although they do not refer to any "legal clauses" per se, they suggest that such institutional arrangements are "a form of guarantee that utilization—at least in formal terms—will take place" (p. 8).

Certainly, underlying the notion of institutionalization is that evaluation findings are discussed and disseminated within and beyond the commissioning organization and are ultimately used in decision making. Indeed, according to Jacob (2005b), an evaluation culture mainly depends on the degree to which it is being used to formulate and implement policies (p. 53) and strategies or program.

In short, for me, institutionalizing evaluation implies having a system of formal arrangements and procedures in place to support commissioning and carrying out evaluations and, ultimately, *using* the findings. The system is developed in response to a legal or institutional requirement to evaluate the effectiveness of public or institutional policies and actions.

Culture, however, is a more qualitative notion concerning values and beliefs. References to evaluation culture and evaluation capacity building are far more prolific and long standing in the literature (e.g., Mayne, 2008; Mihalache, 2010; Owen, 2003; Patton, 2008; Russ-Eft & Preskill, 2009; Toulemonde, 2000; and Neubecker, Ripley, and Russon's Chapter 9, "Building for Utilization," in this book). But the delineation between *culture* and *capacity building* (and to a certain degree even *institutionalization*) is not so clear as DePeuter and Pattyn (2008),

Kuzman (2009), and Labin, Duffy, Meyers, Wandersman, and Lesesne (2012) point out. When trying to identify the interrelationship between *evaluation capacity* and *evaluation culture,* researchers in their extensive reviews of the literature concluded that there was little agreement but a rich heterogeneity *of meaning and proposed indicators.* "Every particular source approaches evaluation capacity and/or evaluation culture from a particular perspective" (DePeuter & Pattyn, p. 3). Indeed, for some authors institutionalization and culture are also conceived as one (e.g., Furubo et al., 2002). The definitions put forward by DePeuter and Pattyn also lack clarity. Culture, they say, is "the pattern of shared beliefs and values of policy makers and evaluators which provide them with rules for behaviour that lead towards a practice of evaluation." But evaluation capacity is more concerned with "the operational aspects and components deemed necessary for conducting an evaluation" (p. 10). In this sense, evaluation capacity is strongly linked to the evaluation practice itself. Yet Boyle, Lemaire, and Rist (1999), for example, argue that evaluation capacity is quite different from evaluation practice.

However, the aim of this paper is not to provide any conclusive definitions but a working definition for framing the later discussion. From my perspective, therefore, and for the purpose of this chapter, evaluation culture refers to a shared set of ideas, values, and beliefs at an organizational level about the evaluation's role, functions, practice, and use of the knowledge generated through evaluations. *Capacity,* I would argue, has more to do with the measures and strategies used to establish "good practices" for commissioning, doing, and using the evaluations. In this sense, institutionalization could be considered one of the measures that can be used to build capacity. But whether or not institutionalization guarantees effective use of the knowledge is questionable (e.g., Constandriopoulos, 1999).

INSTITUTIONALIZING EVALUATION IN SWITZERLAND'S FEDERAL ADMINISTRATION

Switzerland is a multiethnic, multilingual, multicultural, and multireligious nation shaped by the will of its people. It has been a federal state since 1848. Its political system comprises three levels: the Confederation, the cantons (26), and the communes. The Confederation has specific responsibilities in a limited number of areas such as foreign policy, national security, monetary policy, environment, transportation, and health, which are explicit in the Federal Constitution. Federal responsibilities are administered by the Federal Chancellery and seven departments, which in turn are responsible for some 90 federal agencies. Each canton has its own constitution, parliament, government, and courts. Each canton has a number of political communes. The cantons determine the degree of autonomy of their communes and their responsibilities can therefore vary quite considerably. In addition to the tasks allocated to them both by their canton and the Confederation, the communes also have their own powers in various areas.

Since the late 1980s, the evaluation of federal measures and activities has gradually been institutionalized. The Federal Department of Justice and Police has been a significant player in developing the legal framework to support the systematic evaluation of federal actions. The new Federal Constitution of 1999 introduced an article (article 170) stating, "The Federal Assembly shall ensure that the effectiveness of federal measures are evaluated" (The Federal Authorities of the Swiss Confederation, 1999). Essentially, there are currently two central agencies responsible for overseeing and evaluating federal policies; the Parliamentary Control of the Administration (PCA) was established in 1990 and is responsible to the Federal Assembly in matters of performance audits and evaluations. It supports Parliament's monitoring and evaluation of the measures taken by the federal administration. The Evaluation Unit within the Swiss Federal Audit Office assesses the execution and impact of federal measures but particularly those that have financial significance. A careful balance of "top-down" and "bottom-up" processes has also been put into place to "empower" the federal administration to develop its own practice, experience, and evaluation system. Each of the federal agencies can therefore determine how to report on the effectiveness of its measures and actions. The following section considers the challenges and strategies used by one federal agency to respond to the task.

A FEDERAL AGENCY'S EXPERIENCE WITH INSTITUTIONALIZING EVALUATION AND DEVELOPING AN EVALUATION CULTURE

This section starts with describing the organizational context and the development over time of an evaluation service within a particular federal agency in Switzerland. This descriptive part is then completed with a short account of the service's main functions, tasks, and responsibilities as they are today.

The Federal Agency in Context

The Swiss Federal Office of Public Health (FOPH) is part of the Federal Department of Home Affairs. It is the national authority on health matters. It also represents Switzerland in international organizations and in dealings with other countries. The Federal Constitution, adopted in 1848, provides the federal state with very limited responsibility in the field of health. As such, the cantons have a high degree of autonomy. The FOPH therefore shares responsibility with the cantons for public health and the development of a national health policy.

Prior to the HIV/AIDS pandemic, the FOPH had less than 100 employees. Its traditional tasks were to protect the population against health hazards and oversee the cantons' implementation of federal health legislation. With the onset of HIV/AIDS, it took a lead role in developing national prevention and health promotion strategies. During the 1990s, the health, accident, and military insurance systems were also integrated into "normal business." Consequently, the number of staff grew rapidly over a relatively short period, from under 100 to more than 500 today.

The FOPH's principal aim is to promote and maintain the good health of all people living in Switzerland. Its tasks and responsibilities cover a wide range of health themes including the following:

- Providing consumer protection (in relation to food, chemicals, therapeutic products, cosmetics, and utility goods)
- Monitoring communicable diseases, food safety, and chemical and radiological protection
- Developing and overseeing national strategies designed to prevent a number of communicable diseases, reduce substance dependence, and promote healthy lifestyles
- Regulating the basic and postgraduate education of doctors, dentists, pharmacists, and veterinary surgeons and awarding the relevant Swiss degrees
- Legislating on epidemiology, biological safety, research on humans and transplantation medicine, and supervising activities in these areas

The Time and Place of Evaluation Within the Agency

The FOPH plays a role in both formulating policy and guiding implementation. It takes a primary role in preparing public health legislation for Parliament; the draft laws are subjected to a wide and formalized consultation process. Once a law has been adopted, its implementation is mainly left to the cantons, municipalities, and nongovernmental partners. The FOPH therefore has a particular interest in using evaluation to gather evidence on the implementation, effects, and effectiveness of public health policies.

Figure 4.1 Evaluation's Optimal Contribution Within the Policy Cycle

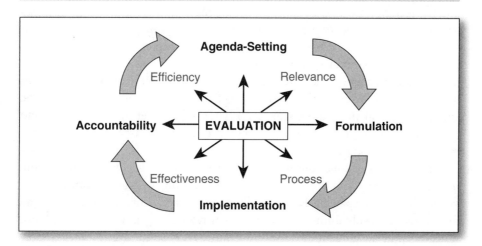

Source: Adapted from *Guidelines for health programme and project evaluation planning,* Swiss Federal Office of Public Health, 1997, p. 19. Used with permission.

Figure 4.1 is an idealized, but somewhat simplified, representation of where evaluation can contribute within the policy cycle. For example, evaluation can be used for prioritizing issues to be put on the political agenda, but it can also have an important role to play in the implementation and accountability phases—for example, to determine to what degree the proposed strategy is (still) relevant. In the FOPH, evaluation is more systematically used in strategic planning (formulation) and operational implementation. For example, many of the prevention strategies and programs are often rolled over to the next four-year legislative cycle; information on weaknesses and potential areas for improvement is equally as important as effectiveness.

Taking Evaluation From an Isolated Activity to an Organization-Wide Service

The Early Years: An Isolated Activity

The FOPH has had an evaluation tradition since 1987, well before the appearance of article 170. In its efforts to combat the HIV/AIDS epidemic and the associated problems linked to the use of illicit drugs, the FOPH developed national prevention strategies to be implemented by cantonal and municipal authorities, and nongovernmental organizations (NGOs). Due to the sensitive and pioneering nature of this work (e.g., promotion of condom use as opposed to abstention or fidelity, needle exchange programs in prisons, medical prescription of heroin), it was agreed from the beginning that commissioning evaluations to external specialists would better ensure their credibility. They addressed a broad range of interest groups (to include politicians, NGOs, cantonal health authorities, the media, target populations, public or taxpayers, special interest groups, and researchers). Thus, while their primary task was to judge effectiveness, they were also required to highlight areas where improvements could be made.

These strategic evaluations were commissioned to a sole supplier, a university institute for social and preventive medicine, covering a period of three to four years and over a span of 17 years. To meet the needs of the different target audiences, the evaluations were comprehensive (taking into account process, outcome, and the epidemiological and behavioral changes over time), comprising multistudies (to analyze specific aspects of the prevention strategies) and using mixed methods. Feedback from the individual studies was provided at the end of each. A synthesis of the overarching lessons drawn from the multistudies was reported at three- to four-year intervals.

The lessons drawn from both the individual and synthesis studies were presented and discussed with the FOPH director and the relevant internal partners, before being presented to the health minister. Press conferences released the news to the public (and politicians) at large. The reports, together with a management statement, were distributed far and wide both within and outside Switzerland.

At a later stage, from 1993 onward, once an internal evaluation service was established, the communication strategy was further developed to *emphasize utilization*: (a) by organizing workshops—to which cantonal and NGO partners were invited—to deliberate on the findings and decide on what actions needed to be taken and (b) by producing different media and formats to report and discuss findings with different audiences. For example, the findings from the evaluation of a project that introduced sterile needle dispensers for drug users in prisons were presented in brochure format and used in training sessions with prison wardens. An HIV/AIDS prevention campaign poster used humor to report the increased use of condoms to the general public and thereby demonstrate the successes of one of the prevention strategy's main objectives. The positive results—increased protective behavior and the decline in new HIV infections—coupled with a wide-reaching communication strategy helped legitimate controversial prevention strategies.

The Emergence of an Internal Evaluation Service

The AIDS and drugs sections staff lacked experience in the commissioning of evaluations and the time and expertise needed to oversee and manage them. For example, the ownership of intellectual property compared with data ownership was not sufficiently discussed or agreed on, the external evaluation team tended to take the lead in the design of the proposed studies and questions, and no terms of reference were drawn up since the studies were contracted out to a sole supplier. In 1992, the Prevention Division was reorganized to include a specialist section (Research, Evaluation, and Training) and evaluation specialists were engaged (150%). The "purchasers" continued to finance the evaluation studies and fund the specialist staff by allocating a proportion of their annual *program* budgets. The amount could therefore vary from year to year.

With the creation of an internal evaluation section, a change of management procedures took place. The time period for all *new* evaluation contracts was gradually reduced to a maximum of two years (although there can still be exceptions), a system of competitive tender was introduced to foster the development of a critical mass of evaluation specialists, partnerships were forged with a range of different institutions—both private bureaus and universities, a database of potential public health evaluators was created, and a set of procedures and standards for the FOPH was provided in the form of "guidelines" and checklists (Swiss FOPH, 1997). A definition of *evaluation*, its purpose and function, was included in the guidelines, as was a glossary of evaluation terms and their meaning. As such, it was hoped that it would develop a common understanding of what evaluation was and what could be expected. Such regulations, procedures, and mechanisms helped build on the existing culture and provided a more formalized, overarching evaluation framework.

But for many years, evaluation remained an isolated activity within one of the several business units. It was generally considered of little direct interest to anyone outside the prevention field and thought to be an expensive activity, even a luxury, particularly in times of economic hardship. However, even though evaluation remained a priority for the prevention field it came under threat several times during FOPH-wide or divisional reorganizations.

External Factors Contributing to Evaluation's Organizational Institutionalization

Although there were already several legal clauses in place to support and justify the use of evaluation for specific health issues, the introduction of the Constitution's Article 170 provided a general legal framework for the federal administration. It also provided an external pressure for generating executive interest in evaluation. Evaluation was becoming a "must." In 2001, therefore, a specialist *Centre de competences en evaluation* (CCE) was set up by the executive to provide an organizational-wide evaluation service. It reported to the head of Management Services, was allocated 4.6 person years, and provided with its own, dedicated budget. As such, the executive determined a strategic role for evaluation and its in-house institutionalization. The CCE drew up a strategic framework (evaluation system) that set out the basic principles on an evaluation's utility and functions as well as the procedures needed to ensure its application. It was approved by the office's executive and provided the CCE with an entry card to new internal clients.

Following another major internal reorganization three years later, the CCE was moved from its executive location to a business unit. It was merged with research management and became a service unit rather than a competence center. However, its attachment to the newly formed Health Policy Unit has helped integrate evaluation into strategic planning and health policy development. It has kept its independent budget although the percentage of staff exclusively working in evaluation activities has been reduced to 3.8 person years.

The Internal Evaluation Services Unit: Functions, Tasks, and Responsibilities

The Evaluation Services Unit (ESU)[1] is responsible for all evaluation-related issues. Its main role is to commission external evaluations on behalf of its internal partners and then manage the contracts; occasionally, it is asked to conduct internal evaluations as well. It ensures that evaluations are designed to render judgment about the relevance, effectiveness, efficiency, coherence, and, sometimes, the sustainability of the strategies and measures developed and launched by the FOPH. Evaluation therefore has four key functions:

1. *As a strategic tool:* Provides evidence to the FOPH's executive and specialist units for strategic development

2. *As a learning tool:* Helps improve performance and effectiveness; in its analysis, evaluation highlights the strengths and weaknesses of the interventions and suggests how and where improvements can be made

3. *As a source of knowledge and expertise*: Strengthens the public health knowledge base about what works, how, under what conditions, why, for whom, and at what price

4. *To ensure transparency*: Makes all evaluation reports public to help clarify and improve understanding of Swiss public health policy, its measures, actions, and effectiveness (for all reports and more on evaluation issues, see www.health-evaluation.admin.ch)

The principle of a multiyear (four-year) evaluation plan is a more recent phenomenon. Evaluation requests from the various sections and divisions are prioritized by consensus within their business unit before being presented for executive approval. The criteria applied are the urgency of the public health issue or its relevance to the FOPH's strategic objectives. The four-year plan is reviewed and revised annually to develop or delete the proposed studies.

The Six-Step Commissioning Process

For each study, the ESU develops the focus and questions in partnership with the requesting internal partner (see Encouraging Greater and Wider Participation in the Evaluation Process subsection later in this chapter for stakeholder involvement issues). The terms of reference are used not only to clarify and agree on responsibilities and tasks but also, more importantly, to determine the potential audiences, what can be expected from the evaluations, and by when. The selection of an external evaluation team is a joint decision between the internal partner and the ESU, the ESU being essentially responsible for methodological issues. The ESU takes full responsibility for the contractual arrangements, overseeing the evaluation process, the quality control, and final acceptance of the report. The internal partners are kept informed of progress throughout the study and review the draft report for possible inaccuracies. But the final report remains the responsibility of the ESU; this includes its dissemination and publication on the website as well as arrangements for presentations and workshop discussions on how to use the information. An action plan for using the findings is drawn up through discussion between the ESU and the "purchasing" internal partner. The latter remains responsible, however, for actually "using," or applying, the findings and recommendations. The ESU has more recently begun the systematic monitoring of partners' use of evaluation findings after at least one year's interval. Figure 4.2 illustrates the ESU's six-step commissioning process. The guidelines and checklists previously developed (Swiss FOPH, 1997) are systematically used by the ESU, internal partners, and evaluators alike to steer the process.

The commissioning process has therefore been institutionalized. Encouraging a partnership in designing the study and selecting the external evaluators

Figure 4.2 The FOPH Six-Step Commissioning Process

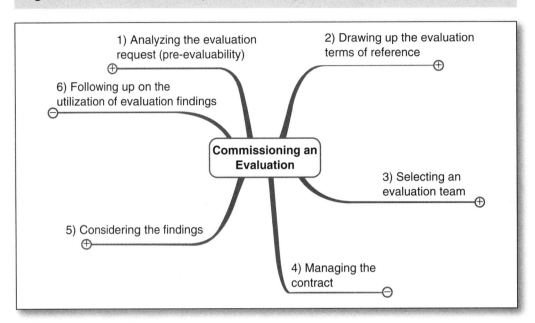

ensures there is shared "ownership" over the process and product. On the few occasions that the ESU itself commissioned a study, little use was made of the report or its findings.

The ESU is now integrated into the FOPH's four-year strategic planning process so that the knowledge generated through evaluations can be taken into account.

The Challenges and Strategies Being Used to Develop an Organization-Wide Evaluation Culture

It took many years for the executive to officially recognize that evaluation could be a relevant and useful tool for the *whole* of the FOPH. Similarly, the principle of providing dedicated, centralized human and financial resources that were independent of the strategic and operational decision makers took considerable time and energy to establish. But these are only some of the indicators that signal the existence of institutionalization and capacity building (of evaluation) and not necessarily an established culture (e.g., Labin et al., 2012). So what else has been and is being done toward building an evaluation culture, and has a genuine culture now been developed? The following section outlines the challenges that had to be overcome and some of the strategies that have or are being adopted.

The Challenges

Since 1992, there have been three major office reorganizations and numerous minor ones within the major business units and divisions. There have also been significant budget cutbacks and a moratorium on engaging new staff. For a decade or more, there has been a general feeling among FOPH staff of having to do more with less. So for each individual, time and prioritizing one's use of time is critical. Participating in evaluation activities, such as developing evaluation questions or the logic of interventions, is a time-consuming process often seen by senior or middle managers to be of secondary importance. Yet as Patton (2008), Love (1993), Stufflebeam and Shinkfield (2007), U.S. General Accounting Office (2003), and many others have convincingly argued, it is through engaging partners in the process of evaluation that a real culture can be developed.

A second major challenge is the office's actual organization. There are four main business areas and 15 divisions, all of which, given the variety of health themes for which they are responsible, operate relatively independently. There is an executive staff comprising the director, vice directors (heads of each of the business areas), and several service division heads such as management services and international affairs; the director has overall decisional power. The strategic objectives are developed in a bottom-up and top-down process and tend to reflect the concerns of the specific units rather than the more general, common issues. The challenge for evaluation is to engage the FOPH's senior managers in themes of an overarching relevance and concern. One possibility, for example, would be to evaluate the different arrangements that exist in all the various FOPH units for delegating specific tasks to others. (The term *delegation* is used here to mean when all or part of the functions and/or tasks assigned to it by the legislative or executive branches are transferred to a third party.) This is done not only to reduce the burden on the FOPH for its ever-increasing workload but also to involve important stakeholders in its policies and strategies and extend its spheres of influence. However, this is not without risk to its authority and autonomy. The intention of such an evaluation would be to study the different arrangements and determine what works, for whom, why, under what conditions, and at what costs. However, such a proposal has not as yet been met with much enthusiasm.

A third challenge is the relationship between an evaluation need and the nature of the business units. While evaluation has proven useful and relevant for innovations and work of an experimental nature (mainly in the prevention field), its perceived utility to other business areas, such as consumer protection or epidemiology, was not immediately apparent.

A fourth important challenge is keeping up with a constantly changing environment, which results from changes in the political climate, structural reorganizations, and staff turnover. It is not entirely uncommon for an evaluation to be proposed and commissioned by a middle or senior manager who is no longer the relevant commissioner when the findings are up for discussion. The question of ownership and support for any further action is critical here. Equally, the expanding business areas and subsequent reorganizations have meant that evaluation has been under threat on several occasions. The challenge therefore is to constantly adapt the strategies being used to optimize evaluation's utility.

Finally, throughout the years, the specialist Evaluation Unit has always been located in a subordinate position reporting to the executive through a senior manager. As a result, the image, relevance, and utility of evaluation are reported through the mediation of another's empathy or bias as the case may be. This weakens its power to influence and shape an evaluation culture, especially at the top managerial level. (See Hawkins's Chapter 3, "Evaluation Management," in this book for more on the value of independence for internal Evaluation Units.)

Strategies to Address the Challenges

The ESU has been using various capacity-building strategies to respond to the above challenges. For the purpose of this chapter, it is not possible to describe each and all of these in detail. The four most important of these for engaging organizational commitment and establishing a genuine evaluation culture are discussed below: *communicating* good practices of evaluation's utility, encouraging wider and deeper *participation* in the evaluation process, improving *credibility* and relevance, and informal and formal *training*.

Communicating good practices of utility. In order to engage new business units, initially, the "users," or clients, from the "old" areas (from the prevention field) were called upon to present examples of their successes—how they had used evaluation findings to defend or adapt a particular strategy. Cummings and Worley (2009, p. 206) suggest that disseminating the utility of a change from one unit to another helps reduce counterattacks from the organization as a whole and builds consensus and commitment to the change.

Yet, as much as a strategy of "demonstrating good practices" to promote adoption has advantages, it was not sufficient in itself. As mentioned earlier, new clients argued against evaluation's relevance or utility to such fields as regulation and consumer protection; it was not essential to "justify" such work. Here the federal "institutionalization" card was able to come into its own. Using the new constitutional article requiring a judgment on the effectiveness of measures as mandatory, the office director encouraged each of the business units to experience at least one evaluation. Subsequently, within two years, each had commissioned at least one such study.

The established good practice used in the prevention field for communicating and using evaluation findings (which included drawing up and implementing a work plan to translate evaluation findings and recommendations into action) was systematically advocated for all new evaluations of *strategic significance*. Torres, Preskill, and Piontek (1996) argue that the main objective here for the evaluator (the ESU in this case) is to facilitate organizational learning through engaging partners in face-to-face discussions aimed at stimulating "inquiry, reflection, dialogue and action planning." This is certainly the objective of the six-step commissioning process. But as for reflective "action planning" together with partners, it was found that this cannot always be done immediately when the report is finished. Several weeks are needed to deliberate on how to proceed, even longer when the process is expanded to include external stakeholders. Over time, the ESU learned that the longer the time lapse, the greater the chance that the opportunity for such collaborative action planning is lost (e.g., due to other work pressures or lack of ownership because of middle to senior management staff changes). As a result, in such cases a less participatory approach has been put into place; at the very least, approximately one year later, the ESU asks internal partners to report on how they put the lessons drawn from evaluation findings to best use. These reports provide a brief account of utility to senior management or to the Federal Department of Home Affairs. Such practice has been especially useful when the need for evaluation has been called into question (e.g., during a major reorganization).

Another way for communicating the benefits of evaluation is through institutionalizing its use in strategic and program planning. For example, planners are systematically asked to demonstrate the integration of previous evaluation lessons in their plans for the next phase. Having a member of the ESU take part in the process reinforces this "rule" and also provides further opportunity for discussion and debate.

The four-year evaluation plan provides another ideal mechanism for engaging senior managers in "inquiry, reflection, dialogue, and action planning." Through their involvement in the plan's development, they are compelled to take an active interest in the number and nature of evaluations being commissioned. They have an interest in seeing that their particular business unit is benefiting from the funds available for evaluation and that the studies are relevant to their unit's strategic objectives. But it is through the, albeit occasional, presentation of findings, key policy, and strategic messages that most interest is being generated.

Encouraging greater and wider participation in the evaluation process. It has been argued earlier that organizations can best profit from evaluations if an "evaluation culture" is established and continually developed (e.g., Leeuw, Rist, & Sonnischsen, 1994; Mayne, 2008). But, as previously said, learning from findings is only part of the whole; most learning takes place through integration of stakeholders (internal and external partners) into the evaluation process itself (e.g., Fetterman & Wandersman, 2005; Patton, 2008). The formalized six-step commissioning process ensures the integration of internal, client partners. But for external stakeholders, at what stage should which steps be integrated, and what kind of integration is feasible in a federal agency? In short, how deep and how wide should their participation be?

For the FOPH, the involvement of *external* stakeholders in an evaluation and the intensity of their involvement depend on the importance or sensitivity of the particular strategy in question. A recent example is the evaluation of new financing arrangements in the hospital sector. In such cases, an evaluation advisory committee is systematically set up by the ESU and its internal, client partners to bring the major stakeholders together at the beginning (to comment on the evaluation focus and questions), during the evaluation (to help locate and/or access data, and, where relevant, report back on important information), and at the end (to deliberate over and contextualize the conclusions and recommendations), and finally, to assist with translating findings into action. External stakeholders in this case include, for example, Santé Suisse who represents the health insurance companies, the Swiss Medical Association, and the H+, an association representing hospitals in Switzerland. This practice has been successful in fostering a collective ownership of the evaluation design and procedure and in highlighting contextual issues and data sources that would not otherwise be apparent to the evaluation team.

But there is simply not the time or the will from the FOPH to engage a wide group of external or internal stakeholders *throughout the whole process for every evaluation*. Nevertheless, it is common practice for the ESU to set up an internal advisory group to follow the study's progress from beginning to end. Experience has shown that prudence has to be applied, however, in the breadth of internal partners taking part. In view of work pressures, only those having a direct interest in the object of evaluation will give up their time to take part in this group. In cases where external partners are practically involved in, for example, the implementation of a program or measure, at the very least, their participation is invited in discussions about the practical implications of the evaluation findings.

Much effort has gone into raising awareness about the benefits of evaluation among internal partners in other ways:

- The ESU has encouraged self-evaluations for some minor operational issues, providing consultancy and methodological support. But with limited staff capacity, the ESU can help only a very restricted number of requests per year.
- The ESU systematically presents its services to all newly employed junior and senior managers.
- The ESU takes an active part in strategic planning and developing the four-year evaluation plan in collaboration with its internal partners.
- A series of discussions takes place between the ESU and the head of the unit responsible for the strategy or program being evaluated to ensure that more strategic questions are included.

Improving credibility and relevance. Quality evaluations are arguably needed to ensure credibility (e.g., Bussmann, 2008; Mayne, 1992, 2008). Equally, for evaluations to be credible, they need to be relevant to users' needs (Patton, 2008). Hence, a number of measures have been put into place to ensure the quality, credibility, and relevance of the commissioned evaluations. The most significant are the following:

- *Quality control and (limited) meta-evaluation.* When a draft report is submitted to the ESU, it conducts its own evaluation of the evaluation as a quality assurance measure. The checklists used to support the process are based on the quality standards of the Swiss Evaluation Society (SEVAL) (Widmer, Landert, & Bachmann, 2000). The quality control is complemented by an evaluation of the relevant internal clients' appreciation of the process but more particularly on the perceived utility of the report. Preskill and Torres (1999) and Stufflebeam and Shinkfield (2007) have advocated the value of meta-evaluations to ensure credibility and quality. However, while it is beyond the time and scope of the ESU's resources to enter into the full meta-evaluation they describe, the limited version has proven useful for negotiating quality issues with evaluators and internal partners alike.

- *A system of competitive tender* has been in place for many years. It was introduced by the ESU before becoming an obligation under the General Agreement on Tariffs and Trade (GATT agreement). The GATT rules are now systematically applied in commissioning evaluations. However, the ESU's practice has often been to go even further; most evaluations are posted on the Swiss Evaluation Society's (SEVAL's) website and/or sent to all its members, even for contracts below the minimal sum. But what has this achieved? The original idea was to help develop a mass critique of evaluators and thereby eventually enable choice among a wider pool of competent evaluators. Another objective was to stimulate innovate ideas and approaches in response to the terms of reference. In the early years, "expressions of interest" were received from 15 to 20 evaluators with around 10 submitting full proposals. After several years, however, apart from a few exceptions, considerably fewer proposals were being submitted. As a result, the same institutions or private evaluation bureaus were being commissioned over and over again. This poses a real dilemma; on the one hand, competitive tendering has not resulted in more diversity, and on the other hand, due to one or two below-standard studies, the FOPH is hesitant to take any risk and try out new teams. In part, to some degree, this could be due to a lack of innovative thinking on the part of the FOPH; is it asking the same types of questions and favoring the same type of approach? Some evaluators have criticized the FOPH for being too authoritarian in the methodological section of its terms of reference (ToR). Others have welcomed the clarity of the methodological expectations. There seems no obvious answer, but it is a question that the ESU needs to take more seriously.

Informal and formal training. The list of authors advocating the need, strategies, and means for developing capacity and skills within organizations is extensive (e.g., Mayne, 2006; Patton, 2008; Preskill & Torres, 1999). As Hawkins stated in Chapter 3 of this book,

> On the one hand, expertise in a wide range of evaluation approaches is desirable along with sector and context knowledge, and on the other, an "insider's" insight and understanding of the organization is useful, particularly when it comes to interpreting findings and formulating useful recommendations.

It is argued that thinking "evaluatively," that is, learning to inquire, reflect, analyze, and identify key lessons from evaluations, is an all-important process for optimizing evaluation use. The preceding section described how and to what degree internal and external partners take part in the process as a means of encouraging their thinking and acting evaluatively. Other means are also being used, some of which are briefly described below.

As mentioned above, as part of the quality standards and report's metaevaluation processes, the ESU asks its internal clients to comment on the accuracy of the report's first draft. They are also asked to draw out the strategic messages and provide a critical comment on the usefulness of the evaluation and its findings, as well as their preliminary ideas about how the knowledge might be put to best use. Apart from quality issues, from the ESU's point of view, the process is also aimed at helping develop evaluative thinking; internal and ESU staff alike learn to critique and draw out the lessons and key messages from the findings. This appears to be a somewhat difficult task as demonstrated in the variable quality of such commentaries or "prise de position." Only the better ones are posted on the Internet together with the report.

But in general, the learning experience is better demonstrated through other measures, for example, presentations, workshops, face-to-face discussions, and training courses. To support the application of the office's guidelines on evaluation planning (Swiss FOPH, 1997), the ESU organized a limited number of courses on the basic principles of evaluation for internal clients (Läubli Loud, 2004). These were well attended but not continued given the ESU's other work priorities.

As for evaluators themselves, there are professional development courses and more formal basic and further education events being organized by universities and the SEVAL. The ESU has also attempted, and failed, to make its own contribution to professional development. To stimulate new thinking, in the early years, before there was a mass critique of evaluators, occasionally experts from outside of Switzerland were engaged to accompany the Swiss evaluation teams and constructively comment on the approach and methodological problems that arose. These consultants were contracted by the ESU to offer advice in a collegiate manner, both during face-to-face meetings and in writing. Although the intention was supportive, rather than seeing this as an opportunity to debate methodological challenges with peers, the Swiss external evaluation teams felt threatened and the experiment was abandoned.

As for the ESU's own staff, through attending scientific conferences and, where resources permit, professional development events, members are encouraged to keep abreast of theoretical and practical developments in evaluation and continually build upon their expertise. Monthly team discussions were also organized for several years to debate practical and theoretical issues. Some members continue to take part in the SEVAL interest groups and provide input on management issues to university courses.

IS EVALUATION INSTITUTIONALIZED, AND DOES A CULTURE NOW EXIST?

There is no conclusive agreement in the literature about the meaning of institutionalization, capacity, and culture or which indicators can be used to demonstrate each (e.g., Kuzmin, 2009; Labin et al., 2012). This makes the task of assessing the presence of either that much more difficult! However, DePeuter and Pattyn (2008) have clustered the 17 most commonly used indicators and then attempted to distinguish between those relevant to evaluation capacity and culture (p. 11). Even though they note there is still some overlap, I have reordered the original sequence of their cluster groups and explanations to assess the degree of evaluation's institutionalization and cultural development in the FOPH (see Table 4.1).

Table 4.1 Indicators and Evidence of Capacity and Institutionalization and Culture

Indicator	*FOPH Status*
Culture Related	
Awareness of intrinsic value of evaluation: Policymakers have a positive attitude about evaluation.	Continued divisional support is provided for evaluation and, since 2001, executive support. Recognition has been shown for evaluation's instrumental value in judging effectiveness—such as reporting to the Health Minister on the effectiveness of prevention strategies—but also for highlighting where improvements could be made.
Context dependency: Evaluators and evaluation capacity builders take into account environmental circumstances.	This is the principle criterion used to decide which stakeholders should be represented on the advisory committees to ensure that their needs and views are taken into account. Study designs also usually include an analysis of contextual factors and their influence on process and outcome.
Coverage of policy spectrum: Evaluations take place at each stage of the programming cycle. Evaluations are executed in a wide number of policy domains. A regular flow of evaluations is undertaken.	Reference to the reports and ongoing studies listed on the FOPH's website will show that evaluations are commissioned in a wide range of the business areas, that they cover each stage of the program cycle, and that there is a regular flow of evaluations. http://www.bag.admin .ch/evaluation/01759/index.html?lang=en
Demand: A genuine evaluation demand exists (without referring to a specific "driver" for demand).	Between 1986 and 2010, 112 evaluation reports were delivered to the FOPH. They are all available on the FOPH's website. While most have been in the prevention field, since 2001 there has been growing demand from other business areas as well. The four-year evaluation plan helps keep in check the number of studies that can be accommodated given the ESU's available human and financial resources.

Indicator	FOPH Status
Networking: Networking occurs with evaluation stakeholders in the framework of evaluation associations, et cetera. The label also clusters references to a "Community of Practice."	The ESU team are all members of the Swiss Evaluation Society and take part in the Network of Federal Evaluation meetings.
Ownership: Relevant stakeholders are engaged in the evaluation process. Socialization of evaluation occurs in the organization.	As described in the preceding sections, external stakeholders do take part in the evaluation process. Equally, heads of some of the divisions and business units now take an active part in defining and agreeing the terms of reference. Other examples of the socialization of evaluation at an organizational level are provided in the section on "strategies being used to respond to the challenges."
Political Commitment: There exists genuine political guidance to help develop the evaluation function.	There is a legal framework to support evaluation and provide recommendations on how to proceed to ensure that the effectiveness of federal measures is evaluated. For the most part, responsibility lies with the federal agencies for organizing their own evaluations. The Department of Home Affairs has on occasion co-opted the FOPH's evaluation services to commission and manage evaluations on its behalf (e.g., the H1N1 influenza vaccination strategy). Within the FOPH, its leadership has shown commitment to evaluation by establishing the ESU. It agreed to the strategic framework prepared by the ESU, invited the ESU to take part in strategic development, and asked that it provide a four-year plan.
Legal embedding: A legal framework for evaluation exists.	There is a federal constitutional article (article 170), and more than 10 legal clauses that support evaluation in relation to specific aspects of the FOPH's work.
Use: The effective use of evaluations are practiced and applied.	The FOPH's effective use of evaluation has been acclaimed by several authors (e.g., Balthasar, 2006, 2007; Fornerod, 2001; and Widmer & Neuenschwander, 2004). The FOPH's six-step commissioning process ensures that utilization is built into the design and is followed up throughout the evaluation process.

(Continued)

Table 4.1 (Continued)

Indicator	FOPH Status
Capacity and Institutional Related	
Coupling with policy and management decisions: Evaluations are integrated into policy making. Evaluations are linked with management instruments. Evaluations are generated in a timely manner to make it possible to incorporate them into the decision-making process.	Occasionally an evaluation has been specifically planned for its results to be fed into policy decisions (such as for the revision of legislation on aspects of the health system). Evaluations are generally linked into the project management, monitoring, and strategic planning processes. Their time frame is always designed to be compatible with a policy or internal decision-making agenda.
Data collection mechanisms: The availability of data sources is guaranteed through well-functioning data collection systems.	The FOPH ensures access to the data collected by the Federal Office of Statistics, Social Insurances, and other relevant and reliable sources. Where relevant, it funds monitoring studies for particular data needs.
Diffusion and feedback mechanisms: Procedures exist to accumulate evaluation findings and afford smooth dissemination of reports. The existence of well-functioning communication channels spread the evaluations.	While there is currently no systematic measure in place for accumulating evaluation findings, discussions on how this could be done are in progress. But there are tried and tested procedures for disseminating evaluation reports, discussing findings and recommendations, and drawing up an "action plan" to deal with them.
Financial resources: The necessary financial sources are available to conduct evaluations.	A central, dedicated budget supports the FOPH's evaluation services.
Human resource (HR) capacity (internal/external): Sufficient human resources are available to perform an evaluation (at the organizational level, as well as in the broader evaluation market).	The ESU has limited HR to deal with the various internal evaluation demands: commissioning and managing studies, providing evaluation consultancy to internal partners, and occasional conducting of an internal evaluation itself. The number of staff allocated to the service has varied over time. The Swiss Evaluation Society (SEVAL) has more than 400 members, the majority of which are evaluators.

Indicator	FOPH Status
Organizational anchoring of evaluation function: The evaluation function is structurally embedded in the organization (centralized and decentralized). The evaluation function is structurally embedded in a country's governing system (within the legal and/or executive power).	The ESU is centrally funded and services all business areas in the FOPH.
Quality instruments: Mechanisms to secure the quality of the evaluation process exist.	The ESU has its own guidelines and checklists to support a six-step commissioning process for ensuring quality. These are in line with the Quality Standards of the Confederation and the Swiss Evaluation Society.
Skills to perform evaluation: The necessary technical skills to successfully perform an evaluation are available or are being developed (through training, etc.).	The ESU's staff trained in social science research methods. One staff member holds a master's in evaluation. Professional development activities exist, but participation is subject to availability of funds.

Source: Adapted from DePeuter & Pattyn (2008).

Given the information in Table 4.1, the evidence suggests that an organizational evaluation culture does exist and is framed by the rules, procedures, and resources to support evaluation's practice and development (institutionalization). However, further research would be needed to determine the quality and maturity of the FOPH's evaluation culture. For this, it would be useful to refer to Mayne's indicators in Chapter 1, "Issues in Enhancing Evaluation Use," of this book; that is, the organization

- engages in self-reflection and self-examination (i.e., self-evaluation) [at all levels];
- engages in evidence-based learning; and
- encourages experimentation and change [including risk taking].

The ESU made at least two attempts to conduct such a study with internal partners, but each time, the research had to be aborted; given the limited resources available for evaluation, the FOPH considers that such research is not a priority.

CONCLUSION

Evaluation can be perceived as beneficial, harmful, or adding little value. Our perceptions are shaped, in the first place, by personal experience and context (see, e.g., Bannister & Fransella, 1989; Kelly, 1955; and Hawkins's comments on culture and context in Chapter 3, "Evaluation Management," of this book). The meaning we attribute to experiences is developed and reinforced through our interaction with others. Hence, there are likely to be differences in the collective appreciation of what evaluation is, the potential benefits it can offer, and the role it should play in any given context. Evaluation's institutionalization can be seen as a positive means of supporting results-based management, organizational learning, and a culture of evaluation and evaluative thinking. On the other hand, it can be interpreted as a negative imposition, perceived as a form of control. In times of scarce resources, evaluation activities could be perceived as competing for scarce resources or as a worthwhile investment. There are inevitable tensions, such as these, when evaluation becomes anchored in an institution or organization. Consequently, the way evaluation is introduced, managed, and thus conceived is critical.

This study has attempted to show the interplay between institutionalization and cultural development and the ESU's opportunistic use of the former to establish the latter. The constitutional article provided external pressure to implement evaluation throughout the organization. The FOPH's guidelines, quality standards, commissioning process, and evaluation framework provided the necessary rules to standardize procedures—but their sense and purpose really became much clearer, to internal partners in particular, through their practical application in a specific study. Evaluation's organizational institutionalization helped formally implant evaluation and drive demand, but it worked hand-in-hand with the various strategies adopted by the ESU to avoid its being understood as an unnecessary obligation.

So how much does the structural location of an internal evaluation function help? Love (1993) argues that when evaluation is located at the highest level and reports directly to top management, its staff is more likely to be perceived and supported as an integral part of strategic management. This observation was certainly borne out in the case of the FOPH; with the creation of a centralized service, demand for evaluation grew and broadened, and gradually, as can be seen from the commissioned studies on the FOPH website, the questions are becoming more focused on strategic issues.

But Mayne, Divorski, and Lemaire (1999) argue that when evaluation is institutionalized in the administration, it is less likely to address impact or the continued relevance of a strategy or program. In other words, it is more likely to restrict its questions to those concerned with improvement and learning. While this may well be so in general, there appear to be some exceptions to the rule, as shown in the case presented. The prevention programs always took into account the impact of measures on the population's health, changes in the number of affected cases, new infections, and so on. Also, occasionally some studies were commissioned to evaluate the continued relevance of a strategy or the effects of new laws (e.g., the relevance of the federal radon prevention measures, and the effects of new financial arrangement for psychotherapy treatment). This is due in part to the nature of the federalist political system and the demands of article 170 itself, which requires that the effectiveness of federal measures is evaluated.

In her reappraisal of the literature on improving the utilization of evaluation research, Wimbush (see Chapter 5, "Reshaping Evaluation to Enhance Utilization in Scotland," in this book) argues that during the first decade of the 21st century, there has been a resurgence of the "learning culture" with emphasis on "capacity building," teaching organizations to "fish," and "leading them to water" by providing training, resources, and corporate memory and by setting quality standards for the management of evaluation. While this may well be the case, at a policy level in Switzerland, there is still much emphasis on also using evaluation to demonstrate the impact of interventions and, especially, to appreciate what works. The centralized evaluation services of Parliament and the Federal Audit Office have limited resources, and they cannot deal with all the issues of the entire administration. By and large, the various federal agencies themselves are expected to take responsibility for evaluating the effectiveness of their measures.

But more generally, institutionalizing the function at the highest level within a vacuum does not necessarily ensure effective use (e.g., Love, 1993). Resistance to taking ownership of the process and findings or accepting even constructive criticism along with time pressures and other priorities are some of the reasons mentioned for not getting involved (e.g., see Santamaria Hergueta, Schnur, and Thapa's Chapter 8, "Evaluation Policy and Practice in a Changing Environment," in this book). Taking on board constructive criticism and making changes depend on whether or not there is an established learning and evaluation culture (e.g., Russ-Eft & Preskill, 2009). So perhaps it is less to do with evaluation's structural location and more to do with how the internal service recognizes and can use opportunities to facilitate and institutionalize change. There are likely to be differences initially in the collective appreciation of what evaluation is and the role it should play when introduced into an organization or context.

A myriad of factors both within and outside an organization arguably combine to help or hinder the development of an organization-wide evaluation culture. The intent of this chapter has been to show how institutionalization can be used to develop such a culture or reinforce the elements of an existing one, and vice versa. The role that an internal Evaluation Unit can assume here is imperative. Identifying new or adapting proven strategies to new situations must be ongoing, especially in light of structural reorganizations and changes in the political context.

DISCUSSION QUESTIONS

1. What are the advantages and disadvantages of introducing and institutionalizing top-down evaluation?

2. What measures would you use to foster a demand for evaluation within a nongovernmental organization?

3. How would you go about developing an internal evaluation culture in an organization that lacks a learning culture?

4. What are the advantages and disadvantages of using external evaluators instead of internal evaluators for developing an evaluation culture?

NOTE

1. The ESU is also responsible for research management, and its official name is Evaluation and Research. However, since this chapter focuses on its evaluation activities, it is referred to hereafter as the Evaluation Services Unit—the ESU.

REFERENCES

Balthasar, A. (2006). The effects of the institutional design of the utilization of evaluation: Evidenced using qualitative comparative analysis (QCA). *Evaluation, 12*(3), 354–372.

Balthasar, A. (2007). *Institutionelle Verankerung und Verwendung von Evaluationen* [Evaluation institutionalization and use]. Zürich, Switzerland: Rüegger Verlag.

Bannister, D., & Fransella, F. (1989). *Inquiring man: The psychology of personal constructs.* London, UK: Routledge.

Boyle, R., Lemaire, D., & Rist, R. C. (1999). Introduction: Building evaluation capacity. In R. Boyle & D. Lemaire (Eds.), *Building effective evaluation capacity* (pp. 1–22). New Brunswick, NJ: Transaction.

Bussmann, W. (2008). The emergence of evaluation in Switzerland. *Evaluation, 14*(4), 499–506.

Constandriopoulos, A-P. (1999). Is the institutionalisation of evaluation sufficient to guarantee its practice? *Cadernos de Saude Publica, 15*(2), 229–259.

Cummings, T. G., & Worley, C. G. (2009). *Organization development and change* (9th ed.). Mason, OH: South-Western Cengage Learning.

DePeuter, B., & Pattyn, V. (2008) *Evaluation capacity: Enabler or exponent of evaluation culture?* Paper presented at the 2008 conference jointly organized by the French and German Evaluation Societies, Strasbourg, France. Retrieved June 14, 2012, from http://www.evaluatieplatform.be/doc/paper%20-%20De%20Peuter%20&%20Pattyn.pdf

The Federal Authorities of the Swiss Confederation. (1999). *Federal Constitution of the Swiss Confederation of 18 April 1999.* Retrieved from http://www.admin.ch/ch/e/rs/101/index.html

Fetterman, D. M., & Wandersman, A. (2005). *Empowerment evaluation principles in practice.* New York, NY: Guilford.

Fornerod, S. (2001). *A quoi et à qui servent les* évaluations? *Une recherche sur la place des évaluations dans les processus de décision et d'apprentissage dans l'administration fédérale* [What does evaluation offer and for whom? Research into where evaluations feature in the decisional and learning processes of the Federal Administration (Unpublished master's thesis)]. Institute of Higher Education in Public Administration (IDHEAP), Lausanne, Switzerland.

Furubo, J-E., Rist, R. C., & Sandahl, R. C. (Eds.). (2002). *International atlas of evaluation.* New Brunswick, NJ: Transaction.

Guba, E. G., & Stufflebeam, D. L. (1970). *Strategies for the institutionalization of the CIPP evaluation model.* An address delivered at the Eleventh Annual Phi Delta Kappa Symposium on Educational Research, Ohio State University, Columbia, OH.

Hartz, Z. M. A. (1999). Institutionalizing the evaluation of health programs and policies in France: Cuisine *internationale* over fast food and *sur mesure* over ready made. *Cadernos de Saude Publica, 15*(2). Retrieved November 24, 2011, from http://www.scielo.br/scielo.php?script=sci_arttext&pid=S0102-311X1999000200002&lng=en&nrm=iso&tlng=en

Jacob, S. (2005a). *Institutionnaliser l'évaluation des politiques publiques. Etude comparée des dispositifs en Belgique, en France en Suisse et aux Pays-Bas* [Institutionalizing policy evaluation. A comparative study of dispositions in Belgium, France, Switzerland and Holland]. Brussels, Belgium: Peter Lang.

Jacob, S. (2005b). La volonté des acteurs et le poids des structures dans l'institutionalisation de l'évaluation des politiques publiques (France, Belgique, Suisse et Pays-Bas) [The commitment of actors and importance of structural organization for institutionalizing policy evaluation (France, Belgium, Switzerland and Holland)]. *Revue française de science politique, 55*(5–6), 835–864.

Jacob, S. (2005c). Réflexions autour d'une typologie des dispositifs institutionnels d'évaluation [Reflections on a typology of institutional evaluation dispositives]. *Canadian Journal of Program Evaluation, 20*(2), 49–68.

Kelly, G. A. (1955). *Personal construct theory.* New York, NY: Norton.

Kuzman, A. (2009, December 15–17). *Evaluation capacity building strategy: Towards a mature profession.* Paper presented at the Conference on National Evaluation Capacity, Casablanca, Morocco. Retrieved July 6, 2012, from http://web.undp.org/evaluation/workshop/nec/2009/documents/papers/Kuzmin.pdf

Labin, S. N., Duffy, J. L., Meyers, D. C., Wandersman, A., & Lesesne, C. A. (2012, January 27). A research synthesis of the evaluation capacity building literature. *American Journal of Evaluation.* Retrieved July 6, 2012, from http://aje.sagepub.com/content/early/2012/01/27/1098214011434608

Läubli Loud, M. (2004). Setting standards and providing guidelines: The means toward what end? *Evaluation, 10*(2), 237–245.

Leeuw, F. L., Rist, R. C., & Sonnischen, R. C. (1994). *Can governments learn? Comparative perspectives on evaluation and organizational learning.* Brunswick, NJ: Transaction.

Love, A. J. (1993). Internal evaluation: An essential tool for human services organizations. *Canadian Journal of Program Evaluation, 8*(2), 1–15. Retrieved September 12, 2011, from http://www .evaluationcanada.ca/secure/08-2-001.pdf

Mayne, J. (1992). Institutionalizing program evaluation in action-oriented evaluation in organizations. In J. Hudson, J. Mayne, & R. Thomlison (Eds.), *Action oriented evaluation in organizations* (pp. 21–27). Toronto, Ontario, Canada: Wall & Emerson.

Mayne, J. (2006). Studies are not enough: The necessary transformation of evaluation. *Canadian Journal of Program Evaluation, 21*(3), 93–120.

Mayne, J. (2008, November). *Building an evaluative culture for effective evaluation and results management* (Brief No. 20). Rome, Italy: Institutional Learning and Change (ILAC).

Mayne, J., Divorski, St., & Lemaire, D. (1999). Locating evaluation: Anchoring evaluation in the executive or the legislature, or both or elsewhere? In R. Boyle & D. Lemaire (Eds.), *Building effective evaluation capacity* (pp. 23–52). New Brunswick, NY: Transaction.

Mihalache, R. (2010). A developing evaluation culture in Romania: Myths, gaps and triggers. *Evaluation, 16*(3), 323–332.

Owen, J. (2003). Evaluation culture: A definition and analysis of its development within organizations. *Evaluation Journal of Australasia, 3*(1), 43–47. Retrieved July 12, 2011, from http://www .aes.asn.au/images/stories/files/Publications/Vol3No1/evaluation_culture.pdf

Patton, M. Q. (2008). *Utilization-focused evaluation* (4th ed.). Thousand Oaks, CA: Sage.

Preskill, H., & Torres, R. T. (1999). *Evaluative enquiry for learning in organizations*. Thousand Oaks, CA: Sage.

Russ-Eft, D., & Preskill, J. (2009). *Evaluation in organizations: A systematic approach to enhancing learning, performance, and change* (2nd ed.). New York, NY: Basic Books.

Stufflebeam, D. L. (1997). *Strategies for institutionalizing evaluation: Revisited: Vol. 18. Occasional Paper Series*. Kalamazoo, MI: Evaluation Center, Western Michigan University.

Stufflebeam, D. L., & Shinkfield, A. J. (2007). *Evaluation theory, models and applications*. San Francisco, CA: Jossey-Bass.

Swiss Federal Office of Public Health (FOPH). (1997). *Guidelines for health programme & project evaluation planning*. Berne, Switzerland: Author. Retrieved November 3, 2011, from www.bag .admin.ch/evaluation/02357/02362/index.html?lang=en

The World Bank (2009). *Institutionalizing impact evaluation within the framework of a monitoring and evaluation system*. Washington, DC: Independent Evaluation Group, International Bank for Reconstruction and Development, World Bank.

Torres, R. T., Preskill, H. S., & Piontek, M. E. (1996). *Evaluation strategies for communicating and reporting: Enhancing learning in organizations*. Thousand Oaks, CA: Sage.

Toulemonde, J. (2000). Evaluation culture(s) in Europe: Differences and convergence between national practices. *Vierteljahreshefte zur Wirtschafsforschung, 69*(3), 350–357.

U.S. General Accounting Office. (2003). *Program evaluation: An evaluation culture and collaborative partnerships help build agency capacity* (Report to Congressional Committees No. GAO-03-454). Retrieved November 24, 2011, from http://www.gao.gov/new.items/d03454.pdf

Varone, F., & Jacob, S. (2002, October). *Institutionalising policy evaluation: A comparison of Western democracies*. Paper presented at European Evaluation Conference, Seville, Spain.

Widmer, T., Landert, C., & Bachmann, N. (2000). *Evaluation standards of SEVAL: SEVAL standards*. Retrieved August 23, 2012, from http://www.seval.ch/en/documents/SEVAL_Standards_2000_en.pdf

Widmer, T., & Neuenschwander, P. (2004). Embedding evaluation in the Swiss federal administration: Purpose, institutional design and utilization. *Evaluation, 10*(4), 388–409.

CHAPTER 5

RESHAPING EVALUATION TO ENHANCE UTILIZATION IN SCOTLAND

The Role of Intermediary Bodies in Knowledge-to-Action Strategies

Erica Wimbush

CHAPTER TOPICS

- Applying knowledge-to-action (KTA) strategies to evaluation utilization
- Challenges and changes to an Evaluation Unit's practice in promoting knowledge use
- A review of the success of the different measures adopted by an Evaluation Unit to enhance policy learning and knowledge use

---

The systematic assessment of the performance of public policies and programs is seen as central to public accountability and democracy. It is a core professional skill for those working in government and other public bodies. In the United Kingdom, the use of evidence within policy making became institutionalized during the Blair years of "modernizing" government (Cabinet Office, 1999a, 1999b). This new demand for understanding "what works" gave rise to an industry of evidence gathering and synthesis for policy making (Davies, Nutley, & Smith, 2000) plus a new stream of evaluation studies to assess the

---

Note: This chapter was written during a one-year fellowship (2009–2010) with Professor Sandra Nutley at the University of Edinburgh Business School and funded by the ESRC Knowledge Exchange program and NHS Health Scotland.

impacts of ambitious area-wide, partnership-based policy initiatives. The many challenges faced in undertaking this policy-relevant research and promoting evidence utilization were addressed in several reviews, most notably by the Kings Fund (Coote, Allen, & Woodhead, 2004), the Treasury (Wanless, 2004), and others (Davies et al., 2000; Petticrew et al., 2005). The challenges identified included the lack of a learning culture in government, among evaluators and practitioners in the field, the paucity of relevant and timely evidence on effectiveness and cost-effectiveness, and the need for more impact evaluation research. In the latter case, it was acknowledged that there are formidable methodological challenges in assessing the impact of complicated social programs implemented within complex settings.

From a knowledge utilization perspective, it is argued that the rapid development of utilization practice has run ahead of the development of conceptual frameworks to underpin the design of strategies and assessment of progress (Best et al., 2009; Graham & Tetroe, 2007). The literature on improving knowledge utilization has been growing steadily, albeit often in parallel disciplinary worlds and led primarily by the academic sector. Making effective connections between the two worlds of utilization theory and practice has been slow. This in part reflects the system drivers, the lack of time and resources for collaborative reflection and knowledge coproduction, combined with a lack of incentives and capacity to publish on the part of those steeped in the worlds of policy and practice. In this situation, academics act as the "knowledge filters" and rely on information obtained through, for example, research interviews which are then interpreted through a particular conceptual lens and reflected back to policy actors and practitioners, ideally in ways that enhance their understanding of their world, but all too often using language and concepts they fail to recognize.

This translational problem has been recognized. One response has been to develop a new cadre of knowledge-exchange-and-transfer professionals, a group of "hybrids," or "boundary spanners," who act as intermediaries, enabling connectivity, dialogue, and collaboration across the research-policy-practice boundaries. For example, in the United Kingdom, the Economic and Social Research Council (ESRC) Knowledge Exchange scheme funds secondments or placements that enable greater cross boundary movement (mostly the movement of academics into policy and practice settings) and learning through a period of immersion in the other-world culture of public policy, public management, or academia. There has also been significant investment in an institutional infrastructure for knowledge exchange with the creation of broker organizations or knowledge mobilization intermediaries (KMIs). Examples in the United Kingdom include Knowledge Transfer Partnerships, Innovation and Knowledge Centres, and Genetics Knowledge Parks. Cooper (2012) argues that KMIs have a distinctive boundary-spanning role and operate predominantly in the "white space" in between organizations, professional groups, and sectors in order to enable connectivity and facilitate interactions. For many KMIs, their role in knowledge mobilization (KM) is part of a much broader remit. In the United Kingdom, additional drivers for research utilization are now embedded in the public funding of academic research in terms of its impact or contribution to social, cultural, public policy, and economic well-being (Research Excellence Framework, www.ref.ac.uk).

This chapter is a result of an ESRC funded Knowledge Exchange Placement Fellowship to a university business school environment. It applies some of the most relevant knowledge utilization concepts to the experience of the challenges addressed by an Evaluation Unit within Scotland's public health agency. The organization plays an intermediary role between evidence, policy, and practice in the public health field through its statistical research evidence and evaluation functions and as a commissioner of evaluations of national health improvement policies that are implemented locally. When the agency was established in 2003, a core goal for the evaluation team was to improve the quality and utilization of evaluations and performance data so that health improvement policy and practice is better informed and more effective. As such, the evaluation research outputs are typical of Mode 2 forms of knowledge production in that inquiry is problem based, and the findings are solution focused and created with dissemination and implementation in mind (Denis, Lehoux, & Champagne, 2005; Gibbons, 1995). Evaluations are typically a joint creation between internal evaluation staff, program implementers, and decision makers, allowing for a deliberative process and consideration of contextual factors. Thus, a key difference between research and evaluation is that the purpose of evaluation (and also action research) is essentially tied into, and part of, the future development of the program or organization being studied. Thus, the evaluator and the evaluation are more integral to the program development and learning process than a researcher might be. The implications for utilization are significant with evaluation having an immediate relevance and audience while research often has to work hard at making the connections with possible users. Conversely, evaluators have to work hard to ensure an independent analytical perspective of a program in order to assess its merit or worth, while being close enough to understand the complex dynamics of the program and its implementation context.

This chapter presents an account of an Evaluation Unit's experience of shaping and delivering an evaluation strategy over a period of eight years. The chapter provides an initial overview of the methodological and utilization challenges faced and reflections on what was achieved, why some things failed, and the lessons learned. It draws on "real-life" examples from the perspective of an evaluation team in a national public health agency that occupies an intermediary position between national level policy making, local policy implementation, and the workforce of public health professionals. Four strands of work are selected for consideration: the changing organizational models of knowledge-to-action practice, the introduction of policy reviews as a means of enhancing evidence use and policy learning, the development of theory-based approaches to impact evaluation, and finally building evaluation capacity. The extent to which the conceptual models help to make sense of these experiences is then discussed with some conclusions about the role of intermediary bodies in knowledge-to-action strategies.

CONCEPTUAL FRAMEWORK

This sections sets out the thinking behind four key challenges that the Evaluation Unit's strategy sought to address: enhancing knowledge utilization, operating in a political-policy environment, creating an evaluative learning culture, and addressing the methodological challenge of attribution.

From Knowledge Utilization to Coproduction

Academic thinking and conceptual models on how to improve the influence, utilization, and impact of research, including evaluations, have evolved considerably since the late 1990s (Best et al., 2009; Nutley, Walter, & Davies, 2007; Weiss, 1979). As Mayne points out in the introductory chapter in this volume, a key milestone in the evolution of thinking was the early typology of research utilization by Weiss (1979), followed by Nutley, Walter, & Davies (2003), where research use was conceptualized as a continuum from conceptual use at one end to more instrumental uses at the other. A parallel body of literature on research utilization has grown up in relation to evaluation research where the emphasis was as much on organizational learning and developing an evaluative culture as on maximizing the impacts of research on policy and practice (Cousins & Earl, 1995; Patton, 1997; Preskill & Torres, 1999; Russ-Eft & Preskill, 2009; Torres & Preskill, 2001).

A useful overview of thinking about the processes for moving evidence and knowledge from practice to action is provided by Best et al. (2009). They describe three generations of knowledge-to-action (KTA) thinking: The initial generation used linear models that envisaged a simple one-way process of knowledge transfer where knowledge parcels are passed from research producers to research users. The language of knowledge *utilization* and *uptake* are indicative of this conceptual model. The move to relationship models of knowledge "exchange" recognized the significance of multiple sources of knowledge (research, policy, practice) and moved to a more interactive model of knowledge generation based on dialogue, linkage, and exchange. For example, the Canadian Health Services Research Foundation pioneered this approach and brought researchers and decision makers together throughout all phases of the knowledge development and use cycle to facilitate the generation of relevant knowledge and the use of relevant evidence in decision making (Lomas, 2000). The mechanisms of networks, collaborative partnerships and co-location-funding arrangements are typically used to bring together different forms of knowledge and are key features of knowledge exchange practice. Building on these ideas, a third generation integrative model is now evolving based on systems thinking and ecological models of knowledge production. A systems approach typically involves (a) the coproduction of mental models by researchers and practitioners; and (b) these shared models highlight the importance of integrated, multilevel interventions (and the interactions among them) to address complex problems and situations (Best el al., 2009). In summary, "knowledge products are seen as embedded within relationships of linkage and exchange, which in turn are embedded within a larger system that is shaped by culture, structures, priorities, and capacities" (Best et al., 2009, p. 2). Advocates of the model propose the "coproduction" of knowledge with systems capacity that supports collaboration, linkage, and exchange (Best et al., 2009).

In the case study examples that follow, the evolution of knowledge utilization practice within the national agency mirrors this process. However, the influence of the wider external policy environment plays a strong role in the take up of evidence-based knowledge and deserves separate attention.

Policy Windows

Recognition of knowledge as "embedded" in wider systems does not necessarily shed light on the political environment within which this coproduced knowledge is ultimately deployed. Even gold-standard coproduced knowledge may fail to be taken up if the political wind is not conducive. There is some research-on-use literature where the concepts of acceptance and adoption are generally examined, but the political science literature on the role of ideas in the policy process explores the political context for research acceptance. This suggests that the acceptance of scientific evidence or ideas by policymakers requires a receptive political environment whereby decision makers have the motivation and opportunity to translate evidence into policy. Kingdon (1995) suggests that three conditions must coincide: (a) policy issues that require attention, (b) evidence about potentially effective solutions available to the policy community, and (c) changes in the political system that affect receptivity to the evidence. Cairney (2009) looks at the case of translating new evidence on passive smoking into smoking ban policies across the devolved political systems of the United Kingdom. Although the same evidence was available and the same policy was adopted by the four governments, the nature of the "window of opportunity" (timing, motive, and opportunity) differed in each country. The policy window was dependent on a wide range of actors, institutions, and factors: most importantly, differences in policy competence, the role of parties within parliament, reactions to public and media opinion, levels of pressure group activity, and reactions to international policy developments.

This body of thinking suggests that identifying these predictable but transitory "policy windows" are a necessary dimension of effective knowledge utilization strategies. In the case study examples that follow, this is particularly relevant to understanding the relatively low uptake of the recommendations from our policy reviews, despite an increasingly collaborative approach to knowledge coproduction.

Organizational Learning, Evaluative Learning Culture, and Capacity-Building

In the evaluation literature on improving utilization, there is an emphasis on the importance of developing an evaluative learning culture across stakeholder groups and within organizations and processes to facilitate knowledge acquisition and evaluative thinking (Russ-Eft & Preskill, 2009; Torres & Preskill, 2001). This emphasis on organizational learning is also taken up in the recent overview of research use by Nutley et al. (2007). Both literatures stress the limits of understanding utilization as an individual learning issue and the importance of organizational culture in understanding how knowledge is created, acquired, shared, and used. Attention is focused on how knowledge is "managed" and the facilitation of individual and collective learning through, for example, participative approaches to evaluation where knowledge and learning is coproduced (Greene, 1988; Wadsworth, 1998). Extending the lessons about organizational learning processes beyond the boundaries of single organizations or programs to "whole system" learning processes appropriate for multiagency collaboration and partnership-based delivery is less well understood, although not entirely neglected (e.g., Solomon & Chowdhury, 2002; Williams & Sullivan, 2011).

In the case study examples that follow, attempts to build an evaluative learning culture at individual, organizational, and systems levels were closely intertwined with the Evaluation Unit's capacity-building activities where the goal was developing the capacity to both create and use evaluative information (Mayne & Rist, 2006). According to Rogers (2004) and McDonald, Rogers, and Kefford (2003), this involves both "teaching them to fish" (e.g., providing the training, resources, corporate memory, and community of practice to support *conducting* evaluations) and "leading them to water" (e.g., reassuring incentives and training to encourage the *use* of evaluative information).

Methodological Challenges of Impact Evaluation: Assessing Attribution in Complex Systems

As noted above, the challenges faced by the Evaluation Unit were methodological as well as about fostering knowledge utilization. The primary methodological challenge concerned the issue of attribution—assessing the impact of complicated programs implemented within complex settings. In the field of public health evaluation, randomized controlled trials are the design of choice for evaluating the efficacy of interventions, because they provide the most robust way of minimizing selection or allocation bias. But randomization is often impossible or too difficult for practical or political reasons. Examples where "natural experiments" have been used successfully to assess policy impact are relatively rare (Hawe, Shiell, & Riley, 2004; Melhuish, Belsky, Leyland, & Barnes, 2008), and what constitutes a good natural experiment is not clear (Petticrew et al., 2005).

Addressing cause and effect within complex systems and real-life settings where there are numerous factors and multiple actors influencing the intended outcome is recognized as an important methodological challenge (Forss, Marra, & Scwartz, 2011; Mayne, 2011; Shiell, Hawe, & Gold, 2008). To what extent are any observed changes the consequence of the actions of a particular policy or program? Since the late 1990s, the use of theory-based evaluation is the main methodological approach to emerge that helps to address the issue of causality. It has made a significant contribution to evaluation methodology in terms of understanding change processes and mechanisms and the importance of broader contextual factors. These are also of vital importance for understanding the transferability of social interventions from one country or setting to another. In the United Kingdom, the methodological development of theory-based approaches to evaluation began in the early 2000s with the application of realistic evaluation (Pawson & Tilley, 1997), the Aspen Institute's theories of change (ToC) methodology (Connell & Kubisch, 1995; Connell, Kubisch, Schorr, & Weiss, 1998), and the more general use of "program theory" (Rogers, 2008) to the evaluation of complicated and complex programs. This is the main area and context for methodological development considered in this chapter. An important point is that the participatory approach adapted to theory-based approaches to evaluation brought significant added value in terms of fostering an evaluative culture as well as evaluation practice (Wimbush, Montague, & Mulherin, 2012).

In the next section, the experiences of Scotland's public health agency in developing and implementing a utilization-focused strategy for evaluation are outlined as a way of exploring the application of these concepts in real-life settings. It is not an exhaustive account of its work but focuses on four strands of work that illustrate some key challenges and innovations to enhance learning and knowledge utilization.

EXPERIENCES AND LESSONS FROM SCOTLAND'S PUBLIC HEALTH AGENCY

Scotland has had a national body for public health and health education promotion since the early 1980s. Today, the agency is called NHS Health Scotland, formed in 2003 from a merger of two predecessor bodies, the Health Education Board for Scotland (established 1993, with around 60 staff) and the Public Health Institute for Scotland (established 2001, with around 20 staff). It now employs about 300 staff members and has an independent board. The corporate strategy (2008–2011) had four key objectives:

1. Advancing understanding of Scotland's health and how it can be improved

2. Providing timely, evidence-based inputs to health improvement policy and planning

3. Increase capacity and competence in the delivery of health improvement programs

4. Improve the quality of dissemination of evidence, learning, and good practice

Evidence gathering and utilization is thus seen as a core role for the organization. The agency operates as an intermediary organization, enabling connectivity and interactions between the Scottish Government (national level policy making for health improvement), the bodies charged with improving health at a local population level (i.e., the 15 local health boards, local government, and their Community Planning partners), and the professional public health workforce. The agency is responsible for providing advice and expertise to these groups and in-house teams based on epidemiological analysis, reviews of effectiveness evidence, and evaluations of policy implementation. The organization can be seen as having a "knowledge broker" role within the wider system of individuals, organizations, and partnerships concerned with health improvement. Using Nutley's framework (2003), the brokerage role of the organization spans the following:

- *Knowledge management:* Facilitating the creation, dissemination, and use of public health evidence relevant to current policy and practice
- *Linkage and exchange:* Brokering the relationship between knowledge "creators" and "users," through research-policy-practice dialogue and joint working, learning networks and training
- *Capacity building:* Making analytical data and evidence accessible and actionable for decision making and improving the workforce capacity to plan, generate, and use evaluation information

NHS Health Scotland reflects the importance attached to evidence-based policy and the shifting balance of investment elsewhere in the United Kingdom.[1] When established, one third of the new public health agency's human resources, or staff, was dedicated to public health evidence and analysis. Sixty percent of this resource (17 posts, or job positions) was concentrated in advising policymakers and practitioners on what works to improve health, based on reviews of the existing international research evidence (systematic reviews, reviews of reviews, evidence-based guidance). The remaining public health resource was concerned with analyzing Scotland's population health data (six posts) and coordinating the evaluation of local implementation of policies to improve Scotland's health (six posts).[2] The interdependence of these three elements of public health evidence in the policy cycle was acknowledged (see Figure 5.1)

Figure 5.1   NHS Health Scotland: Evidence in the Policy Cycle

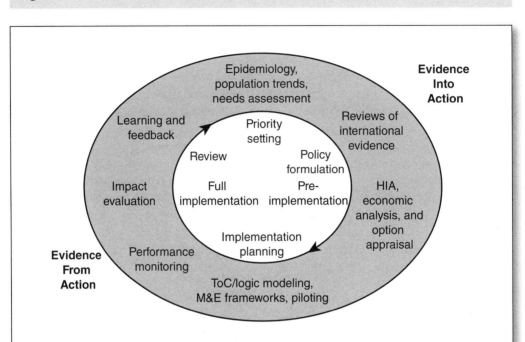

Source: NHS Health Scotland, 2004

Note: HIA = Health Impact Assessment; ToC = Theory of Change

and resourced with a commitment to strategic leadership and continuous improvement.

The rest of this chapter focuses on the evolution of the evaluation function from 2004 to 2012 to enhance the utilization of evaluative thinking and learning on policy and practice.[3] A strategic approach to this work was formulated during 2004 after a process of consultation with national and local stakeholders (see box on the next page).

In the next section, four main strands of the team's work are selected for review: (a) changing organizational models of knowledge utilization, (b) initiating a series of policy reviews as a means to enhance policy learning and knowledge utilization, (c) developing theory-based approaches to assessing impact, and (d) building evaluation capacity.

Aim

The aim of this strand of NHS Health Scotland's work is to contribute to more effective planning and delivery of health improvement policy through a systematic and coordinated approach to providing feedback and learning from evaluations of policy implementation and pre-implementation policy appraisal.

Objectives

1. Advance knowledge and understanding about the effectiveness of health improvement policy implementation in Scotland

2. Improve policy implementation processes by strengthening capacity and skills around program planning, monitoring, and evaluation

3. Develop a culture of learning, innovation, and experimentation within which evidence, evaluation, and review are integral parts of policy planning and delivery

Source: http://www.healthscotland.com/understanding/evaluation

---

Knowledge Utilization: Changing Organizational Models

Despite the rise of knowledge broker organizations, few studies have specifically focused on the role of intermediary organizations, such as NHS Health Scotland, in facilitating the use of research evidence in policy making and practice although the need for this is recognized (e.g., Davies et al., 2000; Nutley et al., 2007). NHS Health Scotland was an active participant in a European Commission (EC) funded project "Getting Evidence into Practice" (2003/2004) that sought to develop European protocols for delivering effective practice in improving population health. This work identified four necessary strands of knowledge utilization activity:

1. Systematic reviews of research and collation of research evidence

2. Developing and disseminating guidance on effective practice based on reviews of the evidence

3. Developing the capacity to deliver effective practice

4. Learning from implementing effective practice

In June 2005, NHS Health Scotland commissioned a panel of experts to conduct an internal review of its own work on getting evidence into policy and practice (EIPP) to guide the future integration of the inherited work strands. The review also took into account the wider evidence base on knowledge utilization and organizational learning (Percy-Smith, Speller, & Nutley, 2006). The review made several recommendations including the following:

- *Mainstream the EIPP function across the organization:* A need to move away from having isolated "pockets" of EIPP projects to mainstreaming the EIPP function across the whole organization, unified by a common approach—for example, identifying good practice from shared learning, developing a protocol for what counts as evidence for different purposes for use across the organization, and establishing a protocol for the collection of case study evidence from practice
- *Moving to an "embedded" model of practice change:* A need to move away from the individual-oriented research-based practitioner model toward an "embedded" organizational approach to practice change where EIPP work is used to engage and influence the relevant organizations and/or professional bodies, rather than the individual practitioners

Little progress was made in implementing these recommendations for five years. The original three learning networks were dissolved and human resource mainstreamed as part of NHS Health Scotland's standard public health adviser role in evidence synthesis. The practice of evidence dissemination and learning exchange was continued by the organization's implementation support group. There was little impetus to develop a common approach to EIPP practice across the organization until new windows for development arose in 2011 and 2012. A national review of knowledge-to-action (KTA) across the health service in Scotland coincided with the redevelopment of NHS Health Scotland's corporate strategy, which created within the organization the reflective space for thinking about new ways of working.

The national level health service review was a response to concerns about the loss of libraries and the need to modernize and reposition them as part of a multidisciplinary KTA function. For NHS Health Scotland, the review triggered a process of internal review, involving reflection and cross-organizational dialogue in relation to library modernization and the wider KTA role of the organization. This has resulted in a more explicit and embedded KTA process within the core business of the organization. It is seen as central to achieving the corporate outcome of enhanced evidence-informed decision making as articulated in the new corporate strategy. The KTA process is shown visually in Figure 5.2 as combining knowledge management with knowledge utilization

Figure 5.2 NHS Health Scotland: The Wider Knowledge-to-Action Function

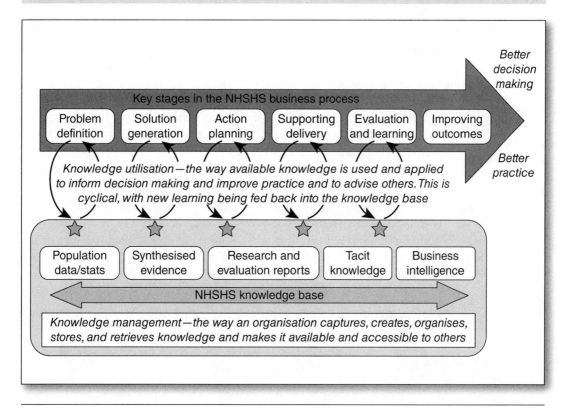

Source: NHSHS Board Paper 37/11. © NHS Health Scotland

throughout the key stages in NHS Health Scotland's business process with the goal of influencing decision making in policy and practice contexts. It is recognized that the KTA process needs to be supported by an organizational culture where evidence and learning are valued and by new technological platforms that enable knowledge management and collaborative working.

Policy Reviews: Enhancing Policy Learning and Knowledge Utilization

To date, there has been near total neglect of the review stage of the policy cycle and the potential scope for evidence use and lesson learning. When establishing the new Evaluation Unit in NHS Health Scotland, a series of policy reviews was initiated for health improvement policies where local implementation had been underway for at least five to six years and where there was an appetite among policymakers to "refresh" the policy. The policy review process was intended to address inadequacies in the existing practice of monitoring policy performance solely in terms of hitting national-level targets for population-level health status or behavior change. The policy review process introduced a systematic and transparent process of evidence gathering, research synthesis, and stakeholder engagement. Three policy reviews have been conducted since 2005 in the areas of food and diet (Lang, Dowler, & Hunter, 2006), mental health and well-being (Hunter, Barry, & McCulloch, 2007), and physical activity (Halliday, 2009).

Although the approach was continually refined over the course of the three policy reviews, the core methodology comprised the following:

1. *Review panel:* The panel conducted the review, led the deliberative process, and analyzed the information and evidence gathered together by the Secretariat (NHS Health Scotland's policy evaluation team); they reported to the Scottish Government policy lead (civil servant responsible for policy development in a particular area).

2. *Progress and impacts:* Progress to date with policy implementation and evidence of impacts was assessed, using population-level data on outcomes, program evaluations, and new research commissioned to assess community-level and service impacts.

3. *Horizon-scanning:* Scotland's policy and progress were benchmarked against other countries and international trends; any new evidence or guidance was identified that may necessitate adjustments in policy focus or direction as well as any new opportunities to enhance or accelerate existing action (e.g., the Commonwealth Games in Glasgow in 2014).

4. *Stakeholder engagement:* A consultative and deliberative process of engagement involved a number of relevant individuals, groups, and organizations (e.g., Scottish Government officials, national agencies, Community Planning Partnerships, and the implementation workforce) to evaluate the picture of progress and change, to reflect on areas of success and challenge and lessons learned, and to agree on key priorities for the future.

5. *Recommendations for the future:* Based on the lessons learned from progress with implementation and impacts, any gaps in policy implementation and any alignments or accommodations necessary were made in the light of new evidence and opportunities.

The methodology evolved over the three reviews. Most importantly, as the NHS Health Scotland policy team, we moved away from using a review panel of academic experts (assisted by a secretariat) that could provide independent and expert scrutiny of the policy and its implementation. By the third review, membership of the review panel brought together key stakeholders and combined academic expertise, the policy lead, and key implementation bodies (users), and the secretariat. It was chaired by a key public figure, an international sportsman and broadcaster (and the original chair of the policy Task Force) with a reputation as an advocate of the policy under review. Unlike the previous two expert panels, this combined panel devised a communications plan for the review to maximize the coverage of its messages among a wider group of stakeholders.

Under the initial expert-led model, policy leads were involved only in formulating the terms of reference, selecting the panel, and giving evidence; policy learning was limited, and there was a lack of ownership of the findings, even a defensive attitude. When the policy lead was centrally involved in the review panel, it improved policy ownership and utilization, although the take-up of recommendations and receptivity to policy change was still largely determined by political and other contextual factors. For example, the coincidence in timing of the Scottish Diet review report with the window offered by the publication of data on national dietary targets helped to escalate the relevance of that review and provided a well-evidenced performance story that complemented the national target data. In the case where no national targets existed (mental health and well-being), the profile of the review was much lower.

The stakeholder engagement dimension of the review process was retained over the course of the three reviews, although the nature of the process varied with each panel. While all three included a series of engagement events to deliberate on the panel's preliminary analysis, the Scottish Diet Review and the Mental Health Improvement Review also included a number of full day "hearings" with the panel for two-way dialogue about the evidence presented and to familiarize the experts' panels with the contexts of policy and its local implementation and key stakeholders (professional groups, researchers, industry bodies, etc.). The number of hearings was drastically reduced by the third review, not only primarily to speed up the process but also because the familiarization process was unnecessary for the panel.

In contrast to the policy reviews, another less successful attempt to improve knowledge utilization and policy learning was via the synthesis of process evaluation findings across a number of major national evaluations to identify recurring policy implementation problems. This was a desk-based synthesis, and the work did not engage users in knowledge generation and learning. The potential users were identified and engaged in discussions only after the synthesis paper was produced. This led to responses from invited participants that suggested a lack of ownership for any improvement action arising. As such, this form of knowledge production was far less successful.

Theory-Based Approaches to Assessing Impact: Contributions and Influence

Within the context of Scotland's public health policy, the most significant application of theories of change (ToC) was to the evaluation of two of the national demonstration projects (Have a Heart Paisley and Starting Well) and a successor program (Keep Well) by policy evaluation teams at Glasgow and Edinburgh Universities (Blamey & Mackenzie, 2007; Sridharan, 2006). While the full application of ToC in a research context elicited a mixed response from the research, policy, and practitioner communities (Craig et al., 2005), its much cruder application to program planning and evaluation in the form of logic modeling has met with a more enthusiastic response, although the underlying theory of change approach is often misunderstood and oversimplified (Birckmayer & Weiss, 2000; Taylor & Newberry, n.d.). At best, logic modeling is used as a tool that assists in the development of a shared understanding of "program theory" thus helping communication and collaboration between program staff, decision makers, and evaluators, and as a starting point to set expectations of performance. At worst, it provides a one-off visual snapshot of a program from a particular stakeholder perspective or is an overly detailed and confusing picture where everything links to everything else. In our experience as the NHS Health Scotland evaluation team, we found it is less common for logic models to be used beyond an initial planning stage and to inform risk management, monitoring and evaluation, and reporting and collecting learning. This was confirmed by a recent review by Coryn, Noakes, Westine, and Scroter (2011).

The potential for this situation to change came with the introduction of outcomes management and accountability across the public sector in Scotland as part of the concordat between central-local government in late 2007. The policy evaluation team became closely involved with the Scottish Government and local health boards in shaping and embedding the new outcomes approach to planning and performance (Craig, 2013). This context provided the foundations for introducing a more structured approach to theory-based impact evaluation that is being applied within the context of local partnership performance. The concept and basic methodology of contribution analysis was developed by John Mayne in Canada for assessing the performance of government policies and public programs within the context of results-based management (Mayne, 2001, 2008, 2011). Contribution analysis provides an alternative way of thinking about the problem of attribution to the traditional positivist approach of proving causality via a counterfact. It does not attempt to prove that one factor (the policy or program) "caused" the desired outcome but instead uses a process of logical argumentation to assess the contributions a policy or program is making to observed changes in outcomes. Mayne's ideas and methods have been further developed in practice through the work of Montague (Montague, 2000, 2009) who sets out the theory of change in the form of a results chain(s), which is then sequenced over time in the form of a results plan.[4] The main output is an evidence-based performance story about the contributions of a program, organization, or policy toward influencing a set of desired population outcomes, such as improved health.

The methodology of contribution analysis is still evolving, but the main argument is that it is reasonable to conclude that the intervention is making a difference if the following occurs:

1. There is a theory of change set out that shows how a set of planned activities and outputs will result in a series of outcomes over time, together with the evidence, risks, and assumptions underlying this change sequence.

2. The implementation of the planned activities can be demonstrated.

3. There is sufficient evidence gathered to support the theory of change, that is, the evidence shows that the sequence of expected changes is occurring.

4. Other factors influencing the outcomes have been assessed and accounted for (Mayne, 2011).

A participatory approach to applying contribution analysis has been developed and used in the context of local partnership planning. Examples of applications are given in Wimbush et al. (2012) who argue that, as a participatory process, contribution analysis strengthens both conceptual and practical understanding of planning and managing for outcomes and the implementation and change theories, thus, helping to build outcomes thinking, evaluation practice, and collaborative capacity within and across participating partner organizations.

Evaluation Capacity-Building: Institutions, Management, and Professional Skills

As noted earlier, improving evidence utilization cannot be separated from the broader notion of knowledge development and the need to generate practice-based evidence. Building capacity for evaluation as a route to improving the supply and use of practice-based evidence was an important objective for the policy evaluation team. It was also the one that presented the greatest challenges due to the sheer scale and scope of the capacity-building task as well as understanding what constitutes "quality" and what "capacities" are needed across the system and by whom.

Managing knowledge coproduction. Managing stakeholder relationships with funders, decision makers, those implementing the program, and those responsible for evaluation is an important aspect of the team's role in managing commissioned evaluations. As commissioners, we recognized the need to develop an effective linkage, sometimes brokerage, role with these groups and to create spaces for dialogue and challenge. In addition to its formal research governance role, the advisory groups that were established for all commissioned evaluation research came to play an important role in knowledge translation and coproduction in terms of the following:

- Regular channel of communication between the key stakeholders, those with a shared interest in evaluating and improving program performance, to agree on the focus of the evaluation, key evaluation questions, and any changes to schedules
- Developing a mutual understanding about the program in question, its theory of change and implementation contexts (including partnerships), and sharing and discussing emergent learning about the program
- Forging constructive and collaborative working relationships between stakeholders on, for example, information gathering and data sharing as well as resolving any problems arising between parties
- Developing a shared narrative and vocabulary about the program goals and the expected results

An evaluation advisory group is usually set up at the point where a brief for the evaluation is being drafted for the purposes of commissioning an external research team to conduct the evaluation research on the basis of competitive tendering. For the latter, as commissioners, we learned to stipulate in the tender requirements our expectation that a collaborative team approach was favored as well as the use of a theory-based evaluation framework. Where we wanted the evaluation team to be involved in the process of developing a shared understanding of the program's theory of change, prior to developing and agreeing on a detailed monitoring and evaluation plan, we divided the commissioning process into two stages: acceptance of an initial preliminary proposal, with the full contract signed on acceptance of a more detailed research proposal based on an agreed theory of change. While evaluation research expertise is seen as paramount in the selection of an appropriate evaluation team, the ability to build relationships and trust, especially with the program team, is also seen as essential and assessed during the initial stage. While data collection, analysis, and writing are primarily the responsibility of the contracted research team, there are many instances when joint publications have been developed that involve other stakeholders in the advisory group.

Institutional capacity and academic leadership. In evaluation, these were regarded as necessary and desirable but lacking in Scotland. There was no clear body of expertise applied to evaluation to help guide the work of the new evaluation team. We commissioners sought to remedy this within the health sector via a short-term (three-year) funding arrangement with Edinburgh University to establish an evaluation program. This created a valuable partnership that served to extend our internal capabilities, allowed the demonstration of high quality and innovative evaluation practice (e.g., program explication processes, using reach as an early indicator of inequalities, use of concept-mapping as an integrative tool in multicomponent evaluation studies), and the creation of regular learning opportunities via the annual Evaluation Summer School (a way of creating a community of evaluation practice across the research, policy, and practice areas). While the expectation was that our investment in a single senior post would be sufficient seed funding to found a much broader evaluation program by attracting other grant funding, this was not realized. The program was vibrant but remained focused on a single post that disappeared at the end of the funding period. Recognizing the gap, in 2008, a new academic unit was established by the Medical Research Council (the Scottish Collaboration for Public Health Research and Policy) with a remit to build interorganizational capacity to initiate and undertake high quality and policy relevant intervention research. The collaboration is led by a Canadian epidemiologist and is now nearing the end of its first period of funding.

In addition to these institutional arrangements, there was a need for a cross-sectoral professional network for evaluators of public policies and programs for the purposes of learning exchange and continuing professional development. In collaboration with the Scottish Government and other national agencies, as evaluation team members, we contributed to supporting the formation of the Scottish Evaluation Network (linked to the UK Evaluation Society) as well as to developing a new evaluation leadership and capacity-building resource within the third sector (Evaluation Support Scotland).

Professional skill set. One of the goals of the evaluation team was to strengthen the workforce and system capacity to plan, act, manage, commission, and learn from high quality evaluation work, in different contexts and for different purposes. The need to reappraise the skills required by the team eventually became apparent. Recruitment to professional roles in the evaluation team is based on qualifications and experience in public health and/or social research, in particular conducting evaluation research. As the team's work program developed (theory-based approaches, improving utilization, evaluation support roles) and extended into new areas (outcomes planning and performance management), new knowledge and skills became necessary within the evaluation team:

- The facilitation skills required to fulfill a brokerage role, such as facilitating the process of developing a shared theory of change using logic modeling or results chains; skills to design and manage evaluations in such a way as to actively facilitate learning within the organization and across stakeholder groups
- The interpersonal skills required to strengthen relationships and trust across stakeholder groups and to maintain their engagement over the period of the evaluation
- Knowledge, skills, and credibility in the field of performance management, in particular results-based management

These have been incorporated progressively in recruitment for existing posts, by gradually adapting knowledge and skills profiles and personnel specifications, through individual and team development, and through the creation of a new senior post specializing in the work on outcomes and performance. The Evaluation Summer School is designed to provide an intensive period of professional development for the team each year, working alongside others who apply, commission, or use evaluations in other contexts.

DISCUSSION

Multiple Competing Models

To understand change processes, systems thinking (and complexity theory) suggests we commissioners and scholars need to understand not only the new knowledge product (an intervention, a program, or policy) but also the implementation context in which it will operate (institutional, geographical, cultural, political) (Best et al., 2009). Our experience suggests this type of thinking is apparent in certain strands of evaluation methodology, such as theory-based evaluation and participatory and action-oriented approaches, which become more appropriate where multilevel programs and strategies are being implemented within contexts characterized by complexity and collaborative multiagency partnerships. However, these approaches coexist with the more traditional evaluation methodologies, using, for example, cluster randomized trial designs, and these are increasingly adapted to include a recognizable theory of change for the intervention that is replicable across sites (Hawe et al., 2004; Hawe, Shiell, & Riley, 2008; Hawe, Shiell, & Riley, 2009).

While systems models may reflect a new direction of thinking and methodological development, our experience in the public health field suggests a gradual move away from linear one-way models of knowledge utilization toward models based on relationships, multiple sources of knowledge, and linkage and exchange mechanisms. The policy reviews provided an example of a move from a simple linear utilization model, where the independent panel had the role of knowledge creators who delivered their expert report to the intended policy users who were marginal to the learning process, to one where the review panel incorporated key stakeholders and the review served as a forum for exchange, debate, and learning for panel members, with engagement events to extend that process more widely. The need to create spaces for dialogue and shared learning between evaluation stakeholders has also become an important dimension of both formal and informal evaluation work. A further example was the gradual organizational shift away from a research-based practitioner model to an embedded model of practice change.

However, the change process is not simply a matter of one model of knowledge production replacing another, but brings the coexistence of several competing models. This situation is echoed by researchers who work in the knowledge production-and-utilization area, such as Swan, Bresnen, Robertson, Newell, and Dopson (2009). They also note that tensions can exist within as well as across constituent communities and, second, that mobilizing a new model of knowledge production may produce its own contradictions that can, paradoxically, lead to the simultaneous resurrection (and reinforcement) of preexisting models.

The Impact of Competing Models of Knowledge Development on Evaluation Capacity Building

Evaluation capacity building is seen as a vital part of any KTA strategy and was an integral part of our evaluation strategy. The delivery of this aspect of the strategy took time to progress since needs were complicated to define and open-ended (how much is enough?). While all evaluations are broadly about improving knowledge about public policies and programs, they can serve different purposes and have different underlying models of knowledge development. This in turn has implications for what is defined as *quality* and *good practice* in evaluation and therefore what capacities are required. Borrowing Chelimsky's (1997) thinking on the three main purposes of evaluation helps to illustrate the competing perspectives:

1. Evaluation for program improvement directly links evaluation to learning processes and is founded upon a relationship model of knowledge development. For example, within the field of international development, those adopting a "development as social change" model of practice eschew methods-driven approaches to evaluation.

   Assessment and learning go beyond methods to a way of being in relationships that matter. Therefore, critical for ensuring that assessment and learning serve the social change process is the quality of relationships and establishing a trusting (internal) learning environment. (Guijt, 2007, p. 6)

2. The knowledge-building purpose of some evaluation research puts the emphasis on accumulating and storing high-quality effectiveness evidence from interventions research through initiatives, such as the Cochrane or Campbell Collaborations. A linear dissemination model of knowledge production prevails where the knowledge creators (typically external evaluators who produce research reports, publications, and systematic reviews) are separate and independent from knowledge users.

3. The accountability purpose of monitoring and evaluation also tends toward a one-way knowledge generation process. Performance information is typically prescribed by and generated for funders and donors and this is reported upward via a formal and ritualized annual review process. Self-evaluation processes within organizations often extend beyond the accountability requirements of reporting to funders.

In practice, the distinctions are not so neat and these models coexist. For example, where performance information is used for internal improvement purposes, a two-way coproduction model may operate, depending on team relationships and the organizational learning culture. However, different stakeholder perspectives on knowledge generation and what constitutes good evaluation practice can give rise to conflicts over quality and negatively impact on the evaluation's influence and utilization. For example, Spicer and Smith (2008) describe this situation as characteristic of the evaluation of the Children's Fund where independent local evaluations commissioned by the partnerships were highly contested and had limited influence on program design and implementation. The importance of establishing early dialogue and engagement between evaluators and stakeholders is therefore paramount. In terms of evaluation capacity building, awareness of competing models is helpful for managing the multiple stakeholder perspectives and interests.

Reflections on Enhancing Policy Learning Through the Policy Review Process

As an intervention at the end stage of the policy cycle, the introduction of a more systematic and engaged process of policy review was expected to widen and enhance opportunities for policy learning. In practice, this was more limited than anticipated for two reasons related to contextual factors:

- The focus on past policies attracts less political interest than new policies in development with direct association with a current minister
- A key driver for policy learning is peer competition (the motivation to keep up with other equivalent countries), but this requires comparable national indicators and implementation contexts

This suggests that more attention to the peer competition motivation in the design of the policy reviews might make policy learning more effective. Furthermore, strengthening the links between individual and organizational learning in the review process could be enhanced further.

LESSONS LEARNED

The main lessons learned over the last eight years are summarized below. The categories used are derived from Cherney and Head's (2011) nine components of an organizational environment that support the utilization of evidence in decision making in both policy and practice contexts:

1. *Communication:* Creating reflective spaces for policymakers and practitioners enables them to interrogate, think over, and discuss new evidence that they can relate to their own experience and understanding that ultimately contributes to program and service or policy redesign.

2. *Clarification:* Working with policymakers, program implementers, and/or service managers to apply theory-based approaches to planning and evaluation has helped to coproduce "mental models" of how a program is designed to address a particular problem and how it is intended to work (often at multiple levels); this then enables the deployment of evaluative feedback on how it is actually working and what adaptations might be required.

3. *Competency:* The core focus on the knowledge and skills to conduct and use high-quality evaluations needs supplemented with the skills of facilitation to enable individual agents or teams to plan and design service or program implementation for intended outcomes and to integrate the use of existing evidence and evaluative feedback into the process.

4. *Capacity:* Traditionally, this concerns the organizational or system capacity to generate and use evaluation information; however, if this is seen as part of a wider KTA process of evidence-informed decision making, then capacity-building also encompasses the ability to store and manage accumulated knowledge and learning so that it is retrievable by others at a later date.

5. *Climate:* Having an external policy climate that is conducive to using evidence in policy and practice is a critical enabling factor and has been given further impetus by the introduction of outcomes thinking in public service management and accountability systems; an emphasis on continuous quality improvement in business processes has also helped to create a supportive internal climate for organizational learning and improvement.

6. *Commitment:* While officially individuals or policy units may endorse these reform principles, individual-level and organizational commitment is necessary to translate these into practice and manage the long-term process of change. For this reason, it is critical to have champions who provide leadership at multiple levels in the system and who can effectively drive the change process with the wider context in mind.

7. *Collaboration:* A collaborative approach to knowledge generation is an essential prerequisite for utilization. However, uptake is also strongly mediated by the external policy environment; therefore, the acceptance of ideas and evidence needs to coincide with windows of opportunity in the external environment.

8. *Innovation and experimentation:* The role of evaluation in testing innovation and encouraging experimentation makes important contributions

to evidence-based policy and practice in two main ways: in policy areas where there is a high level of uncertainty about what actions might be effective in addressing a problem and in modifying programs or services that are shown to be effective elsewhere in local conditions.

9. *Monitoring and review:* With enhanced use of evidence in decision making now recognized as a core dimension of corporate strategy, developing systems for monitoring this process and outcome will become an integral part of the organization's performance reporting and improvement process.

CONCLUSIONS

This chapter has explored the extent to which concepts related to systems thinking on knowledge utilization help to make sense of some of the experiences and challenges of a national public health agency and helped to shape an evolving evaluation strategy. It does not provide a comprehensive picture of the national agency or the evaluation function, but it gives an analytical account of some key strategic and methodological challenges. However, the lessons may well have resonance for other Evaluation Units, especially those within organizations with a role in knowledge mobilization for policy and practice contexts. The concepts considered offer insights as to why some aspects of the work were successful and why certain ideas took root, while others took more time to progress, and some failed to thrive.

Making explicit the different assumptions that underpin different mental models of knowledge development and the fact that the models coexist and compete, helps to shed light on the tensions that are often encountered between different stakeholder groups involved in evaluation. They generate different criteria for assessing the quality of evaluation work and what constitutes good practice. Since an important goal of evaluation capacity-building work was to improve the quality of evaluations undertaken, to progress in this area, it becomes essential to be clear about what types of evaluation are needed in what circumstances. It also shapes understandings about what types of skills and learning processes are required internally and across the wider system.

There is some evidence of a move toward systems thinking and a more embedded model of knowledge development, both at an organizational level and across the wider system of public service delivery. It builds on (rather than replaces) a preexisting relationship model and the mechanisms of linkage and exchange. The move is in part due to the recognition of the wicked nature of the health-improvement policy area, in particular addressing the inequalities dimension. The policy implementation response has been to develop complicated multilevel programs delivered by multiagency partnerships within a complex and dynamic environment. While this has created methodological challenges, it has also brought opportunities to experiment with theory-of-change approaches to evaluation and to strengthen program planning. The advent of an outcomes-based approach to public management and accountability provided the opportunity to embed and integrate these evaluation approaches with performance management, to move toward telling a credible contribution story and away from an exclusive focus on performance targets.

An important factor in success has been to combine, within our organization's strategic approach, an acceptance of innovation and experimentation alongside the more routine elements of evaluation practice. In essence, this has meant a license to try out new approaches (e.g., introducing policy reviews, initiating the Evaluation Summer School, trying logic modeling, and adapting commissioning and management practices)—while being alert to opportunities afforded by policy windows to accelerate new ideas and practices, such as came with the concordat and national performance framework and the focus on outcomes. There are costs and risks with this approach since it requires the ability to respond quickly and flexibly to new opportunities; but if successful, it will generate new areas of work and sometimes new areas of skills and expertise. Where there is a fixed or established evaluation resource, these new developments can be challenging and seen as an undesirable added workload. The readjustments to planned work programs and team skills need to be acknowledged and managed.

DISCUSSION QUESTIONS

1. To enhance the use of evaluation in policy, Scotland's experience illustrates the "coming together" of several factors. Which of these are evident in your country or state?

2. Review panels were constituted to assess policy performance with a view to changing or improving policies. Membership, mainly academic in the beginning, evolved to bring in a broad range of stakeholder representation. What new challenges do you think arose from introducing a broader membership? Which stakeholder groups would you include in such a review panel?

3. In Scotland's example, one third of the new public health agency's resources was dedicated to public health evidence and analysis, of which 60% (17 posts) concentrated on advising policymakers and practitioners on what works to improve health (systematic reviews, reviews of reviews, evidence-based guidance). The remaining public health

resource (40%) was concerned with analyzing Scotland's population health data (6 posts) and coordinating the evaluation of local implementation of policies to improve Scotland's health (6 posts). What percentage of the public health agency's budget is dedicated to establishing evidence on policy implementation and effectiveness?

4. The use of an evaluation advisory group is often used to accompany commissioned evaluations as a means of enhancing the use of evaluators' findings. However, there are various reasons why such a group might be constituted. Can you think of three reasons for constituting such a group and what you would hope could be achieved?

NOTES

1. For example, the national public health agency in England, the Health Development Agency (2004), had recently been restructured to focus solely on reviewing public health evidence and producing evidence-based guidance as a new arm of the National Institute for Clinical Excellence (NICE).

2. By 2012, the size of the Evaluation Unit had increased to 11 posts.

3. The evaluation team grew from six posts in 2004 to 11 posts in 2012. The work of the team is largely external facing, although some in-house advice on organizational performance and self-evaluation processes is also provided. Evaluation staff are directly involved in the planning and design of evaluations of national policies and programs, commissioning and managing external contractors, and handling reporting and dissemination aspects; in recent years at NHS Health Scotland, we have increasingly coordinated and conducted the evaluation work ourselves, using routine data. Evaluations are planned and managed on behalf of the Scottish government, with internal program teams and sometimes with local health boards.

4. It is recognized that there are many other complementary methods, tools, and frameworks that can be used as part of the process, such as logic models with linked summaries of evidence, the RE-AIM framework, partnership continuum, and inequalities indicators.

REFERENCES

Best, A., Terpstra, J. L., Moor, G., Riley, B., Norman. C. D., & Glasgow, R. E. (2009). Building knowledge integration systems for evidence-informed decisions. *Journal of Health Organization and Management, 23,* 627–641.

Birckmayer, J. D., & Weiss, C. (2000). Theory based evaluation in practice: What do we learn? *Evaluation Review, 24*(4), 407–431.

Blamey, A., & Mackenzie, M. (2007). Theories of change and realistic evaluation: Peas in a pod or apples and oranges? *Evaluation, 13*(4), 439–455.

Cabinet Office. (1999a). *Modernising government white paper* (Cm 4310). London, UK: Stationery Office.

Cabinet Office. (1999b). *Professional policy making for the twenty first century.* London, UK: Strategy Policy Team, Stationery Office.

Cairney, P. (2009). The role of ideas in policy transfer: The case of UK smoking bans since Devolution. *Journal of European Public Policy, 16*(3), 471–488.

Chelimsky, E. (1997). Preface: The coming transformation in evaluation. In E. Chelimsky & W. R. Shadish (Eds.), *Evaluation for the 21st century: A handbook* (pp. 1–26). Thousand Oaks, CA: Sage.

Cherney, A., & Head, B. (2011). Supporting the knowledge to action process. *Evidence and Policy,* 7(4), 471–488.

Connell, J. P., & Kubisch, A. C. (1998). Applying a theory of change approach to the evaluation of comprehensive community initiatives: Progress, prospects, and problems. In K. Fulbright-Anderson, A. C. Kubisch, & J. P. Connell (Eds.), *New approaches to evaluating community initiatives: Vol. 2. Theory, measurement, and analysis* (pp. 15–44). Washington, DC: Aspen Institute.

Connell, J. P., Kubisch, A. C., Schorr, L. B., & Weiss, C. H. (1995). *New approaches to evaluating community initiatives: Vol. 1. Concepts, methods and contexts.* Washington, DC: Aspen Institute.

Cooper, A. (2012). *Knowledge mobilization intermediaries in education* (Unpublished doctoral dissertation). University of Toronto, Ontario, Canada.

Coote, A., Allen, J., & Woodhead, D. (2004). *Finding out what works: Building knowledge about complex community-based initiatives.* London, UK: Kings Fund.

Coryn, C., Noakes, L., Westine, C., & Scroter, D. (2011). A systematic review of theory-driven evaluation practice from 1990 to 2009. *American Journal of Evaluation, 32,* 199–226.

Cousins, J. B., & Earl, L. M. (Eds.). (1995). *Participatory evaluation in education: Studies in evaluation use and organizational learning.* London, UK: Falmer Press.

Craig, N. (2013). Seeing the wood and the trees: Using outcomes frameworks to inform planning, monitoring and evaluation in public health. *Journal of Public Health, 35.*

Craig, P., West, P., Wimbush, E., Magee, C., Kennicer, M., & Rossi, M. (2005). *National Health Demonstration Projects—Evaluation task group review: Final report.* Edinburgh, UK: Scottish Government. Retrieved August 2, 2012, from http://www.scotland.gov.uk/Publications/2005/04/07105005/50064

Davies, H. T. O., Nutley, S. M., & Smith, P. C. (2000). *What works? Evidence based policy and practice in public services.* Bristol, UK: Policy Press.

Denis, J. L., Lehoux, P., & Champagne, F. (2005). A knowledge utilization perspective on fine-tuning dissemination and contextualizing knowledge. In L. Lemieux-Charles & F. Champagne (Eds.), *Using knowledge and evidence in health care* (pp. 18–40). Toronto, Ontario, Canada: University of Toronto Press.

Forss, K., Marra, M., & Scwartz, R. (Eds.). (2011). *Evaluating the complex: Attribution, contribution and beyond.* New Brunswick, NJ: Transaction.

Gibbons, M. (1995). The emergence of a new mode of knowledge production. In U. Felt & H. Nowotny (Eds.), *Social studies of science in an international perspective* (pp. 55–66). Proceedings of a Workshop, Institut für Wissenschaftstheorie und Wissenschaftsforschung, Universität Wien [Institute for Scientific Theory and Research, University of Vienna], January 13–14, 1994, Vienna, Austria.

Graham, I. D., & Tetroe, J. (2007). How to translate health research knowledge into effective healthcare action. *Healthcare Quarterly, 10*(3), 20–22.

Greene, J. (1988). Stakeholder participation and utilization in program evaluation. *Evaluation Review, 12*(2), 91–116.

Guijt, I. (2007, November). *Assessing and learning for social change: A discussion paper.* Brighton, UK: Institute of Development Studies.

Halliday, E. (2009). *Five year review of "Let's make Scotland more active": A strategy for physical activity.* Edinburgh, UK: NHS Health Scotland. Retrieved August 2, 2012, from http://www.healthscotland.com/documents/3223.aspx

Hawe, P., Shiell, A., & Riley, T. (2004). How far "out of control" should a randomised trial be? *British Medical Journal, 328,* 1561–1563.

Hawe, P., Shiell, A., & Riley, T. (2008). Important considerations for standardising complex interventions. *Journal of Advanced Nursing, 62*(2), 267.

Hawe, P., Shiell, A., & Riley, T. (2009). Theorizing interventions as events in systems. *American Journal of Community Psychology, 43,* 267–276.

Health Development Agency. (2004). *Learning from effective practice: System and standards.* London, UK: HDA.

Hunter, D., Barry, M., & McCulloch, A. (2007). *A review of Scotland's national programme for mental health and wellbeing, 2003–2006.* Edinburgh, UK: NHS Health Scotland.

Kingdon, J. (1995). *Agendas, alternatives and public policies* (2nd ed.). Harlow, Essex, UK: Addison-Wesley Longman.

Lang, T., Dowler, E., & Hunter, D. (2006). *Review of the Scottish Diet Action Plan: Progress and impacts 1996–2005.* Edinburgh, UK: NHS Health Scotland.

Lomas, J. (2000). Using linkage and exchange to move research into policy at a Canadian foundation. *Health Affairs, 19*(3), 236–240.

Mayne, J. (2001). Addressing attribution through contribution analysis: Using performance measures sensibly. *Canadian Journal of Program Evaluation, 16*(1), 1–24.

Mayne, J. (2008). *Contribution analysis: An approach to exploring cause and effect* (ILAC Brief No. 16). Retrieved August 2, 2012, from http://www.cgiar-ilac.org/files/publications/briefs/ILAC_Brief16_Contribution_Analysis.pdf

Mayne, J. (2011). Contribution analysis: Addressing cause and effect. In K. Forss, M. Marra, & R. Scwartz (Eds.), *Evaluating the complex: Attribution, contribution and beyond* (pp. 53–96). New Brunswick, NJ: Transaction.

Mayne, J., & Rist, R. C. (2006). Studies are not enough: The necessary transformation of evaluation. *Canadian Journal of Program Evaluation, 21,* 93–120.

McDonald, B., Rogers, P., & Kefford, B. (2003). Teaching people to fish? Building the evaluation capability of public sector organizations. *Evaluation, 9,* 9–29.

Melhuish, E., Belsky, J., Leyland, A., & Barnes, J. (2008). Effects of fully-established Sure Start Local Programmes on 3-year-old children and their families living in England: A quasi-experimental observational study. *Lancet, 372*(9650), 1641–1647.

Montague, S. (2000). *Circles of influence: An approach to structured, succinct strategy.* Retrieved August 2, 2012, from http://www.pmn.net/library/Circles_of_Influence_An_Approach.htm

Montague, S. (2009, May). *Structured contribution analysis: A brief dialogue and practical demonstration.* Paper presented to Evaluation Summer School, NHS Health Scotland, Edinburgh, United Kingdom.

NHS Health Scotland. (2011). *Library modernisation and the new knowledge services* (HS Board Paper No. 37/11). Retrieved January 14, 2013, from http://www.healthscotland.com/documents/5567.aspx

Nutley, S., Walter, I., & Davies, H. T. O. (2003). From knowing to doing: A framework for understanding the evidence into practice agenda. *Evaluation, 9*(2), 125–148.

Nutley, S., Walter, I., & Davies, H. T. O. (2007). *Using evidence: How research can inform public services.* Bristol, UK: Policy Press.

Patton, M. Q. (1997). *Utilization-focused evaluation* (3rd ed.). Thousand Oaks, CA: Sage.

Pawson, R., & Tilley, N. (1997). *Realistic evaluation.* London, UK: Sage.

Percy-Smith, J., Speller, V., & Nutley, S. (2006). *Evidence informed policy and practice: A review of approaches used in health improvement in Scotland.* Edinburgh, UK: NHS Health Scotland.

Petticrew, M., Cummins, S., Ferrell, C., Findlay, A., Higgins, C., Hoy, C., . . . Sparks, L. (2005). Natural experiments: An underused tool for public health. *Public Health, 119*(9), 751–757.

Preskill, H. S., & Torres, R. T. (1999). *Evaluative inquiry for learning in organizations.* Thousand Oaks, CA: Sage.

Rogers, P. (2004, November). *Leading horses to water: Challenges in building evaluation capacity.* Paper presented to U.K. Evaluation Society Conference, Glasgow, Scotland.

Rogers, P. (2008). Using programme theory to evaluate complicated and complex aspects of interventions. *Evaluation, 14*(1), 29–48.

Russ-Eft, D., & Preskill, H. (2009). *Evaluation in organizations: A systematic approach to enhancing learning, performance and change* (2nd ed.). Cambridge, MA: Perseus.

Shiell, A., Hawe, P., & Gold, L. (2008). Complex interventions or complex systems? Implications for health economic evaluation. *British Medical Journal, 336*(7656), 1281–1283.

Solomon, M. J., & Chowdhury, A. M. (2002). Knowledge to action: Evaluation for learning in a multi-organisational global partnership. *Development in Practice, 12* (3–4), 346–354.

Spicer, N., & Smith, P. (2008). Evaluating complex, area-based initiatives in a context of change: The experience of the Children's Fund Initiative. *Evaluation, 14*(1), 75–90.

Sridharan, S. (2006, September). *Explicating Have a Heart Paisley Phase 2 interventions.* Edinburgh, UK: Research Unit in Health, Behaviour and Change, University of Edinburgh.

Swan, J., Bresnen, M., Robertson, M., Newell, S., & Dopson, S. (2009, November 6). *When policy meets practice: Colliding logics and the challenges of "Mode 2" initiatives in the translation of academic knowledge.* Paper presented at ESRC Research Seminar Series, Making Sense of Knowledge Production; Seminar 2: Co-Producing Knowledge, St Andrews University, Scotland, United Kingdom.

Taylor, A., & Newberry, J. (n.d.). *Boxing ourselves in: When do program logic models become a hindrance to crossing boundaries?* Powerpoint presentation at the Centre for Research and Education in Human Services, Kitchener, Ontario, Canada. Retrieved from http://evaluation canada.ca/distribution/20051027_a_taylor_andrew_newberry_jason.pdf

Torres, R. T., & Preskill, H. (2001). Evaluation and organizational learning: Past, present, and future. *American Journal of Evaluation, 22*(3), 387–395.

Wadsworth, Y. (1998, November). What is participatory action research? *Action Research international* (Paper 2). Retrieved January 10, 2013, from http://www.montana.edu/cpa/news/images/articles/hires/img200603291143660763-1.pdf

Wanless, D. (2004). *Securing good health for the whole population (Wanless report).* London, UK: HM Treasury.

Weiss, C. H. (1979). The many meanings of research utilisation. *Public Administration Review, 39*(5), 426–431.

Williams, P., & Sullivan, H. (2011). Lessons for leadership in learning and knowledge management in multi-organisational settings. *International Journal of Leadership in Public Services, 7*(1), 6–20.

Wimbush, E., Montague, S., & Mulherin, T. (2012). The applications of contribution analysis: Outcome planning and impact evaluation. *Evaluation, 18*(3), 310–329.

CHAPTER 6

FROM DISCRETE EVALUATIONS TO A MORE HOLISTIC ORGANIZATIONAL APPROACH

The Case of the Public Health Agency of Canada

Nancy L. Porteous and Steve Montague

This chapter describes the experience of the Public Health Agency of Canada in augmenting the traditional focus on one-off evaluation studies of individual programs to take a more holistic, organizational approach to our evaluative work.

Note: The authors thank the staff, past and present, of Evaluation Services and the Centre for Excellence in Evaluation and Program Design at the Public Health Agency of Canada for their contribution to this model. Thanks especially to Mary Frances MacLellan-Wright, Adriana Newbury, and others across the Agency who participated in the development of the logic models displayed in Figures 6.2 to 6.4. Thanks also to Paula Walters-Dazé for developing the visuals in Figures 6.1 and 6.5.

Evaluators get entrenched in thinking at the program level. In fact, evaluators are trained to think at the program level. As evaluators, we do good work on the technical front, but too often the quality and usefulness of our evaluations suffer due to a lack of broader organizational understanding and hence an inability to connect our work to the bigger strategic picture.

Not only does the quality and usefulness of individual evaluations suffer, but there are also missed opportunities at the organizational level—opportunities to contribute our unique set of evaluation competencies to organizational learning and development in a more general way, perhaps an even more profound way.

> Evaluators must *operate at the system level* in addition to the level of individual programs that they have traditionally addressed. This is where internal evaluation teams must shine. They must aggregate knowledge across the organization to draw lessons about what works and what does not work with their client base and their subject matter. This is a difficult task because we evaluators have been trained to address our methodologies to individual programs, but this is not where we will find our maximum value added. Many professionals in the organization can offer advice on individual program performance; few have a perspective wide enough to profess across the variety of approaches adopted by the organization. (Gauthier et al., 2009, p. 33)

In the following sections, we discuss the context in which the Public Health Agency's evaluation function developed and the reasons for the shift to a more holistic, organizational approach. We then consider the strategies adopted to connect to the broader organizational picture as well as some of the challenges faced along the way. The four strategies discussed are

- keeping well informed about the organization,
- creating an organizational-level logic model,
- developing a multiyear evaluation plan for the organization, and
- focusing on cumulative evaluative learning across the organization.

In our view, these strategies not only enhanced the quality and usefulness of our evaluation studies for accountability purposes but also contributed to the organization's ability to learn and develop. On the surface, these strategies may seem rather simple and obvious; however, they are not always so straightforward. This brief introduction to these practical approaches may be of particular interest to those new to evaluation generally and/or internal evaluation specifically.

CONTEXT

Public Health Agency of Canada

The Public Health Agency of Canada is part of the national Health Portfolio along with Health Canada, the Canadian Institutes of Health Research, and several other small agencies. The Public Health Agency was created from areas within Health Canada in 2004 following the severe acute respiratory syndrome (SARS) outbreak to respond to the Canadian government's commitment to increase its focus on public health and its capacity to manage public health events. In fiscal year 2011 to 2012, the Agency had about 3,000 employees and an annual budget of approximately $620 million. The Agency is focused on preventing and controlling chronic and infectious diseases, preparing for and responding to public health emergencies, and building public health capacity in Canada. The Agency has regulatory responsibility for quarantine activities as well as pathogen control and safety.

The focus of the Agency's strategic plan for 2007 to 2012 is strengthening links between information gathering, knowledge development, and public health action. The strategic plan (Public Health Agency, 2007, p. 8) describes the Agency's role as follows:

> While health care service delivery is primarily a provincial/territorial responsibility, the responsibility for public health is shared across all jurisdictions. The federal government plays a key role in conjunction with provincial/territorial and local governments, as well as other sectors. In these areas, federal efforts are intended to provide added value, distinct from and complementary to other jurisdictions' activities. These efforts include the following:
>
> - *National leadership.* The requirement to set national standards and guidelines, mobilize partnerships, coordinate national efforts, or build consensus, such as coordinating and leading disease and risk factor surveillance at the national level or developing a national public health human resources strategy
> - *Critical mass.* Where the federal government possesses highly specialized technical expertise to provide advice and services to build national capacity, such as the public health science capacity housed at the Agency's laboratories or its surge capacity in the event of an emergency
> - *Economies of scale.* Similar to critical mass, where significant existing capacity makes it more affordable to build on existing investments, such as the Level 4 biosafety facilities at the Agency's National Microbiology Laboratory

- *Public good investments.* Where costs are centralized but the potential benefits are widely shared, as with the Agency's work on sharing and communicating knowledge within the public health community in Canada and abroad

Evaluation in the Government of Canada

In the Government of Canada, departments and agencies are subject to the Treasury Board Secretariat of Canada's Policy on Evaluation (renewed in 2009). Some of the key features of this policy that have influenced the design of the Public Health Agency of Canada's internal Evaluation Unit include the following:

- *Clients or users:* The head of the organization is the primary client (in this case, the chief public health officer of Canada) although the Treasury Board expects that evaluations will also serve Canadians, Parliamentarians, Ministers, central agencies, and program managers.
- *Focus of evaluations:* Five core issues must be addressed in every evaluation.

  Relevance

  1. Continued need for program

  2. Alignment with government priorities

  3. Alignment with federal roles and responsibilities

  Performance

  4. Achievement of expected outcomes

  5. Demonstration of efficiency and economy

- *Coverage:* Each program must be evaluated at least every five years
- *Transparency:* All evaluations and their accompanying management response and action plans must be made easily available to Canadians in a timely manner (i.e., posting on the Internet)

Evaluation at the Public Health Agency of Canada

As mentioned above, the Public Health Agency of Canada was created from existing areas within Health Canada. The Agency inherited Health Canada's decentralized model for evaluation in which the majority of program evaluations were conducted by evaluators located in program areas. A small corporate Evaluation Unit has been in place at the Agency since 2006. Called the Centre for Excellence in Evaluation and Program Design, it was first housed alongside a center that administered transfer payments (i.e., grants and contributions) within a program branch; then, it reported to an assistant deputy minister responsible for corporate services (such as human resources and finance).

In the past, because there was a specific government-wide requirement to do so, evaluations within the Agency almost exclusively examined grant and contribution programs. Grant and contributions programs existed in health promotion and disease prevention areas; as a result, there were limited formal program evaluations in any of the science, emergency, or regulatory areas of the Agency. Under the decentralized model, evaluators in program areas typically commissioned studies to external consultants. The strength of the decentralized model was that evaluators situated in program areas knew the programs and its stakeholders well and they were in close proximity to provide technical assistance and facilitate evaluation use. The challenge was the real and perceived potential for lack of objectivity due to the evaluator's location in a program area. An evaluator was often line reporting to the manager responsible for the programs they evaluated.

At this time, under the decentralized model for the evaluation function, the Centre for Excellence in Evaluation and Program Design was not a "doer" of evaluation but rather a reviewer of evaluations. The unit supported evaluations in the program areas by providing technical assistance at the front end of evaluations and by carrying out quality assurance reviews at the back end. The unit had only a few staff.

In early 2010, the Agency's evaluation function transitioned from the decentralized model (in which programs conducted evaluations) to an entirely centralized model, led by the corporate Evaluation Unit renamed Evaluation Services. The Evaluation Unit is currently co-located with the internal audit unit overseen by a Director-General of Audit and Evaluation who reports directly to the head of the organization.

The decision to centralize the evaluation function was driven in large part by senior management's desire to have the evaluation of programs carried out with more distance from programs. Centralized evaluation functions are the norm in the Canadian federal government and reflect the requirements of the Treasury Board's policy on evaluation. The unit's salary budget in fiscal year 2011 to 2012 supports a staff of 20 employees; the operating budget is approximately $750,000. All budget allocations are ongoing (as opposed to time- or project-limited) and managed directly by the Evaluation Unit (i.e., the unit is not dependent on transfers from the program areas that are being evaluated). The vision for the Evaluation Unit is that evaluative evidence is valued and used systematically in planning and decision making throughout the Public Health Agency of Canada.

As a result of centralization, the evaluation team expanded and now consists of an executive director and her executive assistant, an associate director, and 17 staff dedicated to evaluation activities (three managers as well as 14 evaluation analysts) for a total of 20 staff in the unit. This is in addition to the Director-General of Audit and Evaluation and her executive assistant. See Table 6.1 for a breakdown of the planned investment of staff time in the four broad activity areas of the unit. Almost all evaluations are conducted in-house by Evaluation Unit staff. Staff tell the management team that they appreciate the opportunity to do the hands-on work of conducting evaluations. This is a consciously determined part of the management team's staff recruitment and retention strategy; there has been little staff turnover since the centralization of the function and the move to the in-house conduct of evaluations. External subject matter or technical experts are routinely engaged, depending on the

Table 6.1 Planned Time Allocation

Evaluation Unit Activity	% of Human Resources
Conduct evaluations (agency programs as well as interdepartmental initiatives) For each evaluation project, the following is our target for time investment: • Planning—25% • Conducting—50% • Reporting, approvals, and dissemination—25%	75.0
Contribute to planning, performance, and reporting (assist with logic models, advise on performance measurement, feed evidence into policy and funding proposals as well as corporate reports and expenditure reviews, etc.)	7.5
Stewardship of the function (evaluation plan, evaluation committee, follow-ups on management response and action plans, development of tools and processes, keeping abreast of agency and government-wide issues, training, liaising with central agencies)	7.5
Management and administration	10.0

nature and needs of the evaluation project. Consultants are engaged for parts of some evaluations, for example, literature reviews, aspects of data collection, and components of report writing.

The Evaluation Unit has developed an electronic planning support tool that tracks staff time (analogous to recording billable hours in the private sector). This information is used to monitor the actual investment of time on projects and tasks against our estimates. The time tracking tool is used to calculate the staff costs associated with each project; when we present an evaluation report to senior management, we tell them how much it cost the organization. We also use these data to sharpen our forecasts for future projects. The duration of most evaluation projects is between six and 18 months; the pressure to conduct evaluations more quickly continues to increase. We are constantly balancing rigor with relevance.

Within the Evaluation Unit, there is a continuum of analyst positions from junior to senior evaluation analyst. Distinctions among the levels of positions align well with the Treasury Board Secretariat of Canada's Competency Profile for Federal Public Service Evaluation Professionals and the Canadian Evaluation Society's Competencies for Evaluation Practice. Staff come from a variety of discipline backgrounds, such as economics, social sciences, and health sciences (including a physician and a nurse). With the transition from the decentralized to the centralized model for the conduct of evaluations, we made a conscious effort to recruit evaluators with experience in program areas from both head-quarters and regional offices. In addition, we deployed a staff member from the strategic policy unit of the Agency. The philosophy of the management team is that this diversity of experience enriches the unit. Most analysts have at least a master's degree; however, only a few have completed graduate-level programs specifically in evaluation.

Based on assessments of learning needs, a professional development plan is in place for the unit. This year, for example, it included in-house training on qualitative data analysis software (NVIVO), evaluation ethics, writing briefing materials, evaluation report writing, and "public health policy 101." In addition, staff participate in learning events and conferences organized by evaluation associations, such as the Canadian Evaluation Society. Access to professional development opportunities is a deliberate part of the management team's staff recruitment and retention strategy. Staff tell us they appreciate the support for their ongoing learning.

The Evaluation Unit operates using a matrix management approach. Analysts have a line-reporting relationship to a manager for administrative purposes, but they may report to one of the other managers for specific evaluation projects.

We try to balance two broad principles in assigning staff to tasks and projects.

- Principles that honor the evaluation function by striving to find the best fit to provide high quality products on time and on budget
  - Match staff skills, knowledge, and experience to the assignment
  - Meet reporting deadlines
  - Demonstrate efficiency in use of human and financial resources
- Principles that honor individual team members by striving to provide equitable opportunities
  - Support professional development goals of staff
  - Accommodate areas of staff interest
  - Balance workloads
  - Respect ability or inability to travel or work overtime, as required

With this context in mind, the following sections outline the strategies we implemented, and the challenges we faced, to move toward a more organizational focus.

STRATEGY 1: KEEP WELL INFORMED ABOUT THE ORGANIZATION

Like most organizations, the Public Health Agency of Canada is operating in an increasingly complex and rapidly changing environment. In order to stay on top of what is going on within the organization, we have been deliberate and intentional in connecting with colleagues in other parts of the organization and systematic in monitoring key discussions, documents, and decisions.

If not aware of senior management preoccupations and concerns as well as plans and priorities (both those that are relatively formal and announced across the organization as well as those that are not widely known across the organization), we feared that we would be unaware of important aspects of the context surrounding a particular program to be evaluated. As a result, we would fail to identify key evaluation issues and questions; thus, our evaluation products would not be relevant to senior management.

Connect Regularly With Key Colleagues

There are a number of important areas and issues with which to be familiar, including those in Table 6.2.

Table 6.2 Organizational Issues to Be Monitored

Areas Within Organization	Examples of Issues to Monitor
Policy	Stakeholder expectations, political sensitivities
Planning	Priorities and commitments
Performance measurement	Results
Internal audit	Risks
Finance	Resources
Communications	Public opinion, media interest

There are informal and formal approaches to liaising on these issue areas. On the informal front, individual evaluators in the unit look for opportunities to get to know their colleagues across the organization and build good working relationships. On the formal side, the Public Health Agency has networks of policy analysts, planners, and performance measurement specialists who meet to discuss topics of interest. Participating in these networks is an excellent way for Evaluation Unit staff to develop and maintain solid organizational and situational awareness. It is important for us to be aware of what networks exist and to make the case that an evaluation perspective can add value. We have to prioritize which groups are most critical to the Evaluation Unit and determine the appropriate intensity of staff involvement. This latter point is important for two reasons. First, time is always at a premium, and we do not want to divert too much time and attention away from conducting evaluations and carrying out other evaluation-related activities. Second, our evaluator role demands some distance from the entities we will eventually be evaluating. We are mindful of the role we play in these networks and the extent to which evaluation staff are becoming a part of the processes, products, or programs they will eventually need to evaluate (see further discussion on distance and independence in the Summary, Discussion, and Implications sections of this chapter).

Connecting regularly with key colleagues and networks is beginning to pay off in two important ways. First, we have key contacts when we need the "scoop" on the latest developments within the organization. Second, with strong working relationships as well as good situational and organizational awareness, our Evaluation Unit members are in a better position to proactively insert ourselves into any processes that could benefit from evaluative thinking. Evaluators have many skills (e.g., asking questions, relying on evidence, analyzing, facilitating, etc.)

and tools (e.g., logic modeling) that are of great value to the organization; but, unfortunately, we are not always or often seen as the first "go-to" people.

Continually Monitor Key Discussions, Documents, and Decisions

To keep an eye on what is happening across the organization, we also believed it was important for our internal Evaluation Unit to engage in a systematic process of ongoing environmental scanning and analysis, including

- being aware of the governance structures and reporting relationships within the organization and taking stock of items on the agenda and forward agenda;
- reviewing minutes and records of discussion and decision from governance committees;
- being familiar with policy, program, and budget and reporting cycles and reviewing draft and final plans and reports as they are available; and
- being aware of any formal or informal changes in senior management priorities—for policies and programs as well as management and administration.

In addition to monitoring current discussions, documents, and decisions, it is also critical that staff in our unit know where and how to access this information retrospectively. Often, evaluators rely on program staff to provide key program documents. Unfortunately, with high turnover rates and variable information management practices, program staff do not always have the full picture—especially the corporate memory of program history. As a result, evaluators need to know what systems exist in the organization to help them mine this information. Staff in our unit monitor databases that contain information on governance committees (issue sheets and presentations by and about the program area as well as records of discussion and decision), executive correspondence and briefing notes, as well as notifications of web postings and other publications.

We have discovered that knowing where to find information is especially important when evaluating an entity that cuts across many parts of the organization and is not limited to a well-contained program area. There is not a single repository of information; evaluators must search for and piece together information from multiple sources. The evaluation of the Canadian Health Portfolio's response to the H1N1 pandemic in 2009 and 2010 illustrates the need to engage in extensive mining of existing information (www.phac-aspc .gc.ca/about_apropos/evaluation/reports-rapports/2010-2011/h1n1).

- The communications team provided critical information regarding web analytics, public opinion research, and media analyses.
- The corporate secretariat, which manages all senior management governance bodies, granted access to meeting materials. They also had records from meetings with other federal government departments.
- The emergency operations center provided extensive information on response efforts—all e-mails as well as daily situation and epidemiological reports.
- The strategic policy directorate housed the materials from meetings with provincial and territorial partners as well as international organizations and other national governments.
- The respiratory disease and immunization program area shared crucial subject matter information.

Approaches and Lessons Learned

On our unit work plan, we assign specific team members to be responsible for being the main point of contact with key areas within the organization (e.g., the communications or strategic policy units), and we divide the responsibility for serving on internal or external networks and work groups.

Similarly, we assign individuals to be responsible for monitoring key discussions, documents, and decisions. We experienced a number of challenges but have been experimenting with ways to address them. First, ongoing environmental and organizational scanning is important, but when faced with urgent deadlines for evaluation deliverables, inevitably, these are the tasks that get bumped down the priority list. As a management team, we try to reinforce the importance of this activity by requesting short briefings on the content of specific documents with an analysis of the implications for our evaluation function or specific evaluation projects; in other words, we create a deadline! The second challenge related to the shared accountability for the task. Instead of assigning one individual to a few specific documents, we assigned four team members to the strategic analysis of a large set of regularly produced documents. In the end, little got done. We revised our work plan to identify specific individuals for specific documents. Third, we did not establish a formal mechanism for feeding this information into team learning. We discovered it needs to be formalized as a standing item on the team meeting agenda and integrated into the evaluation project planning and management processes. We regularly invited staff from other areas of the organization to come to one of our team meetings to explain their role in the organization and describe the pressures they face (e.g., finance, legal services, public opinion research, strategic policy). In addition to the regular Evaluation Unit team meeting, which is typically one and a half hours every two weeks, there is also a staff-driven unit Lunch and Learn event once a month for discussing evaluation lessons learned across projects and a new "incubator" series to exchange ideas about how our Evaluation Unit's tools and practices can be improved.

Benefits

Maintaining organizational awareness has been critical for our unit at two levels: (a) for enhancing the quality and usefulness of specific evaluations and (b) for injecting evaluative thinking into other aspects of the organization—to influence organizational culture and learning, one has to be aware of what is going on in the organization at all levels. These two benefits mutually reinforce each other (see Table 6.3).

Table 6.3 Two Main Benefits of Maintaining Organizational Awareness

	Benefits ← →	
Gathering important intelligence that will help sharpen the focus of an evaluation, broaden its data collection, and enhance analysis ↓ Improves quality and usefulness of individual evaluations		Integrating evaluative thinking into key discussions, processes, analyses, documents, and decisions across the organization ↓ Enhances organizational learning and development
	Illustrative Quotes	
"Since evaluation systems are context dependent, they must take into account constituents' needs, wants, and expectations plus other variables such as . . . political forces, media interests . . . organizational mission, goals, and priorities; organizational governance, management, protocols, and operating routines; and the organization's history and current challenges" (Stufflebeam, 2002, p. 1).		"Internal evaluators are often excluded from major decisions or so far removed from critical information networks that they don't know about new initiatives or developments in time to build in an evaluation perspective up front" (Patton, 2008, p. 219). "Front-end analysis is the unfulfilled wish of most evaluators: to be asked to examine relevant issues before organizations commence program interventions" (Sonnichesen, 2000, p. 212).

By investing time in keeping well informed about the organization, we have developed valuable insider knowledge about some aspects of the organization. Over time, we aim to gain a solid grasp on the overall organizational culture and how it might be evolving; the Agency's history and current context; past, current, and emerging pressures and priorities; the players and small "p" politics; as well as the way things work, including subtleties and nuances sometimes lost on someone external to the organization. If we stay on top of what is going on in the organization, we anticipate that there will be more likelihood that we will be able to identify opportunities (both formal and informal) to exert influence in the planning, implementation, and reporting cycle (see Figure 6.1).

Figure 6.1 Evaluation's Role in the Planning, Implementation, and Reporting Cycle

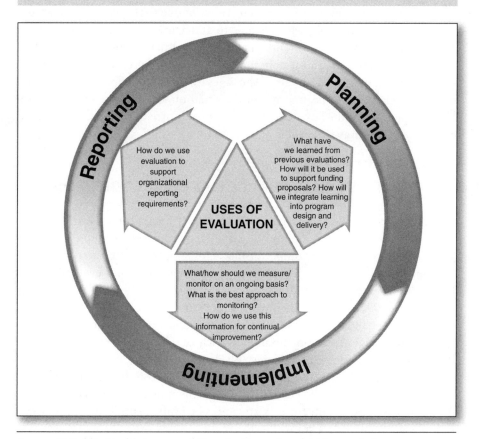

Source: © Public Health Agency of Canada. Reproduced with permission.

A good example of the need for evaluator involvement in broader organizational exercises concerns a recent Canadian government-wide expenditure review and deficit reduction exercise (see www.actionplan.gc.ca/initiatives/eng/index.asp?mode=3&initiativeID=301). Each federal department was required to identify savings of 5% to 10% of their budgets. In the Public Health Agency of Canada, a member of the Evaluation Unit participated in the analysis stage of the review by playing a challenge function and injecting information from previous evaluations, where available. This helped ensure that evaluative evidence was in fact one of the inputs into the decision-making process. Equally important, however, was the value to the Evaluation Unit of being involved in the exercise. We were involved in discussions which revealed various perspectives across the organization—issues and concerns, as well as perceived success stories. This provided us with invaluable insight into future directions within the organization. In this case, it also meant that we were privy to information that only a limited number of staff were aware of due to the confidential nature of the exercise. As a result, we were able to anticipate potential changes within the organization about six months prior to any official announcements. This enabled us to factor that information into current evaluation work. There were several very important and direct linkages to evaluation projects currently underway. Had we not been aware of the situation, there was a very high likelihood that we would have delivered completely irrelevant and meaningless evaluations several months later.

STRATEGY 2: CREATE AN ORGANIZATIONAL-LEVEL LOGIC MODEL

Organizations often lack a corporate-level, results-focused framework that can be used as a basis to develop and describe strategy, design and re-design programs, measure and report on performance, or simply describe activities.

Logic models can assist. They are a common planning and evaluation tool for describing the theory and assumptions underpinning individual programs (Porteous, 2009; Porteous, Sheldrick, & Stewart, 1997, 2002). Although less prevalent, logic models are also extremely valuable visuals to depict the overarching results logic for an organization as a whole (Harrison, 2007; Montague & Porteous, 2012; Taylor-Powell, Jones, & Henert, 2003).

An organizational-level logic model has contributed to helping to galvanize a results focus at the Public Health Agency. As mentioned earlier, when created, the Agency was carved off from existing areas within Health Canada, so it was business as usual amid a transition to creating a new organization. There was not the luxury to stop and take the time to build from scratch an overarching results framework to underpin the work across the organization. Programs and organizational units brought pieces from their past (logic models, plans, performance measurement strategies, etc.), and at the same time, new programs and organizational units were created. The Agency has a solid five-year strategic plan with a well-articulated vision, mission, and mandate all premised on an information-knowledge-action continuum. What was missing, however, was a real articulation of how that information-knowledge-action continuum operated within the Agency. As a result, there was little consistency in the results stories across programs.

An organizational review and assessment of the Agency by external consultants found that some staff did not necessarily know how, or feel like, they fit into the bigger organizational picture. The review recommended that the organization develop a logic model. Over the course of many months, the Evaluation Unit developed a logic model, working with Montague as an external consultant and a working group of staff members from various parts of the organization. It began with a review of the dozens of existing logic models for programs and organizational units within the Agency followed by consultations with management teams across the organization. With each consultation and working group discussion, the draft logic model was refined to capture the main thrusts of the feedback.

The key elements of the logic model for the Public Health Agency of Canada in Figure 6.2 include program activities, *reach* (a technical term used in evaluation—a measure of the percent of the target population that is in touch with the program), and (expected) outcomes. This symbolic picture was intended to be pitched at a high enough level to be broadly representative but focused enough to clearly distinguish important relationships and sequences. It incorporates several notable innovations in logic modeling: spheres of influence (Montague, Young, & Montague, 2003); explicit inclusion of reach (Montague, 2000; Montague & Porteous, 2012; Montague, Porteous, & Sridharan, 2011); and framing stakeholder engagement as an outcome rather than a process or activity (Porteous & Birch-Jones, 2007, based on work with Montague). Of course, like any logic model, it is just a depiction of the theory behind what the organization does for whom and why. It is not intended to capture all nuances, and it no doubt oversimplifies and "linearizes" the complex systems within and around the organization.

The model shows how information and assistance emerges from both organizational activities and from constructive engagement with stakeholders—influencing both organizations and institutions (left side) *and* individuals and communities (right side) along a progressive chain of outcomes. The chains are interconnected and often work in multiple directions across different stakeholders.

Figure 6.2 Logic Model for the Public Health Agency of Canada

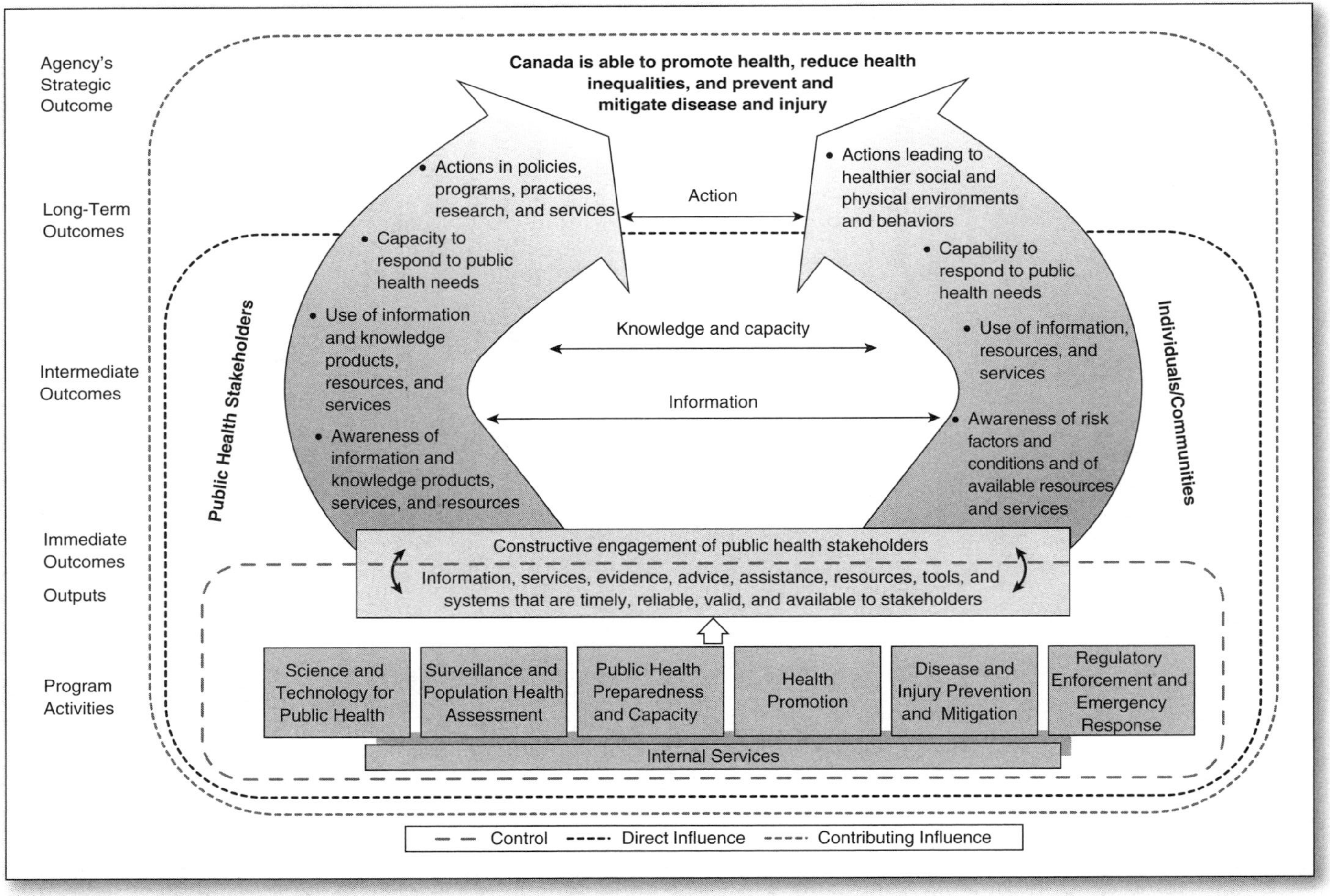

Source: © Public Health Agency of Canada. Reproduced with permission.

The intent is that this progressive, nonlinear, and often iterative chain should help promote health, reduce health inequalities, and prevent and mitigate harm and injury.

The idea underpinning this work was that a high-level results logic could help Public Health Agency employees understand how their activities bring about change to achieve the organization's ultimate outcomes. It can also help employees and stakeholders understand the chain of results between the expenditures, activities, and outputs for which the organization is accountable and over which it has direct control, as well as the results, which it can only influence directly or indirectly. In addition, the approach should help fill gaps in terms of recognizing expected change processes in institutional intermediaries and showing both quantitative and qualitative engagement with key stakeholders as an early and important foundation for the organization's success.

Such an approach offers a common thread to various results stories across the organization. Conceptually, it is a series of linked or nested models, depicting various levels in the organization from the highest level down through organizational units or functions as well as individual programs or activities. The general organizational-level logic model is intended to inspire more detailed logic models, results frameworks, and strategy descriptions within the organization. As such, specific logic models and descriptions will likely embellish, alter, deviate from, or occasionally ignore parts of the overall model. See Figure 6.3 and Figure 6.4 for examples of drill downs from the organizational level to specific horizontal functions that cut across the organization.

Challenges and Benefits

Throughout the process of developing the logic model, there was resistance from one area within the Public Health Agency. They questioned the concept of an organizational logic model for two main reasons: because they believed a logic model's value was limited to the program level; and they thought an Agency-wide logic model would duplicate existing tools, such as the Agency's program activity architecture (a government-wide requirement to have an inventory of programs and their activities and subactivities), as well as the corporate performance measurement framework. Discussion focused not necessarily on the substance of what the logic model was trying to convey but rather the concept and what to call it. We experimented with many labels for this tool: strategic road map, framework, or model; operating environment; and so on. In the end, we settled on *results storyline*. Ironically, while discussions about the merit of an organizational logic model were happening at a

Figure 6.3 Logic Model for the Policy Function at the Public Health Agency of Canada

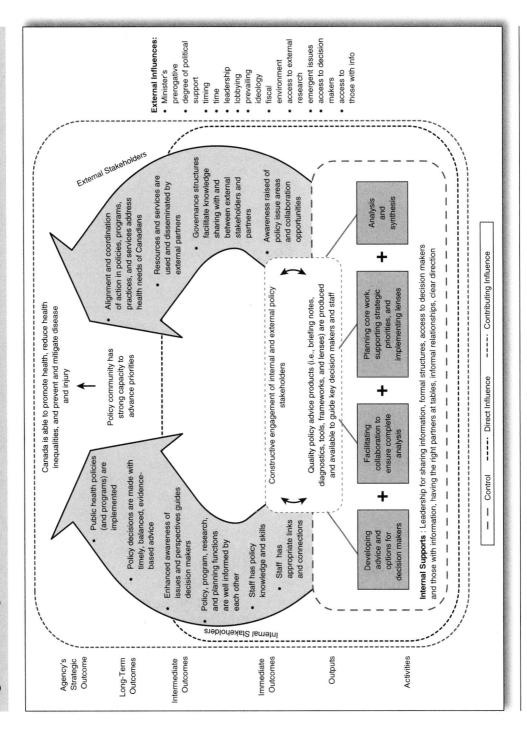

Source: © Public Health Agency of Canada. Reproduced with permission.

Figure 6.4 Logic Model for the Science and Research Function at the Public Health Agency of Canada

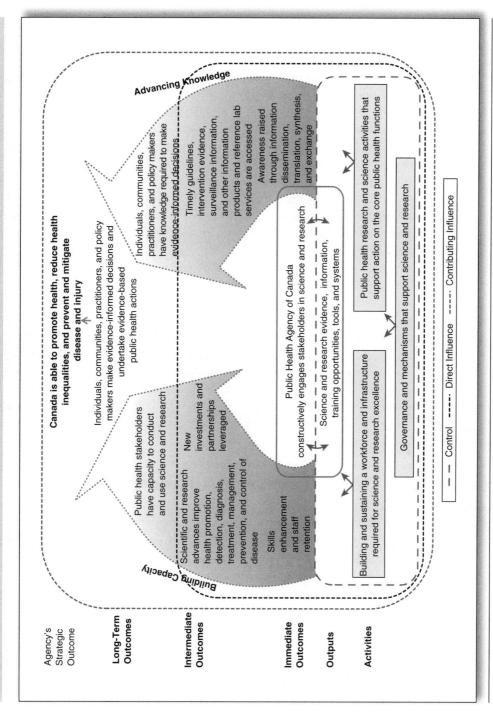

131

senior level, program staff across the Agency were already using the "draft" logic model as a tool for program planning and performance measurement.

Developing an organizational-level logic model adds value at two levels. First, at the level of individual evaluations, it helps situate a program being evaluated in its broader organizational context, in other words, showing how it is connected within the bigger organizational picture. In very practical terms, it has been useful at all stages in our evaluation processes, for example, as a guide to help understand program level theory, to identify the most critical evaluation issues, to address and stimulate thinking about specific evaluation questions, to identify and understand stakeholders, as well as to assist with analysis and reporting. The logic model has also been helpful in developing our organizational evaluation plan, identifying critical policy instruments, functions, themes, or program clusters to evaluate (see Strategy 3 in this chapter).

Second, at the organizational level, the logic model offered an evaluative, results-focused framework that can be used for multiple purposes across the organization: staff orientation and training, internal and external communications, program design and redesign, operational and strategic planning, as well as various types of analysis and reporting. Most importantly though, it is a catalyst for conversation and a diagram to spark dialogue about the theory behind what the organization is trying to accomplish. Over time, such a tool should cultivate more coherence and consistency in the Agency's results storyline—up, down, and across the organization. This is a very tangible contribution of evaluation to an organization's approach to results-based management.

STRATEGY 3: DEVELOP A MULTIYEAR EVALUATION PLAN FOR THE ORGANIZATION

As pointed out in the introductory chapter of this book, an evaluation may not get used because it is not timely and/or not relevant for the organizational decisions at hand. That is, it is delivered too late to input into decision making, and/or it misses critical evaluation issues and questions.

Developing a multiyear organizational evaluation plan is now a well-established practice in many institutions to address this challenge (for example, see guidance for Canadian federal government departments from the Treasury Board of Canada Secretariat, 2011). An evaluation plan maps out the approach to addressing organizational information needs over the longer term to ensure that timely evaluations can actually be used at significant policy, planning reporting, and/or budgeting moments within the organization.

An evaluation plan lays out

- the universe of possible evaluands;
- an approach to prioritizing and scheduling evaluations (typically risk-based);
- the actual schedule of evaluation projects along with estimated budgets and timelines; and
- the priorities for other evaluative work, such as supporting the development and implementation of program performance measurement strategies.

At the Agency, our internal Evaluation Unit tries to anticipate the organization's high-level decision-making needs so that useful evaluative information can be delivered, during key policy, planning, reporting, or budget "windows," such as approval of new policies or programs, budget allocation or reallocation, or renewal of programs. Prioritizing and scheduling evaluations is done using a risk-based approach. Risks are related to the following dimensions (Treasury Board of Canada Secretariat, 2011).

- The stakes associated with poor program performance are
    o health and safety of the population;
    o political implications; or
    o media attention.

- Program characteristics include
    o materiality (size of budget);
    o reach (how many people and/or organizations are involved or impacted); or
    o complexity (number and type of delivery partners, legal context, etc.).

- The extent to which the organization is already aware of issues within the program show
    o managers have identified challenges;
    o stakeholders have expressed concerns; or
    o findings from previous evaluations, audits, and/or other types of reviews point to concerns about program relevance and/or performance.

We have observed many benefits to evaluation planning, both at the organizational level (in terms of engagement and coordination) and for the Evaluation Unit itself:

Engagement of the Organization in Evaluation

- Provides the basis for consultation on evaluation needs and priorities—given that the policy agenda, development and updating of the evaluation plan allows for open dialogue about the most pressing needs for evaluative analysis

- Assists in identifying higher order evaluation issues, or "learning" questions, for the Agency as a whole (we have integrated these questions into multiple evaluations)
- Helps to ensure evaluation coverage of all areas within the organization, not just those that are easier to evaluate or have been evaluated in the past
- Raises awareness of the evaluation function across the organization
- Allows program areas ample time to prepare for an evaluation (for example, program documents are organized and available, performance measurement and administrative data are collected and analyzed, financial data are tracked, lists of program stakeholders are complied, and so on)

Coordination

- Allows the Evaluation Unit to proactively coordinate with other plans and priorities such as the Agency's internal audit plan or stakeholder engagement plan
- Ensures evaluations are scheduled in the context of other major oversight and reporting requirements, such as external audits and/or reports to central agencies or Parliament

Management of the Evaluation Unit

- Ensures that the Evaluation Unit is not continually reacting or responding to ad hoc requests
- Supports budgeting and work planning within the Evaluation Unit
- Encourages accountability for delivering evaluation products on time

An obvious drawback to formal and fixed evaluation plans is the lack of flexibility to respond to shifting needs and priorities within the organization or changes in the resources available within the Evaluation Unit. The approach used within the Canadian federal government to deal with this challenge is development of a "rolling" five-year plan, which is updated annually (Treasury Board of Canada Secretariat, 2011).

In developing the Agency evaluation plan, we include a placeholder for requests from senior management for special studies and to identify crosscutting (that is, multiprogram) evaluations. Each of these points is addressed below.

Special Studies

We discovered early on that it is necessary to leave flexibility in the evaluation plan for accommodating senior management requests for special studies.

An important factor in institutionalizing evaluation within organizations is "establishing and maintaining a quick response mechanism to address emergency evaluation needs" (Stufflebeam, 2002, p. 1). This is especially important for organizations like ours that respond to crises (such as health, defense, and humanitarian assistance organizations). The emergency management area in the Agency routinely carries out "after action reviews," following major training exercises or significant events involving the emergency operations center (such as chemical, biological, and radio-nuclear events, disease outbreaks, or natural disasters). However, there are sometimes concerns about lack of objectivity or the fact that these reviews examine only the response of certain areas within the organization rather than the organization as a whole. When we as the internal Evaluation Unit carry out a review, it has been seen as more objective (for examples of these types of review, see www.phac-aspc.gc.ca/about_apropos/evaluation/reports-rapports/2010–2011/h1n1 or www.phac-aspc.gc.ca/fs-sa/listeria/2008-intro-lessons-lecons-eng.php).

Although these types of "lessons learned reviews" employ systematic evaluative approaches, they have not been viewed by central agencies as an evaluation per se because they did not address all five of the evaluation issues required by the Treasury Board policy on evaluation (as described in the Context section). However, this type of evaluative work is very valuable to the organization. Responding with quality evaluative work under tight timelines has done much to raise the profile and credibility of our internal Evaluation Unit. Quick studies with sound methods and objectivity are seen as deeply relevant and allow management to respond in a timely fashion to areas requiring improvement (Hamilton, Roulston, & Porteous, 2010).

Crosscutting Evaluations

In addition to planning for program-specific evaluations, our evaluation plan considers crosscutting, organizational-level evaluations. These crosscutting evaluations could examine organizational issues from a number of different perspectives, including the following:

- Policy instruments (e.g., financial incentives, regulatory control regimes, information programs, and hybrid combinations)
- Functions (e.g., policy, science and research, knowledge translation)
- Themes (e.g., international activities, publications, field services)
- Clusters of similar types of programs (e.g., programs with similar modes of delivery or those working toward common long-term outcomes or programs aimed at the same target group)

At the Public Health Agency, the organizational-level logic model has been a valuable tool in helping to identify crosscutting evaluation priorities (see Strategy 2 in this chapter).

This type of crosscutting approach can be useful for learning as a whole within the organization by examining issues that touch on multiple program areas. In this sense, the evaluation can be less threatening to an individual program manager and can help engage the broader management team in tackling common areas for improvement.

The downside, however, is that crosscutting evaluations might be "rolled up" to such a high-level of analysis that they lose meaning and relevance. It may be difficult for program managers to ascertain the precise implications for them at a program level.

Related is the issue of accountability for action in response to evaluation recommendations. For large crosscutting evaluations, it is likely that no single manager is accountable. In these situations of shared accountability, we have found that it is important to designate an overall senior management lead for coordinating follow-up on evaluation recommendations. Then, for each major action item, even if accountability for action is shared, one senior manager should be designated as accountable for ensuring coordination of action as well as tracking of and reporting on implementation of action plans. This is especially critical for evaluations that cut across organizations, sometimes referred to as joint, horizontal, or interdepartmental evaluations. For an example, see http://www.phac-aspc.gc.ca/about_apropos/evaluation/reports-rapports/2010–2011/h1n1/pdf/mrap-mrpa-eng.pdf.

STRATEGY 4: FOCUS ON CUMULATIVE EVALUATIVE LEARNING ACROSS THE ORGANIZATION

Within an organization, programs may experience similar types of challenges in implementing activities, reaching target groups, or achieving outcomes. Evaluations may highlight these challenges. However, by responding to the findings and recommendations in a piecemeal fashion program-by-program and evaluation-by-evaluation, systemic issues facing the organization may not be addressed. The same lessons are learned over and over by individual programs, but as a whole, the organization does not learn and develop.

Common themes tend to emerge over time from evaluations and other types of reviews conducted in similar settings. Below are a few examples from the Canadian federal government context.

- Evaluations of interdepartmental or joint initiatives echo consistent findings about difficulties with governance structures and in communication and coordination across partners.
- Many program evaluations reveal a paucity of performance measurement data and a lack of reliable longitudinal data on program expenditures.
- Evaluations of transfer payment programs (i.e., grants and contributions) often comment on the challenges around the timeliness of funding.
- Evaluations of emergency response efforts routinely uncover the need for further clarity of roles and responsibilities among the various players.

To capture common themes, our internal Evaluation Unit has put in place a formal and regular approach to systematically review all Public Health Agency evaluations and other types of assessments. An analysis of findings and recommendations across evaluations has helped uncover issues, such as the examples listed above, with respect to design, delivery and implementation, reach, and achievement of results within the organization. A synthesis across evaluations also carries more weight with senior management than findings and recommendations from a single evaluation; trends across evaluations are more difficult to ignore. Realist synthesis highlights the extent to which mechanisms work (for whom) in different conditions and contexts (Pawson, 2006). Such an approach raises awareness of systemic issues, so they can be addressed.

Some managers feel defensive when evaluations point out areas for improvement in their programs. We have found that it is important and helpful for them to know that other managers are facing similar challenges. By working together, they may be able to tackle broader system-level issues that affect their programs and increase the chances that the issues will be resolved and stay resolved over time.

We have implemented a similar process for the management action plans that respond to evaluation recommendations to examine what patterns exist in the ways in which the Agency addresses evaluation recommendations. An analysis of action plans and the extent to which they were implemented (or not) provides useful insight to the Evaluation Unit and to the rest of the organization. For instance, it can inform how the evaluation team frames evaluation recommendations in the future (i.e., more actionable).

With this type of formal approach to review and synthesis, it is easier to feed this information into the planning-implementation-reporting cycle as shown in Figure 6.1.

Yes, we evaluate individual programs, determine whether they achieve their objectives, and identify ways they could work better. At some point, the accumulation of knowledge about what works and what does not work should lead to an ability to provide guidance for policy and program development. This is where internal Evaluation Units should shine: they should be the corporate memory about program performance, and their expertise should be used to make the best decisions in a critical moment like now. (Gauthier et al., 2009, pp. 23–24)

Benefits

As our Evaluation Unit became more conscious of the broader patterns in findings from past evaluations, we have been able to explore these issues in related evaluations. This allows evaluations to go deeper into these issues, to be more sophisticated in questions and analysis, and to track if efforts to address these challenges within the organization are making a difference.

It is very difficult for an individual program manager to tackle system-wide challenges; however, if approached from an organizational or corporate perspective, there is greater likelihood that common issues can be resolved. This approach can lead to implementing broader, organization-wide changes that will make improvements across programs.

Mayne and Rist (2006, pp. 95–96) have argued that "studies are not enough" and that evaluators must play a significant role in "creating analytic streams of evaluative knowledge." They argue, "There will need to be a movement away from a singular focus on producing more and more one-off evaluations and toward a synthesis and integration of evaluative knowledge into management practices and policies." They believe evaluators should take the lead in creating evaluative information.

SUMMARY

Despite the traditional focus on conducting one-off evaluation studies of individual programs, this chapter shares one internal Evaluation Unit's experience in trying to take an organizationally more holistic approach to its evaluative work. Based on our early experience, we believe that doing so has enhanced the quality and usefulness of individual evaluations (due to the evaluators' more comprehensive understanding of the organizational context and its players) while at the same time it has added value to the organization (because of the evaluators' unique set of skills and experience). Table 6.4 summarizes the key points of this chapter.

Table 6.4 Summary of Key Points

Challenges		Strategy	Benefits	
Evaluations	Organizational Learning		Evaluations	Organizational Learning
Evaluations overlook key issues and do not gather and analyze critical information	Key organizational processes ignore findings and recommendations from previous evaluations	① Keep well informed about the organization	Being up-to-date on latest developments increases likelihood that an evaluation will be relevant and actionable	Increases opportunities to infuse evaluative thinking and/or evidence
Evaluation is disconnected from overall results framework of organization	No common thread ties together program logic and monitoring across organization	② Create an organizational-level logic model	Situates evaluation of any program in broader context	Provides a multipurpose, results-focused framework
Evaluations are not timely or relevant	Evaluative information not available during key policy, planning, reporting, or budget windows	③ Develop a multiyear evaluation plan for the organization	Improves management of the Evaluation Unit	Adds greater engagement of the organization in evaluation and an increase in coordination with other functions
Evaluative evidence does not inform public policy	Learning happens only at the program level, not across the organization as a whole	④ Focus on cumulative evaluative learning across the organization	Allows for deeper analysis of common issues experienced across the organization	Highlights patterns and trends across programs and bolsters case for improvements

DISCUSSION

An obvious question is how much time does all of this take? The time required to implement these four strategies within an organization is not insignificant. It is, in fact, quite substantial. However, investing time up front in implementing these strategies should reduce the level of effort required for various aspects of an actual evaluation process, and it should also significantly improve the quality and usefulness of the eventual evaluation report. In order to test these assumptions, as mentioned earlier, our unit implemented an activity reporting system to track staff time spent on each stage of an evaluation project as well as the activities associated with each of the four strategies outlined in this chapter. With only a little over a year into our time tracking system, it is too early to confirm a payoff.

Another important question is how an Evaluation Unit and individual evaluators can maintain independence and integrity in the evaluation function while striving to be a full organizational player. There are a number of ways to maintain the independence of the work of an internal Evaluation Unit. Mayne (2012) describes four general practices to enhance independence:

- Using independent evaluators
- Using external reviewers
- Involving a broad range of stakeholders in the evaluation process
- Governance and oversight of the evaluation function

At the Public Health Agency, the governance of the overall evaluation function, as well as individual evaluation projects, involves a number of these mechanisms. The visual in Figure 6.5 illustrates these:

- The routine use of external subject-matter reviewers as well as external technical experts in evaluation
- The involvement of different types of organizational stakeholders in providing input to the evaluation
- The pivotal role of the organizational-level evaluation committee chaired by the chief public health officer (head of the organization) and composed of the Agency's most senior management (i.e., assistant deputy ministers of the program branches as well as the heads of key corporate functions, such as finance, communications, and strategic policy)[1]

The Evaluation Committee reviews and approves the Agency's five-year evaluation plan, which includes the schedule of evaluations, and is then

Figure 6.5 Evaluation Governance Structure

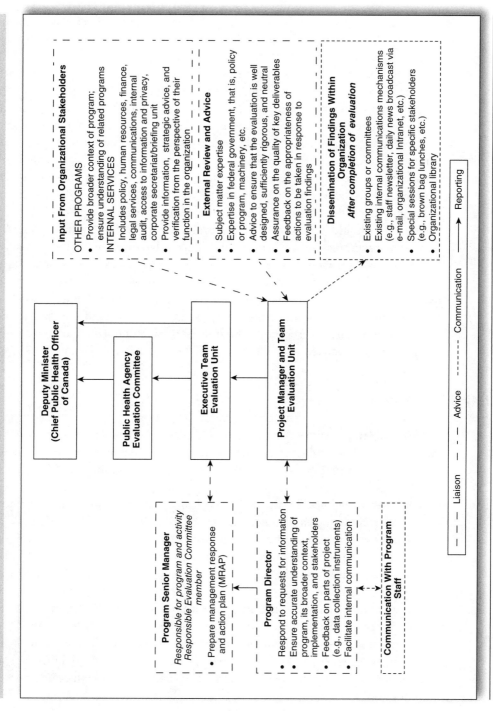

Source: © Public Health Agency of Canada. Reproduced with permission.

involved at every stage of the evaluation process: terms of reference, updates on conducting data collection, preliminary findings and recommendations, and the final report.

One of the interesting advantages evaluators should have in linking to internal management processes without getting co-opted and losing their independence stems from the nature of evaluation itself. Ideally, the function should operate from the "outside-in," starting all planning and performance dialogues, not with a focus on what "we" the organization and its partners are doing, but rather a focus on what is happening "out there" in terms of issues, phenomena, risks, and practices in target communities and their constituent and surrounding systems. This should help evaluators to stay somewhat more detached intellectually from the potential biases involved in internal "inside-out" thinking. Indeed, it should be the role of the evaluator to be the "critical friend" to internal programs and initiatives, providing a language and a lens that will continuously promote the asking of "why?" "who do we reach?" and "what difference does this (do we) make?" (Montague & Shepherd, 2011). This perspective fits well with a pluralist approach to evaluation. "Pluralists call on evaluators to increase their proximity to the evaluand and claim that such practice promotes a better understanding of the internal dynamics and contextual factors associated with the evaluand" (Tarsilla, 2010).

IMPLICATIONS

There are implications for evaluation associations, managers of Evaluation Units, individual evaluators, as well as researchers. Below are a few examples.

Several evaluation associations have developed guiding principles, standards, and ethical guidelines (for a sample, see www.ioce.net/resources/eval_standards_guidelines.shtml). Much work has also been done on articulating evaluator competencies (Canadian Evaluation Society, 2010; Ghere, King, Stevahn, & Minnema, 2006).[2] Many of these principles, standards, guidelines, and competencies, however, are geared toward discrete evaluation projects. Consideration should be given to rendering more explicit the importance of a more comprehensive organizational approach to evaluation. For example, with the Canadian Evaluation Society's competency framework, the importance of possessing broad organizational awareness is only hinted at in the situational practice competency (3) and to an even lesser extent in the reflective practice (1) and interpersonal (5) competencies; the technical (2) and management (4) competencies focus exclusively on the conduct of a specific evaluation.

There are also implications for capacity building within the broader evaluation community and within Evaluation Units in specific organizations. Professional development opportunities should include more exposure to

- policy analysis and development;
- program planning and design;
- the budget, planning, and policy cycles of public and not-for-profit organizations;
- models of organizational governance structures; and
- effective strategies for engaging with and communicating to senior managers and elected officials.

In terms of implications for individual career planning, evaluators might benefit from rounding out their technical evaluation experience with exposure to programs, policy, corporate services, or central agencies at various points in their career. Short assignments or cross training in program or policy areas would enrich their evaluation skills. The presence of an evaluator in a program or policy area would be of benefit to the organization as well.

No doubt, there is a need for more research on evaluation theory and practice (Porteous, 2005). Henry and Mark (2003) have proposed a useful set of questions to guide a research agenda for evaluation, posing questions such as, "What difference has evaluation made? What's the value-add of evaluation to policy and program improvement?" and "When and why does evaluation affect important decisions and actions? How can we optimize the use of evaluative work?" In this regard as well, it will be important for researchers to extend their questions beyond an exclusive focus on what difference evaluation has made at the program level to examining overarching organizational differences. What have been the impacts of evaluation and evaluators on organizational learning and organizational culture? Has there been movement toward an evaluative culture?

DISCUSSION QUESTIONS

1. Can you think of any other ways in which evaluators could apply evaluative thinking at the organizational level? What approaches might be missing from the strategies presented in this chapter?

2. Threats to independence and demands on resources are two challenges mentioned at the end of the chapter. What are some of the other possible pitfalls, downsides, disadvantages,

or barriers of taking a more holistic, organizational approach to our evaluative work? How can these be mitigated?

3. These strategies reflect the authors' experience in Canada largely from a federal government perspective. Do you feel the ideas presented are applicable in other cultural contexts and/or organizational settings? What adaptations might need to be made in your situation?

4. A number of implications for evaluator capacity building are covered. In reflecting on your own evaluation competencies and practice, has reading this chapter stimulated any new ideas about your own professional development and/or career plans?

NOTES

1. Unlike the Public Health Agency's Audit Committee, the Evaluation Committee does not currently contain any external members (although the Evaluation Committee's terms of reference allows for this possibility).

2. The Canadian Evaluation Society recently developed a professional designations program, which awards the Credentialed Evaluator (CE) designation.

REFERENCES

Canadian Evaluation Society. (2010). *Competencies for Canadian evaluation practice*. Canadian Evaluation Society. Retrieved June 4, 2011, from http://www.evaluationcanada.ca/txt/2_competencies_cdn_evaluation_practice.pdf

Gauthier, B., Barrington, G., Bozzo, S. L., Chaytor, K., Dignard, A., Lahey, R., . . . Roy, S. (2009). The lay of the land: Evaluation practice in Canada in 2009. *Canadian Journal of Program Evaluation, 24*(1), 1–49.

Ghere, G., King, J. A., Stevahn, L., & Minnema, J. (2006). Professional development unit for reflecting on program evaluator competencies. *American Journal of Evaluation, 27*(1), 108–123.

Hamilton, J., Roulston, J., & Porteous, N. L. (2010). *Going beyond evaluation: The "what," "so what," and "now what"—Learning from the 2008 Listeriosis Outbreak Lessons Learned Review.* Paper presented at the 2010 Annual CES Conference, Going Green, Gold and Global: New Horizons for Evaluation, Victoria, British Columbia, Canada. Retrieved November 15, 2011, from http://c2010.evaluationcanada.ca/index.cgi?_lang=an

Harrison, J. (2007). Connecting the dots: Six steps to implementing an integrated management environment. *Canadian Government Executive, 13*(2). Retrieved June 21, 2011, from http://cge.itincanada.ca/index.php?cid=324&id=10561

Henry, G. T., & Mark, M. M. (2003). Toward an agenda for research on evaluation. *New Directions for Evaluation, 2003*(97), 69–80.

Mayne, J. (2012). Independence in evaluation and the role of culture. In J.-C. Barbier & P. Hawkins (Eds.), *Evaluation cultures: Sense-making in complex times* (pp. 105–138). New Brunswick, NJ: Transaction.

Mayne, J., & Rist, R. C. (2006). Studies are not enough: The necessary transformation of evaluation. *Canadian Journal of Program Evaluation, 12*(3), 93–120.

Montague, S. (2000). Focusing on inputs, outputs, and outcomes: Are international approaches to performance management really so different? *Canadian Journal of Program Evaluation, 15*(1), 139–148.

Montague, S., & Porteous, N. L. (2012). The case for including reach as a key element of program theory [Special issue]. *Evaluation and Program Planning.*

Montague, S., Porteous, N. L., & Sridharan, S. (2011). *The need to build reach into results logic and performance frameworks.* 2011 Fifteenth Annual PPX Symposium, conducted in Ottawa, Ontario, Canada. Retrieved May 14, 2011, from http://www.ppx.ca/download/learning_events/2010–2011/January2011/LE_Jan2011_MontPortSrid.pdf

Montague, S., & Shepherd, R. (2011). *Addressing the public policy evaluation imbalance: Finding a path to relevance.* Paper presented at Evaluation 2011: Values and Valuing in Evaluation, annual meeting of the American Evaluation Association, Anaheim, California. Retrieved November 23, 2011, from http://www.eval.org/eval2011/

Montague, S., Young, G., & Montague, C. (2003). Using circles to tell the performance story. *Canadian Government Executive, 2,* 12–16.

Patton, M. Q. (Ed.). (2008). *Utilization-focused evaluation.* Thousand Oaks, CA: Sage.

Pawson, R. (2006). *Evidence-based policy: A realist perspective.* Thousand Oaks, CA: Sage.

Porteous, N. L. (2005). *Evaluation theory and practice: The critical role of evaluation associations.* Conference Proceedings of Israeli Association for Program Evaluation, pp. 15–31.

Porteous, N. L. (2009). La construction du modèle logique d'un programme. In V. Ridde & C. Dagenais (Eds.), *Approches et pratiques en évaluation de programme* (Chapter 5). Montréal, Quebec, Canada: Les Presses de l'Université de Montréal.

Porteous, N. L., & Birch-Jones, J. (2007). Getting to engagement: What it is and how it can be measured. Paper presented at the Canadian Evaluation Society's annual general meeting, Winnipeg, Manitoba, Canada. Retrieved June 21, 2011, from http://www.evaluationcanada.ca/distribution/20070606_porteous_nancy_birch-jones_jennifer.pdf

Porteous, N. L., Sheldrick, B. J., & Stewart, P. J. (1997). *The logic model: A blueprint for describing programs.* Ottawa Public Health. Retrieved June 23, 2011, from http://www.phac-aspc.gc.ca/php-psp/pdf/toolkit/logic_model_e.pdf.

Porteous, N. L., Sheldrick, B. J., & Stewart, P. J. (2002). Introducing program teams to logic models: Facilitating the learning process. *Canadian Journal of Program Evaluation, 17*(3), 113–141.

Public Health Agency of Canada. (2007). *The Public Health Agency of Canada strategic plan: 2007–2012.* Ottawa, Ontario, Canada: Minister of Health of Canada.

Sonnichesen, R. C. (2000). *High impact internal evaluation: A practitioner's guide to evaluating and consulting within organizations.* Thousand Oaks, CA: Sage.

Stufflebeam, D. L. (2002). *Institutionalizing evaluation checklist.* Evaluation Center, Western Michigan University. Retrieved June 23, 2011, from http://www.wmich.edu/evalctr/archive_checklists/institutionalizingeval.pdf

Tarsilla, M. (2010). Being blind in a world of multiple perspectives: The evaluator's dilemma between the hope of becoming a team player and the fear of becoming a critical friend with no friends. *Journal of MultiDisciplinary Evaluation, 6*(13), 200–205.

Taylor-Powell, E., Jones, L., & Henert, E. (2003). Enhancing program performance with logic models [E-course]. Program Development and Evaluation, University of Wisconsin–Extension. Retrieved June 23, 2011, from http://www.uwex.edu/ces/pdande/evaluation/pdf/lmcourseall.pdf

Treasury Board of Canada Secretariat. (2011). *Guide to developing a departmental evaluation plan.* Ottawa, Ontario, Canada: Centre of Excellence for Evaluation, Treasury Board of Canada Secretariat.

CHAPTER 7

EVALUATION USE WITHIN THE EUROPEAN COMMISSION (EC)

Lessons for the Evaluation Commissioner

Bastiaan de Laat and Kevin Williams

CHAPTER TOPICS

- Evaluation use in large organizations
- Supportive or inhibiting factors
- Lessons for evaluation commissioners

The European Commission (EC) is probably one of the world's most prolific commissioners and consumers of evaluations. Drawing largely on the findings of two empirical studies conducted in 2002 and 2005, this chapter examines how evaluations are used by the EC and highlights some lessons for evaluation commissioners. The chapter starts with an explanation of evaluation development within the EC before going on to consider the users and uses of evaluation. It concludes by drawing out the factors that foster (or hinder) the use of evaluation.

THE DEVELOPMENT OF EVALUATION WITHIN THE EUROPEAN COMMISSION

The European Commission (EC) is the European Union's (EU) executive body. It represents the interests of the EU as a whole (as opposed to the interests of individual member states). The EC's main functions are to set objectives and priorities for action, propose

---

Disclaimers: Any views and opinions expressed by the authors do not necessarily reflect the views and opinions of the EIB or the OECD.

legislation to the European Parliament and Council, manage and implement EU policies and the budget, enforce European law (jointly with the Court of Justice), and represent the EU outside Europe (e.g., by negotiating trade agreements between the EU and other countries). About 23,000 staff work in the various EC departments (Directorates-General [DGs]) or services. Each DG is responsible for a particular policy area and is headed by a Director-General who reports directly to the EC president. It is a specific feature of the EC that it has a programming cycle of seven years—the current one covers the period of 2007 to 2013. Budgetary commitments for this period total nearly €1,000 billion, of which operational costs are a minor share: The vast majority of the budget is dedicated to expenditure programs in areas as diverse as regional development, overseas development cooperation, telecoms, energy and transport networks, support for small and medium-sized businesses, and research, development, and innovation activities. Given the broad scope of EU policies, the types and themes of evaluations vary widely.

EU programs and policies are evaluated at different times in their life cycle—generally during preparation (ex ante), during implementation (interim or intermediate), and when implementation is completed (ex post). The majority of evaluations are contracted out to external evaluators by evaluation functions situated within each DG or, less frequently, by services in charge of implementation. The EC's evaluation activities are centrally coordinated by the Secretariat-General.[1] For 2010 alone, some 150 evaluations and evaluation-related studies were commissioned by the different DGs—excluding those commissioned by other EU institutions, agencies, and bodies, and excluding so-called impact assessment (see below). In addition, the greater part of EU program management is devolved to member states—especially the regional programs (Structural Funds) with related evaluations being commissioned directly by EU national and regional administrations. These evaluations are generally conducted by external evaluators, according to conceptual frameworks designed by the EC.

The practice of evaluation within the European Commission (EC) dates back to the 1980s, with expertise being historically concentrated in the DGs responsible for major expenditure programs. Initially, this was within the areas of development cooperation and research where the responsible DGs developed their own specific evaluation approaches. A significant boost to evaluation capacity within the EC came in 1995 in the area of regional development with the MEANS Programme (European Commission [EC], 1999, MEANS Collection),[2] which was commissioned to address problems of widely varying practices, inconsistent results, and limited use of evaluations for EU-level policy making. The MEANS Programme was ambitious, drawing on the state of the art in evaluation from across Europe and beyond to develop a methodological framework that takes into account the multilevel, multiple stakeholder, and partner context of regional development programs. In 1998, a substantial part of the MEANS framework was adapted for the evaluation of the financial instruments of the EU's Common Agricultural Policy (CAP).

As a result of the organic growth of evaluation within specific EU policy areas, by the end of the 1990s, there were essentially three families of practice within the EC.

- First, there were the project cycle management (PCM) and the logical framework approaches. These were used to evaluate the overseas development projects and later the programs for preparing the accession of new member states. The approach remains strong to this day in the area of EU external policy.
- The use of independent, expert panels was the dominant approach adopted for the evaluation and monitoring of research programs and policy. Experts in scientific and technological fields are called upon to provide peer reviews and expert opinions. This approach has also had an important influence on the development of evaluation practices in other policy areas, such as the information society, where science, technology, and innovation are central.
- For regional development and employment policies in particular, the MEANS Programme's methodological framework played a central role, providing a structured, eclectic approach for the evaluation of the geographically and sector-bound actions implemented through devolved expenditure programs.

Two major developments within the EC in the area of evaluation have since occurred. First, a shift to results-based management, launched in 2000, was accompanied by a broadening of the scope of evaluation beyond expenditure programs to all EC "activities." The second is the emergence of the Better Regulation Agenda, which has given rise to the rapid institutionalization of "impact assessment," a form of ex ante evaluation that is fully integrated into the preparation of major legislative proposals and nonlegislative initiatives.

EVALUATION USE IN THE EUROPEAN COMMISSION

To better understand how the considerable quantity of evaluation produced were being used and how use could be reinforced, the EC conducted two studies, in 2002 and 2005, in which we were involved (Williams, de Laat, & Stern, 2002; de Laat, 2005).

The initial study, predominantly exploratory in nature, mainly comprised a survey of evaluation functions and a series of DG-focused case studies. It was designed to understand the way in which the different DGs organized their evaluation activities, the degree of evaluation institutionalization within them, and how these parameters affected evaluation use. This study also included a scan of the literature on evaluation use available at the time. This scan identified four main types of use.

- *Managing with the support of evaluation.* Evaluation recommendations are directly taken up by decision makers. Patton (1997) calls this the *instrumental* use of evaluation to directly modify programs.
- *Evaluation as a learning experience.* For participants in an evaluation (for example, as members of an evaluation steering group), the experience of participating can lead to an increased understanding of the activities that they manage and the issues involved. This is often referred to as process use, that is, "changes . . . that occur among those involved in evaluation as a result of the learning that occurs during the evaluation process" (Patton, 1997, p. 90).
- *Evaluation as one input among others in policy debate.* Here, policy making is conceived of as an ongoing dialogue, the quality of which may be enhanced by using evaluation results to support more *informed dialogue* or argumentation (Van der Knaap, 1995).[3]
- *Enhancing incrementally the knowledge base of organizations through evaluation.* The "enlightenment view of evaluation" (Weiss, 1999) whereby the incremental knowledge generated through evaluations is fed into policy debates. *Cumulative learning* across many evaluations takes place rather than direct use from particular evaluations. In this type, evaluations rarely lead to direct changes in policy or to specific decisions. Evaluation inputs should not be expected to override political agendas and administrative necessities, which may well push decisions in quite different directions.

The second study, built on the knowledge gained of the EU context in the first study and the different types of evaluation use found in the literature, identified five types of use that were likely to be present within the EC:

- Providing inputs into *priority setting* and choosing between policy options
- Supporting the design of interventions

- Assisting in the efficient *allocation of resources*
- Improving the *implementation* of activities
- Increasing accountability and awareness of achievements

For each of these types of use, to ensure a systematic approach, a series of analytical criteria and corresponding indicators were developed at the start of the second study to help assess whether the type of use existed in any significant way (see Table 7.1).

The criteria listed in Table 7.1 were proposed in a survey questionnaire to 150 EC staff within evaluation functions. In light of the responses, they were subsequently refined and then used to provide a basis for the analysis that took place within 10 case studies (the contents of which are briefly described in the Appendix section of this chapter). The case studies did not focus on individual evaluations (e.g., one specific ex post program evaluation) as the basis for

Table 7.1 Types of Use, Criteria, and Indicators

Type of Use	Criteria *Evaluation results are*	Indicators (Examples) *Evaluations are referred to, or explicitly used, in*
Priority setting	• used to elaborate and support proposals to European Council and European Parliament (e.g., reform communications, framework regulations, other regulations or directives) • used in an internal process (which can be an ex ante evaluation or impact assessment) that leads to new proposals	• European Commission (EC) Communications or their annexes, the adoption process in European Council or Parliament, the APS and CLWP, internal preparation process for new proposals, within (ex ante) "impact assessment"
Design of interventions	• used to describe the implementation of an intervention to European Council and Parliament • taken account of when designing interventions at the level of the EC • supportive of the annual planning cycle	• EC Communications or their annexes • the adoption process in European Council or Parliament • the APS and CLWP

(Continued)

Table 7.1 (Continued)

Type of Use	Criteria Evaluation results are	Indicators (Examples) Evaluations are referred to, or explicitly used, in
Resource allocation	• supporting establishment of EC annual budget (the "financial perspectives") • instrumental in determining the appropriate level of funding within concrete EC proposals • instrumental in determining the appropriate level of funding in EC acts • underpinning financial management decisions • underpinning budget allocation choices within the budgetary and ABM and SPP processes	• (legislative) financial statements and explanatory memoranda • financing acts and decisions • the adoption process in European Council or Parliament • activity statements • APS • operational decisions with financial implications
Implementation	• supporting management decisions on operations-level spending and activities • underpinning the EC's own administration and internal procedures	• individual Annual Management Plans • designing and modifying internal procedures • EC responses or "fiche contradictoire" to (external) evaluation • check and control by Evaluation Units for follow-up of recommendations
Accountability and awareness	• used to account for achievements in the context of decision-making processes • referred to in dealings of the EC with the European Council and Parliament • referred to in dealings with external stakeholders	• AAR and related processes • Communications, Commission working documents • discharge documents • ECA documents or activities • replies to Parliamentary questions • other European Council or Parliament documents • external documents and reports • relevant stakeholder groups

Note: AAR = Annual Activity Report; ABM = Activity Based Management; APS = Annual Policy Strategy; CLWP = Commission Legislative and Work Programme; ECA = European Court of Auditors; SPP = Strategic Planning and Programming.

analysis but on "activity" as defined by the EC's activity based budgeting (ABB) system. Within an ABB activity, several policy activities come together to contribute toward a policy objective or a set of policy objectives. Taking such an approach allowed an assessment of the interplay of *different* evaluations and other activities vis-à-vis a set of related policy objectives. It also allowed a varied set of policy interventions and policy domains to be investigated.

Table 7.2 indicates how often the different types of uses were encountered across the case studies (different cases could have more than one type of evaluation use). This shows that evaluation was most often used to assist implementation (of a program or policy), whereas priority setting in policy making was the least frequently observed type of use.

Table 7.2 Frequency of Types of Use

Type of Use	Frequency (Case Studies)
Implementation	8
Design of interventions	7
Resource allocation	4
Awareness and accountability	4
Priority setting	2

The following sections present the highlights of the two studies and the relevant implications for evaluation commissioners. Although the most recent study was concluded in 2005, the lessons and insights that can be drawn from them, in view of our experience, are still highly relevant today.

TYPES OF EVALUATION USE

The following paragraphs discuss the types of evaluation use observed in the EC, following the order presented in Table 7.2, and present some tentative conclusions and pointers toward the different factors that are important in promoting different types of use.

Evaluation Use to Improve Implementation

The studies suggest that improving the implementation of various activities is the main contribution of evaluation in the EC, that is, instrumental use.

Only in two case studies (both relating to regulatory policy) was this type of use not observed. Instrumental use of intermediate evaluations of expenditure programs, for example, in the area of regional development, was particularly prevalent, as well as a key form of use with regard to the implementation of agreements with non-EU members in the areas of fisheries, the organization of agencies in the domain of education and culture, and humanitarian aid projects.

An interesting "use-rich" example was provided by DG Education and Culture's Leonardo da Vinci Programme, which focuses on vocational training exchanges within the EU. Here, project selection methods were adapted as a direct result of evaluation findings (and their endorsement by the program's management committee). Action plans developed by both the European Centre for the Development of Vocational Training (Cedefop) and the European Training Foundation (ETF), the two EU vocational training agencies working respectively inside and outside the EU, resulted directly from evaluation recommendations.

The cases examined suggest that promoting the use of evaluation to improve implementation requires particular attention to be paid to

- the quality of evaluations, with regard to the production of practical and realistic recommendations; and
- the regular monitoring of progress in implementing the recommendations.

Evaluation Use in the Design of Interventions

Most of the case studies examined evaluations of existing programs at midterm with a view to their possible continuation or the development of a new generation of interventions. These evaluations therefore often focused on design (this section) and implementation (above) issues.

In no case was the design of an expenditure program, a regulatory initiative, or other type of intervention radically altered due to evaluation findings that, most of the time, led to slight changes or reformulations. Two reasons could account for this. First, none of the evaluations in the case studies were specifically commissioned with the aim of supporting the design of an *entirely new* intervention but mainly focused on implementation issues, usually in the context of the continuation or renewal of the same intervention. Second, a radical change to the design of an existing intervention would generally require a change to its legal base, which may well inhibit evaluators from—or their being asked to refrain from—making any radical proposals for change.

In the early 2000s, the institutionalization of *(prospective) impact assessment* as a tool to support the design of interventions was at a relatively early stage and was not covered in either of the two studies. This aspect of evaluation received a major boost as of 2002 when the EC launched its impact assessment (IA) system, creating a unified framework to replace a range of sectoral impact assessment instruments developed in some DGs, mainly with responsibility for regulatory initiatives. The European Court of Auditors (ECA), on the basis of a review of IA reports between 2003 and 2008, concluded that "impact assessment has become an integral element of the Commission's policy development and has been used by the Commission to design its initiatives better" (European Court of Auditors [ECA], 2010, p. 6). However, both the Court and the EC's Impact Assessment Board observe[4] that there has been relatively limited use of *prior* evaluation findings in impact assessments. The Impact Assessment Board in its 2011 report noted that "there is still a need to better plan evaluations, so that they are available in time to be used as input for the IA process" (EC, 2012, p. 26).[5]

In the light of the cases studied, it can be concluded that effective planning is essential to ensure that evaluation results are available in a timely fashion in order to feed them into the design of an intervention. Moreover, the planning of an evaluation needs to take into account whether provisions exist in the legal base of an intervention for making significant changes or whether the legal base itself would have to be changed.

Evaluation Use in Resource Allocation

Overall, any evidence of using evaluation to support resource allocation was difficult to find—contrasting with a recent World Bank report (2009) that claims (impact) evaluation is a useful tool in budget planning and financial management. The studies indicated that the influence of evaluations in relation to budget issues is marginal, especially for EU internal policies and programs. In the case of budget allocations within *external* policies that focus on countries outside the EU, the role of evaluation appeared to be more important. In such cases, evaluation was generally used to support requests for budget increases but not for making the case for reduced spending. This represents something of an issue for evaluation and even more so in times of severe budget constraints.

By contrast, decisions on reallocations within DGs or programs very often appeared to be supported by the use of evaluation results, and past evaluations feeding into ex ante evaluation can be used to help to better determine budget needs for a specific program when it starts to take shape.

Effective planning, which takes into account an organization's budgetary processes (in the case of the EC, very much shaped by the seven-year cycle, with possible adjustments halfway through), is important if evaluations are to inform decisions about resource allocation and budgeting. Moreover, obtaining senior management support for an evaluation is likely to be useful to promote a more symmetrical use of evaluation results in this context.

Evaluation Use in Awareness Raising and Accountability

The use of evaluations for accountability purposes is readily identifiable from the documents reviewed during the studies, especially in EC "communications," and, to a certain extent, in other types such as budgetary discharge documents, replies to parliamentary questions, and so forth. Moreover, as an often overlooked side effect, the actual publication of evaluation results, which is the general rule for the EC, often helps raise awareness of the evaluated intervention. In several cases, an active communication strategy was developed to reach out and involve stakeholders—for instance, by organizing conferences or public hearings—whereas in other cases, reports were simply made available on the Internet.

Inter-DG communication practices organized around evaluations (e.g., by DGs participating in each others' steering groups) also help raise awareness. This was often the case (and an obligation) in evaluations of regulatory initiatives, agreements, and agencies, when multiple DGs often have shared responsibility. This practice is rarer in the evaluation of expenditure programs, unless two or more DGs are jointly accountable for implementation.

The case studies suggest that using evaluations to raise awareness and for accountability purposes requires particular attention at the planning stage to ensure that evaluation results can be appropriately disseminated.

Evaluation Use in Priority Setting and Choosing Between Policy Options

The studies provided evidence to show that evaluation results were systematically used in the policy-making processes in general, but they did not seem to significantly influence the setting of strategic or policy priorities, and while evaluations may have helped to shape priorities, any causal links were difficult to trace. The studies therefore suggest that evaluation does not appear to be an influential priority-setting tool. It could be argued that this is not so surprising since priorities tend to emerge, rise up, and slide down the policy-making agenda as the policy environment evolves in the light of new challenges and related needs. Indeed, the EC did not set out to use evaluation as a tool for helping to set priorities, since its focus has been mainly on retrospectively examining program performance, that is, on their capacity to respond to predetermined policy priorities and related objectives.

Impact assessment provides a means through which evaluation can better support priority setting and the choice of policy options. Two major components of IA are (a) analyzing the raison d'être of proposed interventions and comparing different scenarios, and (b) assessing trade-offs between policy options. Furthermore, the scope of IA includes "upstream" initiatives such as white papers and communications that help define future EU policies. IA thus provides both a support in its own right for strategic development, policy making, and priority setting and a natural channel by which the results of previous evaluations can be used to this end (see above).

Another way of supporting greater use of evaluation in decision-making was the evaluation highlights document prepared by DG Budget and presented to the European Union's Financial Perspectives ad hoc Working Group and to the European Parliament's Policy Challenges Committee on policy challenges and budgetary means of the enlarged Union 2007 to 2013 (see Box 7.1).

BOX 7.1
USING EVALUATION FOR DECISION-MAKING

The [. . .] evaluation highlights have the objective of furnishing institutions, stakeholders, and the general public with relevant evaluation results, as delivered by independent external consultants during the year 2005. The results have been analyzed in a crosscutting manner for each of the relevant headings in the new financial framework (2007–2013), on the basis of criteria such as the effectiveness, efficiency, relevance, or community added value of the interventions. For each heading, crosscutting findings, appearing in several of the evaluations completed this year, have been identified, which could be of interest for *future decision making* [emphasis added] on EU policies.

Source: European Commission, Directorate-General for the Budget. (2005). *Evaluation in the European Commission. Reporting on results. Annual evaluation review 2005.* Brussels, Belgium: Author. Retrieved from http://ec.europa.eu/dgs/secretariat_general/evaluation/docs/eval_review_2005_en.pdf

These findings mean that evaluation *on its own* may not be the most appropriate instrument to inform policy making, priority setting, and strategy formulation and that untenable promises should not be made in this respect. For some areas, there may be more of a tradition of previous evaluations being used for policy making than for the others. If the policy area is characterized by a low level of this type of evaluation use, there may have to be some preparatory work to secure advance support for using an evaluation. When an evaluation is expected to draw on previous evaluations to help shape policy and priority setting, the processing of information can draw on and feed into other procedures and processes so as to take into account the policy-making environment, including the political dynamics in play. Therefore, if an evaluation is conducted to directly inform policy making, it needs to be linked to the broader policy-making, priority setting, or strategy formulation processes. Some form of meta-evaluation, or evaluation synthesis, may be useful here to bring together the lessons of several individual evaluations and to enhance understanding of the broader policy context.

FACTORS SUPPORTING OR INHIBITING EVALUATION USE AND IMPLICATIONS FOR EVALUATION COMMISSIONERS

So far, our analysis has mainly looked at *how* and to what *extent* evaluation has been used in the EC. Now, we will look more closely at the *factors* that appear to play a role in fostering or inhibiting the different types of evaluation use in order to draw out insights that may be useful for evaluation commissioners. The different factors are discussed below in order of their relative importance, as shown by the two studies.

Evaluation Planning and Timing; Purpose of the Evaluation

Without exception, the timeliness of evaluations and evaluation planning in relation to the program or policy cycle turned out to be the most crucial factor for all types of evaluation use. This finding is echoed by the Impact Assessment (IA) Board report for 2011, which points out that timeliness of evaluations is a key issue for IA, hence, for the preparation and definition of policies and regulation more broadly.

In the cases studied, both the reason (for instance a legal obligation) and the purpose of the evaluation (i.e., who should use the results and when, in order to do what) appeared intimately linked—not to say an equivalent factor—to the timeliness of the evaluation. This is because an evaluation can make a significant contribution to a (set of) decision(s) at a certain period in time only, for example, when the intervention is actually being designed (not once it is up and running). Consequently, the commissioner should ensure that the time frame set for an evaluation allows the findings to be delivered at the optimal moment.

It has been a feature of EC expenditure programs that the time frame for their evaluation is specifically incorporated into their legal base; this means that an evaluation has to be carried out at a given point in a program's life, irrespective of what it could be expected to have achieved by then and regardless of whether an evaluation would have anything meaningful to report on, for example, in terms of a program's effects. Some flexibility should therefore be allowed in order to optimize an evaluation's usefulness, though in the firm knowledge of the trade-offs involved, in particular that an evaluation that is well synchronized with the preparation of a new programming cycle might be able to provide only an analysis of implementation. The studies also identified cases where decisions on follow-up programs had to be taken before the evaluations had been completed, due to legal timing requirements or evaluations taking longer than planned.

Over time, some of the EC's services have introduced greater flexibility into the legal provisions of programs with respect to the timing of intermediate evaluations. For instance, the intermediate evaluation of the Leonardo da Vinci Programme on vocational training was advanced by 6 months in order to be useful to the preparation of the new generation of programs from 2007 to 2013.

Recommended practices for commissioners to make evaluations timelier are therefore to

- understand the policy cycle of which the evaluation is part and determine the most useful moment for the delivery of evaluation results accordingly;
- plan evaluations to respond to decision making needs and constraints (e.g., the type of legislative procedure);
- advance the timing of the evaluation, if this will facilitate its use, should there be sufficient flexibility within the relevant legal statutes and/or it is possible to make compromises in terms of data collection and analysis; and
- establish framework contracts with external evaluators to help reduce the length of procurement procedures and, consequently, the overall duration of evaluations.

However, planning should go beyond the issue of timing to identify the type(s) of use an evaluation is expected to serve and provide a framework to ensure an appropriate evaluation design and process. For example,

- with respect to informing decisions on resource allocation and budgeting, the evaluation commissioner should ensure that evaluations are appropriately designed, especially with regard to the analyses of efficiency and, in turn, to inform on cost issues; and
- if accountability is the explicit purpose of the evaluation (e.g., if this is legally required), a steering group may be useful in this context to develop messages on accountability issues as well as raising awareness among stakeholders, while a communication strategy should be drawn up to identify channels, formal and informal, for communicating evaluation results to both internal and external audiences, giving special attention to a wide range of interested stakeholder groups.

Last but not least, the importance of the role of the evaluation function should be underlined. This entity is often the only one that has a clear overview of the entire set of evaluations and evaluation processes within an organization and how these relate to the overall decision-making processes. For this reason, it should help other parts of the organization to understand the importance of ensuring good evaluation planning.

Support of Senior Management

Support from senior management in the use of evaluation findings appeared to be an important factor, though this support is often implicit in nature and little evidence could actually be found regarding senior management's overt support for evaluation or its use. This was especially true in the case of *intermediate* "routinized" and legally obligatory evaluations of expenditure programs for which there was only "silent support" most of the time. Seemingly, it is clear for senior management that these evaluations simply need to be done. As a consequence, the main use of evaluations is very much *instrumental* and at an operational level (see above).

It appears to be difficult for evaluation results to be "filtered up" to the higher levels of senior management, at least in their original form, even if this does not exclude their use "in disguise" (e.g., in policy papers or concept notes which draw on evaluation results). There was, however, some evidence to show that evaluation results were taken up and used by senior management to support budget *increases* and possible resource reallocations. But, as explained above, evaluation use was not primarily seen as being important for making budgetary or financial decisions other than at operational level, that is, within DGs or programs, though this situation is likely to change in the future, particularly as impact assessments are expected to increasingly draw on previous evaluations.[6]

Consequences for the evaluation commissioner are as follows. To secure commitment for evaluation from senior management and thereby optimize its use, the commissioner needs to ensure buy-in and ownership. In part, this may be secured through institutionalizing evaluation within an organization. In such cases, it is important to assign a specific role for senior managers within the institutionalized procedures for defining the production, circulation, and dissemination of evaluation reports as well as the uptake of results—for instance, through the need for a management response to the evaluation to be provided, or, through an obligation to report on the implementation of recommendations, to an appropriately high-level audience, for example, an organization's executive board. Such commitment is easier when an evaluation *culture* already exists within an organization and when there is general acknowledgment of the benefits and value of evaluation by different stakeholders. Such an evaluation culture cannot be created through a single evaluation but is the outcome of a much longer process; moreover, such a culture needs to be continuously nurtured and confirmed (see the "shared model of change" in Wimbush's Chapter 5 as well as Läubli's Chapters 4 and 10 and Neubecker, Ripley, and Russon's Chapter 9 in this book).

In addition, when the commissioner can actively involve senior management in the evaluation process, this can help improve the strategic use of evaluation. Such involvement appears particularly important at the *planning stage* (e.g., sharing and discussing evaluation terms of reference such as in a workshop, so as to nurture demand for evaluation results). Involving senior management in discussing the draft evaluation results can be equally useful. Securing the participation of senior management at these two stages is particularly important for increasing the strategic use of evaluations, including decisions that involve significant resource reallocations, which could involve closing programs when evaluation results show that they do not respond adequately to the needs of beneficiaries (i.e., limited relevance), are not fully achieving their objectives (i.e., limited effectiveness), or they are not achieving their objectives at a reasonable cost (i.e., limited efficiency).

Evaluation Quality

The quality of an evaluation appeared to also be an important factor for the use of findings, and in this context, the evaluation commissioner has an important role to play. However, even when an evaluation is methodologically and empirically sound, this alone will not necessarily ensure that recommendations will be followed up since political factors can be much more influential. Indeed, major political decisions are taken on the basis of poor-quality evaluations—and are often made in their complete absence. The studies support the idea that, within a system where evaluation *is* taken seriously and is effectively *planned to be used* (i.e., its instrumental use, which was increasingly the case at the EC at the time of the studies), it is a condition sine qua non that evaluations use reliable data gathering and analysis procedures to produce credible evaluation results.

Specifically, when using evaluation results to improve implementation, the notion of quality should take into account the need for recommendations to be practical and realistic enough to be taken forward by services responsible for the evaluated program. Theoretical, or abstract, recommendations are generally not useful in any situation. "Strategic" recommendations—which external evaluators, confronted for the first time with a program, are too often inclined to make—should be made only if they are likely to be taken up beyond those responsible for implementation, that is, at a more political level.

Of course, the quality of the evaluation is directly, though not exclusively, related to the expertise of the evaluators, so selecting the right evaluators is an important task for the evaluation commissioner. An important lesson to highlight here is that evaluations require a combination of skills, which the commissioner should identify in the call for tender in order to prevent—as we saw in several cases—the need for undue support from the evaluation function and other concerned services, either because the evaluators are subject experts who are not well acquainted with evaluation or because they are evaluators with insufficient understanding of the subject matter. Ideally, a combination of expertise should be available in the evaluation team. In the case studies, we noted that the teams usually included both evaluation and subject-matter expertise, such as experts in the fields of energy, rural development, fisheries, or food security. However, in one area, we found that demand for evaluation significantly exceeded supply and evaluators were overstretched as a result—which ultimately had an impact on the quality of reports.

BOX 7.2
TWO EXAMPLES: FOOD SAFETY AND HUMANITARIAN AID

For one of the cases, in food safety, interviewees linked the quality of the study to the evaluator's competences or knowledge of the subject matter. In another case, the evaluation was performed by a "pure" evaluator. The quality of the report produced by those with both subject and evaluation expertise was found to be significantly better (and its usability therefore higher) for these highly technical subjects.

A second example where the quality of evaluators, of the evaluation, and of evaluation use was directly linked was in the case of humanitarian aid. Here it was found important to select evaluators with a good understanding of humanitarian aid so that, from the onset, they were able to gain the confidence of the geographical desks and the field-based technical assistants.

Yet engaging evaluators with the relevant expertise is not sufficient—it is the task of the evaluation commissioner to manage relations with the evaluation team in such a way as to ensure the production of a high quality product.

Several actions that the evaluation commissioner can undertake are instrumental in this process:

- Produce sound and clear terms of reference, which include the purpose of the evaluation and its focus in terms of the questions to be answered.
- Assist in selecting the evaluator or evaluation team with the appropriate mix of expertise.
- When particular evaluation approaches are required, including the development and use of more complex methods, this should be clearly specified.
- Provide a clear set of quality standards with which the work should comply, for example, by proposing a template for the report structure, when possible, with an example of what is considered a high quality report.
- Establish a steering group, involving different stakeholders to oversee the evaluation process.

- Set up an external peer review of the evaluation report or meta-evaluation (especially whenever the evaluation commissioner does not have the competence him- or herself to perform this) and possibly also of the terms of reference and intermediate or draft reports.
- Ensure that it is possible to refuse a report which does not comply with quality standards—it should be noted that this is likely to effect the time frame of an evaluation, so it is best to supervise and work closely with the evaluator from the earliest moments of the exercise in order to ensure that any quality issues are dealt with as they arise.

Finally, the scope, quality, and use of evaluations appear to be closely related. Four cases studied suggest that evaluations are more useful when they have a narrow focus, allowing them to examine questions in-depth and provide more precise results. By contrast, wide-ranging evaluations run the risk of being superficial and giving rise to generic recommendations. The depth and precision of an evaluation influences the practicability and feasibility of recommendations in terms of their implementation.

Monitoring the Follow-Up of Evaluation Recommendations

Although this finding cannot be generalized (Peck & Gorzalski, 2009), at the EC it is common practice in most of the DGs to monitor the follow-up of evaluation recommendations (i.e., their implementation). Although no harmonized format seems to exist within the EC to do this, the main steps are generally as follows. At the end of an evaluation, all recommendations are listed and questions are asked of the relevant services, relating to (a) whether a recommendation will and can be followed up, (b) how it will be followed up, and (c) by when. Next, at regular intervals, the realization of this plan is checked by the evaluation function. This is an issue evaluation commissioners should address to enhance the use of evaluation results, particularly in the context of using evaluations to improve implementation. Although this may be viewed by some as giving evaluation functions too much of a policing role, from our experience, it appears to constitute a very important tool to reinforce the use of evaluation results since it allows those responsible for responding to the evaluation to be held to account for progress made. Furthermore, in the interest of accountability and transparency, and to provide an incentive for follow-up to take place, the results of this process can be made public.

Involvement of Stakeholders

The involvement of stakeholders in the evaluation process, particularly potential users, appeared to be a crucial factor for the uptake of evaluation findings, as more recently confirmed by other studies (Johnson et al., 2009; Vanlandingham, 2011). In the two studies, the most important user group was the commissioning DG itself. In other cases, however, potential users may well be more widely distributed within an organization and even beyond, in particular among beneficiaries and funders. A distinction can therefore be made between two major groups of stakeholders: first, those responsible for the direct uptake of evaluation results and, second, those who are not involved in implementation but have a strong interest in one form or another in the intervention.

The studies suggest a "good practice," namely, that those responsible for the implementation of evaluation results are actively involved in the evaluation process; that is, they are consulted on defining the terms of reference, taking part in the steering group, and commenting on draft and final reports. This can strengthen the feasibility and practicality of recommendations and thus increase the likelihood of their use by lead users.

BOX 7.3
STEERING GROUPS

The EC's Annual Evaluation Review 2003 (EC, 2004, p. 15) showed that steering groups for the management of the evaluations had become standard practice. In 2003, around 82% of all completed evaluation projects were conducted under the guidance of a steering group. The number of evaluations without steering groups was continuously declining. In about half of the internal steering groups, European Commission officials from the different DGs are represented. In the other half, they come from the same DG. In nearly half of the cases, steering groups also incorporated external stakeholders, that is, non-EC.

In some cases, a broader range of stakeholders, for example, civil society, was involved in an evaluation process, not as members of a steering group but through expert hearings or public consultations, some of which were facilitated electronically. An example of the latter case was organized by DG Information Society, which organized a broad consultation of the draft, intermediate report of its *Five Year Assessment* of the Information Society Technologies (IST) research program. This process involved the IST policy community, representatives of member states, and beneficiaries of the evaluated program, many of whom used the opportunity to comment on the draft recommendations. This procedure helped to finalize the final report and to disseminate the preliminary results of the evaluation to the relevant stakeholder communities.

More generally, the involvement of a wider range of stakeholders in the evaluation process may also help increase the legitimacy of evaluation findings, thus, easing the path for the implementation of recommendations and other types of evaluation use.

Human Resources

Even though, in the course of the studies, interviewees and respondents did not mention "time investment" as being a particular problem, evaluations are "time consuming" and human resource intensive. On the basis of the study, and in the light of our own experience, we can recommend that, when planning an evaluation, evaluation commissioners should bear in mind that the following activities are highly resource intensive:

- Determining the need, scope, purpose, and questions for the evaluation— drawing up the terms of reference and organizing and participating in steering group meetings; this work is done by the "secretariat" (or manager) of an evaluation, that is, the official who manages the evaluation process from beginning to end and is in closest contact with the evaluator (in the case of an external evaluation); estimated time needed for this function ranges from 20% of the manager's time to peak periods of nearly full time, especially in the beginning of the evaluation project (terms of reference, kick-off meeting, inception report, inception meeting, etc.) and during the drafting phases of the final report
- Taking part in the steering group; members devote time before, during, and after the meetings for reading and preparing comments on documents
- Administrating the formal and contractual procedures of the evaluation project, again especially important in the case of procuring the services of external contractors or when internal evaluations have external components (e.g., external facilitation of workshop)
- Conducting an internal evaluation, including designing, planning, collecting, analyzing, and interpreting data and writing up and presenting the report

Closely linked to human resources, financial resources more broadly are important. In the case studies, no real problems appeared to have been encountered with regard to funding. In other organizations, this can, however, be a real problem, and the evaluation commissioner should be aware of the cost of the various steps of an evaluation, especially when extensive data collection and more complex analytical methods are requested from evaluators.

Dissemination of Evaluation Results

The studies showed that in most cases, active dissemination of evaluation results is not viewed as a priority—"Interested people will read the report anyway so posting it on the internet is sufficient," as one interviewee phrased it. However, targeted dissemination may contribute to the improved awareness, and eventually improved use, of evaluation results. Similarly, it helps increase the acceptability of the evaluation findings by a wider audience than those directly involved with the implementation of an intervention. Broad dissemination to a wide range of stakeholders is particularly important when using evaluations for awareness raising and accountability purposes.

An evaluation commissioner may therefore want to distinguish between the following groups and use different ways of communicating with them:

- Those responsible for the implementation of the intervention, who are usually directly involved in the evaluation process
- Senior management
- Other services within and outside the organization which are involved in implementing the evaluated intervention
- Those responsible for analyzing and summarizing evaluation activity across the organization
- Wider stakeholder groups, including funders and beneficiaries

It should be borne in mind that for the EC, the groups targeted for dissemination are more readily identifiable for expenditure programs as these have clearly defined beneficiaries. This is not usually the case for regulatory and other policy initiatives. To improve the dissemination of evaluation results, the studies found that it is important not to focus on one single evaluation but to synthesize and disseminate the findings from several evaluations around the same program, policy, or theme.

CONCLUSION

This chapter has presented the results of two studies on evaluation use at the European Commission and translated those findings into hands-on recommendations for evaluation commissioners.

Table 7.3 matches the EC's main uses of evaluation with those discussed in the literature, as described above. The table clearly suggests two clusters, one around instrumental use and learning, a second related to the policy debate and enhancing the knowledge base underpinning decisions and public interventions.

Evaluations appeared to be mainly used to improve the implementation and design of interventions and for awareness raising and accountability. Although evaluations appeared to be frequently used for reallocation of resources within a program, this is not the case for budget allocation at policy level or for priority setting—the more recently developed Impact Assessment (IA) instrument seems to be more used for this and, for the time being, does not seem to take into account evaluation results sufficiently. Factors that foster or hinder evaluation use are related to evaluation planning and timing, and, timeliness: to the buy-in of senior management, to the quality of the evaluation and the involvement of potential users and stakeholders in the evaluation process; and these are all important features the evaluation commissioner should consider when setting up and managing an evaluation. Last but not least, the systematic and transparent monitoring of the implementation of recommendations provides a means of reinforcing accountability for evaluation use.

Table 7.3 Mapping of Purpose of Evaluation at EC Versus Evaluation Use as per the Literature

Literature EC	Managing and Instrumental	Learning	Input Into Policy Debate	Enhance Knowledge Base
Implementation	X	X		
Design of interventions	X	X		X
Resource allocation	X			
Accountability and awareness			X	X
Priority setting	X		X	X

The findings presented in the present chapter now allow us to draw up a profile of the "use-oriented" evaluation commissioner.

- The use-oriented evaluation commissioner will ensure that evaluation results are available "on time" to permit their input into the decision-making process. This means designing an evaluation sufficiently in advance and anticipating the full period needed for its completion. It also means that the evaluation commissioner should analyze to what extent an intervention can actually be changed.
- The use-oriented evaluation commissioner will set up a steering group that oversees the work of the evaluators and provides feedback. She or he makes sure that there is buy-in from senior management into the evaluation (which can either be a systematic feature or specific to each evaluation). Such commitment will be more readily obtained if an evaluation culture has already taken root within an organization.
- The use-oriented evaluation commissioner will ensure that quality assurance is a continuous process, starting when the terms of reference are being designed, and that evaluation recommendations are formulated in such a way as to be used by the relevant services for improving program implementation. She or he will have put into place a system for tracking progress in implementing recommendations over time.
- A dissemination strategy for evaluation results can also contribute to increased use. Again, it is the task of the evaluation commissioner to devise the strategy and ensure that it is implemented. Messages should be tailored to stakeholder profiles, differentiating between communicating inside and outside the organization.
- The studies suggest that the influence of evaluation on budgetary decisions, except when reallocations within a program are envisaged, is weak. Wherever evaluations are commissioned to help with decisions about resource allocation and budgeting, they should be appropriately designed, especially with regard to the analyses of efficiency in order to be able to inform convincingly on cost issues. The evaluation commissioner should therefore be well acquainted with the organization or evaluated program's budgetary processes.
- Last but not least, it was found that in some cases that evaluation may not be the most appropriate or, at least, will not be the single, main approach used within policy-making processes. If an evaluation is explicitly conducted with the purpose of use for policy making in mind, the evaluation commissioner should be closely connected to or at least

well acquainted with, the broader policy-making, priority setting, or strategy formulation process and its design, as well as with other methodologies and tools used in that process (e.g., impact assessment, foresight exercises), in order to make sure that the evaluation she or he commissions and the information it yields can be made useful within this broader process.

DISCUSSION QUESTIONS

1. Amid the various uses for evaluation suggested in the literature is "knowledge generation." How would you measure the incremental knowledge generated through an evaluation?

2. What are the pros and cons about using recommendations as criteria for judging use?

3. A number of criteria and indicators were used to analyze the EC's analysis of evaluation use. Some examples of the indicators used for each of the criterion are provided in this chapter. Can you identify any additional ones, especially qualitative indicators?

4. In developing and implementing a communication strategy for disseminating evaluation findings, who should be involved and how? What are the budget implications?

NOTES

1. This coordination function was situated within the Directorate-General for Budget until being transferred to the Secretariat-General in 2009.

2. MEANS stands for Méthodes d'Evaluation des Actions de Nature Structurelle.

3. A more recent contribution in this area is on exploiting policy windows to enhance use (Wimbush, 2010).

4. See the IA Board's report for 2011 (Commission Staff Working Document [SEC(2011)]101 final; see EC, 2012) and the ECA's Special Report No. 3 of 2010 (ECA, 2010).

5. The recent Smarter Regulation initiative of the EC includes the systematizing and reinforcing of the evaluation of legislation, following implementation, and aims to increase the use of evaluations as inputs into IA.

6. Political guidelines for the next European Commission (2009).

APPENDIX

This appendix provides an overview of the cases studied. Most of these reports can be accessed through the European Commission's websites.

DG (European Commission Policy Activity Analyzed in the Study)	Evaluation–Intervention Couples Identified	Main Use of the Evaluation Results	Intervention Types	Evaluation Types	Is Evaluation a Legal Obligation?	Centralized, Decentralized, or Devolved	Evaluation: Internal, External?
DG Enterprise (Encouraging entrepreneurship)	• Intermediate (2002–03) and final (2004–05) evaluation of MAP • Intermediate (2002) and final (2004) evaluation of IDA program • Evaluation of MGS pilot	• Implementation improvement • The MGS pilot action is stopped after the evaluation	• Programs • Pilot action	• Midterm and final evaluations	Yes	Decentralized	MAP midterm internal, others external
DG Employment (Work organizations and working conditions)	• Evaluation of the practical implementation of national legislation transposing health and safety directives	• To account for achievements in the light of the European Union member states implementing the relevant directives	• Transposition of directives	• Ongoing; ex post	There is legal requirement to monitor rather than evaluate	Decentralized	External
DG Agriculture (Rural development)	• Leader—Several evaluations • Objective 5a and 5b and accompanying measures • Different regulations	• Policy making	• Expenditure programs policies • Regulation	• Ex post • Midterm • Impact assessment	Yes	Decentralized, devolved	External

(Continued)

(Continued)

DG (European Commission Policy Activity Analyzed in the Study)	Evaluation-Intervention Couples Identified	Main Use of the Evaluation Results	Intervention Types	Evaluation Types	Is Evaluation a Legal Obligation?	Centralized, Decentralized, or Devolved	Evaluation: Internal, External?
DG Transport and Energy (Conventional and renewable energies)	• Midterm, evaluation of • Energy framework program which consists of SAVE, ALTENER, SYNERGY, CARNOT, SURE and ETAP	• Implementation of current program, internal coherence, future of the program	• Expenditure programs	• Ex post, midterm, ex ante	Yes	Decentralized	External
DG Fisheries (International fisheries)	• Evaluation of fishery agreements between Europe and non-EU members	• Renewal of fishery agreements	• Agreements with developing countries	"Final"	Yes	Decentralized	External
DG Regional Policy (Regional development fund)	• Midterm evaluation of structural funds	• Implementation • Decisions on performance reserve • Capitalization within the DG	• Structural funds (programs)	Midterm	Yes	Devolved	External
DG Education and Culture (Vocational training–Leonardo)	• Midterm evaluation of Leonardo II Programme • Periodical evaluations of Cedefop and European Training Foundation	• Continued implementation of a program • Input to ex ante evaluation and preparation of a new program • Establishment of agency action plan	• Expenditure program • Agencies	Midterm ongoing, periodical evaluation of agencies	Yes, in all cases	Decentralized	External (but the ex ante evaluation making use of the Leonardo evaluation was done internally)

DG (European Commission Policy Activity Analyzed in the Study)	Evaluation-Intervention Couples Identified	Main Use of the Evaluation Results	Intervention Types	Evaluation Types	Is Evaluation a Legal Obligation?	Centralized, Decentralized, or Devolved	Evaluation: Centralized, Internal, External?
DG Health and Consumer Protection (Food safety)	• Evaluation of the food labeling legislation • Evaluation of Regulation 258/97 concerning novel foods and novel foods ingredients	• Legislation • Regulation	• Legislation and Regulation	Ongoing	Yes	Decentralized	External
DG Justice (Citizenship and fundamental rights)	• Midterm and final evaluations of Daphne Programme	• Implementation of ongoing program • Preparation of new program	• Program	Midterm and final	Yes	Decentralized	External
DG ECHO (Humanitarian Aid)	• Evaluation of humanitarian aid interventions		• Program and external funding	Periodical evaluation	Yes	Decentralized	External

Note: Cedefop = European Centre for the Development of Vocational Training; DG = Directorate-General; ECHO = DG for Humanitarian Aid and Civil Protection; IDA = European Program for Electronic Interchange of Data between Administrations; MAP = Multi-annual Programme for Enterprise and Entrepreneurship; MGS = Mutual Guarantee Schemes. Please note that the following are NOT abbreviations but just catchy titles for a series of subprograms within a broader Energy framework program that ran from the mid-1990s until the mid 2000s: SAVE (promotion of energy efficiency), ALTENER (renewable resources), SYNERGY (co-operative program), CARNOT (environmentally sound use of solid fuels), SURE (nuclear), and ETAP (multiannual program of studies, analyses, forecasts and other related work in the energy sector) were subprograms of the Energy Framework Program of the European Union.

REFERENCES

de Laat, B. (Ed.). (2005). *Study on the use of evaluation in the European Commission, dossier 1: Main report, dossier 2: Case studies*. Brussels, Belgium, UK: European Commission.

European Commission (EC). (1999). *MEANS Collection: Evaluation of socio-economic programmes* (6 Volumes). Brussels, Belgium: Author.

European Commission (EC). (2004, May). *Annual evaluation review 2003. Overview of the commission's evaluation activities and main evaluation findings* (Commission Staff Working Document [SEC(2004)]662). Brussels, Belgium: Author. Retrieved from http://ec.europa.eu/dgs/secretariat_general/evaluation/docs/eval_review_2003_en.pdf

European Commission (EC). (2012). *Impact Assessment Board report for 2011*. (Commission Staff Working Document [SEC(2012)]101 final). Brussels, Belgium: Author. Retrieved from ec.europa.eu/governance/impact/key_docs/docs/sec_2012_0101_en.pdf

European Court of Auditors (ECA). (2010). *Special Report No 3/2010—Impact assessments in the EU institutions: Do they support decision-making*? Luxembourg: Author. Retrieved from ec.europa.eu/governance/impact/docs/coa_report_3_2010_en.pdf

Johnson, K., Greenseid, L. O., Toal, S. A., King, J. A., Lawrenz, F., & Volkov, B. (2009). Research on evaluation use: A review of the empirical literature from 1986 to 2005. *American Journal of Evaluation, 30*(3), 377–410.

Patton, M. Q. (1997). *Utilization-focused evaluation: The new century text* (3rd ed.). Thousand Oaks, CA: Sage.

Peck, L. R., & Gorzalski, L. M. (2009). An evaluation use framework and empirical assessment. *Journal of MultiDisciplinary Evaluation, 6*(12), 139–156.

Van der Knaap, P. (1995). Policy evaluation and learning: Feedback, enlightenment or argumentation? *Evaluation, 1*(2), 189–216.

Vanlandingham, G. (2011). Escaping the dusty shelf: Legislative evaluation offices' efforts to promote utilization. *American Journal of Evaluation, 32*(1), 85–97.

Weiss, C. H. (1999). The interface between evaluation and public policy. *Evaluation, 5*(4), 468–486.

Williams, K., de Laat, B., & Stern, E. (2002). *The use of evaluation in the commission services*. Paris, France: Technopolis France.

Wimbush, E. (2010). *Evidence to & from action: The role of intermediary bodies in knowledge to action strategies*. Bern, Switzerland: IRSPM Conference.

World Bank. (2009). *Institutionalizing impact evaluation within the framework of a monitoring and evaluation system*. Washington, DC: World Bank Independent Evaluation Group.

CHAPTER 8

EVALUATION POLICY AND PRACTICE IN A CHANGING ENVIRONMENT

Evolution of the Evaluation Function in the World Health Organization (WHO)

Maria J. Santamaria Hergueta,
Alan Schnur, and Deepak Thapa

CHAPTER TOPICS

- Evaluation within a complex multilateral organization
- Contributing and constraining factors in the institutionalization of evaluation
- Influences and interdependence of policy and practice

This chapter considers the evaluation issues that we have found important from the perspective of the Office of Internal Oversight Services (IOS), the unit responsible for the corporate evaluation function in the World Health Organization (WHO). We describe the evolution of evaluation within the changing environment of a multilateral organization throughout the last nine years. We focus on the context in which evaluation happens and

Note: David Webb, Director, Office of Internal Oversight Services (IOS), World Health Organization (WHO), Geneva, Switzerland, contributed to the revision of this chapter.

Disclaimer: This article reflects the views and opinions of the authors and does not necessarily reflect the views or official positions of the World Health Organization.

on selected factors that have affected the institutionalization and utilization of evaluation within WHO, illustrating them with examples.

This chapter consists of five sections. The first section sets out the context in which WHO organizes its evaluation function. The second section deals with four key factors in the day-to-day work of evaluation commissioners and evaluators—the role and purpose of evaluation, its use and utilization, the ownership of the process and findings, and the institutionalization and culture of evaluation—as well as the challenges and options adopted to address them. The third section discusses our experience of evaluation development in WHO and the lessons learned, and the fourth provides some concluding remarks. Finally, the fifth section proposes some discussion questions.

STRUCTURAL AND FUNCTIONAL ORGANIZATION OF EVALUATION IN WHO

WHO is a specialized, multilateral organization directing and coordinating health-related issues within the United Nations system (Box 8.1). It has a decentralized structure, with offices and decision-making authority at global, regional, and country levels. WHO's global policies, norms, and standards are defined at its Geneva-based headquarters with policy guidance provided by the World Health Assembly. In turn, the regions adapt the standards to meet their region's needs and develop suitable strategies for implementing them at the country level. The regional level has dual accountability both to the Director-General and to their respective regional committees. In a similar way, WHO country teams are accountable both to the Director-General and to their respective regional directors. These three organizational levels coexist within a vertical structure of technical programs in the secretariat. This results in a dynamic interaction between centralized and decentralized authority and decision making within WHO. This dynamism affects the evaluation function, with shared responsibility for evaluation not only at the organizational level (headquarters, each region, and country teams) but also with technical programs working across the geographical dimension.

BOX 8.1
WHO MANDATE AND STRUCTURE

Mandate

WHO is the directing and coordinating authority for health within the United Nations system whose objective is to attain the highest possible level of health for all peoples (World Health Organization [WHO], 1946).

Broadly stated, WHO's core functions include providing leadership on global health matters, shaping the health research agenda, setting norms and standards, articulating evidence-based policy options, providing technical support to countries, and monitoring and assessing health trends.

Structure

WHO is composed of the following:

- The World Health Assembly, the supreme decision-making body for WHO, is attended by delegations from 194 member states. Its main function is to determine global health policies. The Health Assembly also supervises WHO's financial policies and reviews and approves its Proposed Programme Budget. In addition, the Health Assembly considers the Executive Board's report, and provides directives on matters that may require further action.
- The Executive Board is composed of 34 health experts who are proposed by the member states with membership on the board for that year and elected for three-year terms. The main functions of the board are to give effect to the decisions and policies of the Health Assembly, to advise it, and to facilitate its work.
- The Secretariat, headed by a Director-General, is composed of some 8,000 technical and support staff, who work at WHO headquarters, in its six regional offices (for Africa, the Americas, Eastern Mediterranean, Europe, Southeast Asia, and the Western Pacific), and in more than 140 countries where WHO has a permanent presence. The Director-General is elected by the Executive Board and confirmed by the Health Assembly, while the regional directors are elected by the member states in their respective regions through regional committees and confirmed by the Executive Board.

Evaluation in WHO

The WHO results-based management approach (WHO, 2002b) is the basis for assessing its programmatic performance. Within this approach, there is an accountability framework that focuses on managerial, programmatic, and administrative decisions, as well as codes of conduct and independent quality assurance. Evaluation is an integral component of the independent assurance program, together with other forms of assessments, audits, and investigations (WHO, 2006).

As a technical and normative organization, the main work of WHO is to provide guidance and support to its partners on the planning and implementation of health initiatives and programs agreed on globally in the organization's General Programme of Work.[1] These partners include national institutions and organizations in the health and health-related sectors, nongovernmental organizations, and academic and scientific institutions. Exceptionally, WHO implements programs or projects directly. This is the case for pilot experiences that serve as the basis for later scaling up in countries, or special situations in the case of elimination and eradication of diseases and response to emergencies, when the country capacities require complementary competences for a limited period of time. Due to the nature of its work and its institutional setting, WHO is involved in a wide range of evaluations in terms of organizational level, geographic areas covered, technical content, objectives of the evaluation, and target audience.

Evaluations in WHO can be grouped under two broad categories, depending on the entity commissioning them (Box 8.2):

1. Corporate-level evaluations are commissioned by Internal Oversight Services (IOS). They can be thematic, programmatic, or country-centered evaluations. There was an average of five and three corporate evaluations per year during the periods 2003 to 2009 and 2010 to 2011, respectively.

2. Decentralized evaluations are commissioned by individual programs at any level of the organization. At present, it is difficult to estimate how many decentralized evaluations are carried out every year since the reporting of this information by technical programs is voluntary.

BOX 8.2
TYPES OF EVALUATIONS IN WHO

1. Corporate-Level Evaluations (commissioned by Internal Oversight Services)

Thematic evaluations: Focus on selected topics, such as a new way of working, a crosscutting theme, or core function; or address an emerging issue of corporate institutional interest. These are ad hoc exercises that provide insight into effectiveness, relevance, sustainability, and broader applicability. The evaluations of the WHO Fellowships Programme (WHO, Office of Internal Oversight Services, 2004) and WHO's work with collaborating centres (WHO, Office of Internal Oversight Services, 2007) fall into this category.

Programmatic evaluations: Focus on programs at all organizational levels. These are exercises that provide in-depth understanding of how and why results and outcomes have been achieved over several years and how they contribute toward WHO's objectives. The scope of programmatic evaluations may be limited to a regional office program, an inter-country program, or programs implemented by several country offices, or they may be organization-wide in nature. The evaluation of the Child and Adolescent Health and Development program (WHO, Office of Internal Oversight Services, 2006b) is one such example.

Country evaluations: Assess the work of the entire organization in and with a country, in respect to WHO's objectives and commitments. These assessments are an integral part of strengthening WHO's presence in countries and incorporate issues of program effectiveness, process efficiency, and compliance with organizational policies and procedures.

2. **Decentralized Evaluations (commissioned by individual technical programs)**

Programs at headquarters, regional, or country ("country program review") level manage and perform evaluations as part of their program implementation. Programs that are part of a partnership or funded through external resources often require these evaluations to provide evidence of results to stakeholders and to document programmatic processes and lessons learned.

The evaluations that WHO commissions often give rise to two intrinsic issues. The first issue relates to assessing the impact of a policy, strategy, or intervention on people's health. The second issue relates to the evaluation of the normative work, for which the evaluation community is still working on developing robust standards (UN Evaluation Group [UNEG], 2011). Evaluating the institutional impact and attribution of contributions to improving people's health through policy implementation and through setting norms and standards requires methodologies that address complexity (Rogers, 2008) and analysis of contribution toward results rather than attribution of results (Mayne, 2001). However, these methodologies are insufficiently applied (Coryn, Noakes, Westine, & Schroter, 2011) and rarely used because the program framework is not readily available, or the consideration of the period needed to produce results is not appropriate. As a result, these specific evaluation requirements and resources are not always available to the commissioner (Mayne, 2001, Sridharan & Nakaima, 2011).

Evolution of the Evaluation Function in WHO

In large organizational settings, responding to models of professional bureaucracies and organizational change reflects a process of incorporating new ideas or practices into everyday organizational life. Although the introduction of new ideas and charismatic leadership is necessary to provoke change, it is not sufficient. Rather, the processes of systematization and adaptation across the organization shape its culture (Weber, 1968), which are often referred to as knowledge management or organizational learning (Hatch & Cunliffe, 2006).

In WHO, there have been three distinct phases in the development of the evaluation function at the corporate level. These phases illustrate the organizational change of professional bureaucracies, whereby a charismatic idea is translated into practice through routine operations to serve the needs of the organization. At times, the influence of the charismatic idea may diminish until it finds a fertile environment to help take it forward.

The first phase corresponds to the period up to 2003, when the corporate evaluation function was located in the Department of Planning, Monitoring, and Evaluation, under the cluster of general management. The evaluation team consisted of three full-time staff and a number of external consultants, recruited as required. There was no specific, central budget for organizing evaluations. The department's efforts were largely concentrated on institutionalizing the evaluation function within WHO as well as networking and developing an organization-wide evaluation culture. However, given the priority of consensus building and the development of the evaluation framework (WHO, 2002a), the corporate evaluation agenda remained largely unimplemented, with evaluations being left to individual technical programs.

The second phase corresponds to the period from 2003 to 2009, when the evaluation function was transferred to IOS, an independent office within the Director-General's Office, reporting directly to the WHO Executive Board. The evaluation team within IOS consisted of four full-time evaluators in addition to a number of external consultants and staff seconded for specific evaluations. The team had a total annual budget of approximately US$800,000. Until 2006, the corporate evaluative agenda included funding of regional-level evaluations and capacity development and advising on evaluation topics at all levels of WHO. IOS commissioned organization-wide evaluations, several of which proved crucial to WHO's core work, for example, the thematic evaluations of the WHO Fellowships Programme (WHO, Office of Internal Oversight Services, 2004) and of WHO work with collaborating centers (WHO, Office of Internal Oversight Services, 2007), and the programmatic evaluation of Child and Adolescent Health and Development (WHO, 2006). IOS also produced the *Evaluation Guidelines* (WHO, Office of Internal Oversight Services, 2006a) with details on methodology and practices and details on the application of the UN Evaluation Group's norms and standards (UNEG, 2005a, 2005b), as applied to WHO. From 2007 to 2009, there was an increased focus on program accountability and efficiency in the evaluative work performed.

The third phase, starting from 2010, corresponds to a period of consolidation of processes, experience, and methodologies. This third phase has coincided with a financial crisis and reduction of resources for corporate evaluation to about US$400,000 in 2011, increased pressure for transparency and accountability from stakeholders, and with the implementation of a broad initiative of institutional reform. The latter includes the establishment of a new evaluation framework as part of the overall management reform initiative driven by member states (WHO, 2011, 2012)—with an organization-wide evaluation policy based on the lessons drawn from the preceding two phases.

In the last nine years, from a programmatic perspective, IOS has been effective in increasing the number of corporate-level evaluations. However, from an institutional perspective, there has been insufficient progress in fostering an organization-wide evaluation culture, in developing evaluation capacity at all levels, and in promulgating participatory approaches to evaluations. The need to strengthen evaluation in WHO has been well documented in several external and internal evaluations and assessments (Canadian International Development Agency [CIDA], 2009; Department for International Development [DFID], 2011; Multilateral Organizations Performance Assessment Network [MOPAN], 2011; WHO, 2011).

FACTORS INFLUENCING WHO'S EVALUATION PRACTICE

To better understand the role, implementation, and use of evaluation within the organization and the perceptions of technical program staff, IOS conducted a review of the evaluative work at the headquarters in Geneva (WHO, Office of Internal Oversight Services, 2009). The review included a survey of 116 programs, representing 51 departments (response rates 88% and 75%, respectively), 20 semistructured interviews with program managers (18 individual, two group interviews), and analysis of 26 evaluation reports.

The review indicated that most of the WHO's evaluations are commissioned by individual technical programs. Some of these programs, particularly those that depend on external funding and have multiple stakeholders, have institutionalized evaluation, with systematic procedures for commissioning and conducting studies as well as communicating and using the findings. In addition, their collaborative arrangements often require them to follow the accountability frameworks of the external stakeholders, including periodic program evaluations. Such is the case, for example, for the programs on immunization and on prevention and control of tuberculosis, HIV/AIDS, and malaria, as well as the programs on reproductive health, child health, and neglected tropical diseases. Some of these programs commission full-fledged impact evaluations, such as the evaluation of the global initiative on the Integrated Management of Childhood Illness (Bryce, Victora, Habicht, Vaughan, & Black, 2004; WHO, 2003).

The review singled out the following four factors as having a major influence on evaluation practice in WHO:

- Role and purpose
- Use and utilization
- Ownership of the process and findings
- Institutionalization and culture

Evaluation's Role and Purpose

The utility of evaluation depends to a large extent on the perceived *need* to have evaluative information. If there is no demand for evaluation, then there is a risk of it being underused. Similarly, because of the judgmental component of evaluation, it can be seen to be a threat or even a controlling exercise. Demand therefore also depends on having a good understanding about what evaluation is and the different functions for which it can be used. For evaluation to be useful and meaningful within an organization, several authors have stressed the need to develop a shared understanding of what evaluation is and the various ways in which it can be used (Patton, 1996, 2008). A *culture* of evaluation usually means that there is a general organization-wide acceptance of using evaluation for specific functions, as well as an overall recognition that it provides independent evaluative information to help decision making, and support institutional change and development.

The review (WHO, Office of Internal Oversight Services, 2009) showed that despite the presence of a clear definition (UNEG, 2005a) of what evaluation[2] is, program staff understood evaluation to mean a wide range of types of assessments (Box 8.3). Although there was a clear distinction between routine assessments and selected forms of ad hoc consultative processes, the boundaries between country program reviews and evaluations were less distinct. Extensive internal discussions with technical programs on whether one could strictly differentiate country program reviews from evaluations indicated that these reviews are useful to support policy development and program improvement. Therefore, program reviews were accepted by the IOS reviewers as a working concept under the heading of *evaluation*, although they do not fully meet the UNEG definition of *evaluation*. Other agencies within the UNEG are facing similar challenges in drawing the boundaries around what does and does not constitute an *evaluation*. While all UNEG agencies agree to the formal definition of *evaluation*, in practice, most agencies apply working definitions adapted to their day-to-day practices (UNEG, 2007).

BOX 8.3
TYPES OF ASSESSMENTS IN WHO
OTHER THAN EVALUATION

- *Routine monitoring and performance assessment* under the results-based management framework for internal accountability, and program activities tailored for advocacy among stakeholders
- *Global surveys* used for collecting information from countries, to inform and improve global policies, and by technical programs as surveys for program improvement and for advocacy purposes
- *Ad hoc consultative process* by technical program managers to build evidence for their policies and strategies and to provide feedback on performance. Examples are technical advisory groups (TAGs) and the Scientific Advisory Group of Experts (SAGE)
- *Program reviews,* structured and periodic exercises, to identify what needs to be improved in the short and medium term, mostly concerning programs in countries
- *Audits* that focus on compliance and efficiency and, to a lesser extent, on program performance

---

The review also explored the main reasons for programs' commissioning evaluations (Table 8.1). Out of the 44 units and/or programs using evaluations, 29 reported commissioning them to improve the programmatic quality and efficiency, 27 to report on performance, and 14 to guide further programmatic design.

Table 8.1 Reasons Influencing the Commissioning of Evaluations (N = 44 programs)

Reasons (multiple reasons possible for each program)	Number	%
Measure and improve quality and efficiency of program	29	66
Measure and report on performance, achievements, and lessons learned	27	61
Provide guidance for future design of programs	14	32
Satisfy requirement of external donor or sponsor	11	25
Satisfy requirement of advisory body or governing body	5	11
Mobilize additional resources	6	14

Source: Review of the evaluative work at headquarters, WHO, Office of Internal Oversight Services, 2009.

In addition, 16 of these units and/or programs mentioned that the main reason was to satisfy stakeholders' requirements, and six mentioned using evaluations to mobilize additional resources. In most cases, having an evaluation included as part of the donor project is a major indicator of whether or not evaluations are conducted. This does not necessarily imply that all evaluations are donor driven; the technical programs that have developed an evaluation culture may also be the drivers. However, for those programs without such a culture, it is likely that the donor requirement for an evaluation heavily influenced its implementation.

The literature mentions several reasons for commissioning evaluations. They can be broadly categorized in two groups. The first group relates to improving the efficiency of what is already known (exploitation), in particular with respect to knowledge, resources, and procedures. The second group relates to searching for new options and rethinking what is known for improvement of the organization through flexibility and a culture of change (exploration). Thus, the reasons for commissioning evaluations could be used to illustrate the mode of organizational learning in an institution (March, 1991). This could explain why some of the reasons for conducting evaluations mentioned in other organizations did not figure prominently in the WHO review. In particular, one area that was mentioned less often was the contribution that evaluation makes to increased knowledge sharing among staff members, to building staff evaluation capacity, and to promoting group learning (Fleischer & Christie, 2009; Russ-Eft & Preskill, 2009).

Effect of Financial Resources

Half the program managers not commissioning evaluations stated during the review that this was because they did not have sufficient resources for carrying them out. Some responded that they could perform evaluations only if they received additional resources.

Program managers also noted that the available budget affected the scope, breadth, and depth of their evaluation work, and they were forced to make trade-offs in the evaluation objectives. Many of the large programs such as disease eradication and control programs that are funded by voluntary contributions usually earmark funds for program evaluation as part of the original project budget. For these programs, the availability of adequate resources is generally not a significant concern.

Securing resources for corporate-level evaluations in WHO has proved a challenge. One of the ways attempted was to ask country member states to second (temporarily reassign and transfer) their program and evaluation experts at no salary cost to be part of the evaluation team, with WHO funding only the costs related to travel. Overall, the programmatic and evaluation assistance provided was adequate. However, such an arrangement often proved unwieldy as it made the evaluation dependent on the availability and goodwill of agencies for providing their staff at no cost to WHO. The arrangement also proved difficult to manage from a logistics viewpoint. Another challenge faced was the finalization of the report. After the seconded team members returned to their respective countries upon completion of the site visit, it proved difficult to secure their continuing commitment to finalizing the evaluation process.

The WHO review indicated that there were some program features that facilitated the commissioning of evaluations (Box 8.4). Some of these relate to the governance or budgetary structure of the programs and are similar to those mentioned for other organizations (Patton, 1996).

BOX 8.4
FEATURES FACILITATING THE COMMISSIONING
OF EVALUATIONS (*N* = 44 PROGRAMS)

- Multiagency governance of the programs and belonging to a global health partnership
- Budgetary structure of the program, in particular, high proportion of extra-budgetary budget earmarked by the donor

(Continued)

(Continued)

- Inclusion of evaluations as a requirement in donor-funded projects
- Availability of funds for evaluation, as ad hoc funding, or included as a budgetary component of the program
- Full or part-time staff responsible for evaluation in the technical program
- Evaluation culture integrated into the program
- Stage of development of the program (e.g., long operational tradition at country level)

Source: *Review of the evaluative work at headquarters,* WHO, Office of Internal Oversight Services, 2009.

Different Perspectives on Usefulness and Utilization

One of the major challenges faced by institutions is the use of evaluations (Mayne, 2006). This is closely linked to the utility of the evaluation findings (Patton, 2008; Rossi, Freeman, & Lipsey, 1999; Weiss, 1979). At the same time, there is considerable pressure for quality evaluations to guide the public health agenda and engage stakeholders meaningfully. Most of the WHO technical programs with a strong evaluation culture have joined global evaluation networks, reinforcing their technical and leadership profile (*The Lancet*, 2010).

In their study, Russ-Eft and Preskill (2009) refer to "organization members not valuing evaluation" (p. 17) as the number one reason why evaluations are neglected in organizations. This is an aggregate of not understanding what evaluation is, not having evaluation knowledge and skills, and not making time or resources available for evaluation, or, when leaders think that evaluation has no added value for their institution (Russ-Eft & Preskill, 2009).

The review of evaluative work in WHO identified three issues that needed addressing to ensure the utilization of evaluations:

1. The first issue is the "buy-in" from user(s). It is more effective and efficient if buy-in can be obtained from evaluees and senior management at the planning stage. In this area, there is an advantage for technical programs commissioning their own decentralized evaluations since the staff usually view these evaluations as closely linked to program improvement and thus important. With an evaluation culture adopted by the technical program, its staff and senior program management strongly support the evaluation process and take action on the results. When the evaluation teams are composed of experts with

considerable experience in conducting methodologically agreed program reviews, their findings will be readily acceptable, with little distraction from discussions about methodologies (Balthasar, 2011; Patton, 2008).

2. The second issue is the matching of the timing and requirements of evaluations and organizational processes. A criticism from some programs is that evaluation and program cycles are not synchronized. This can result in evaluation reports that arrive too late to be used in program policy discussions, program planning, or new strategy formulation. For example, the program may receive an evaluation report just after a new five-year program strategy has been disseminated. Programs that implement evaluations as part of their program activities, such as the Special Programme of Research, Development and Research Training in Human Reproduction (HRP) and the Special Programme for Research and Training in Tropical Diseases (TDR), generally build in the right time frame to feed back into planning as part of its strategy formulation process.

3. The third issue is the consideration of the methodology best suited to the purpose of the evaluation, the questions to be addressed, and its target audience. There is a dilemma for the organization in deciding between commissioning a "gold standard" evaluation and one that most efficiently and effectively meets the organizational needs. In practical terms, this means finding the appropriate balance between the purpose, scope, timing, and available budget and the available time, resources, methodology, size, and composition of the team (Balthasar, 2011). WHO struggled with this dilemma, designing evaluations so that they can collect the required information within a reasonable time frame yet be cost-effective and useful for the program being evaluated. This dilemma can be made more difficult in the absence of a framework analysis or "baseline" of what the program was set up to do from the beginning and how its achievements will be measured.

Ownership of the Process and Findings

Russ-Eft and Preskill (2009) mention six strategies for implementing evaluation in organizations. Three of these strategies directly focus on the enhancement of ownership of the evaluation through participatory approaches. These three strategies are (a) gaining commitment and support for the evaluation work, (b) involving stakeholders in the crucial aspects of the evaluation, and (c) ensuring an appropriate understanding of the evaluation context. None of these strategies alone suffices to enhance the use of evaluation in organizations; therefore, these strategies must be considered as complementary enablers of institutional change.

The distinction between programs undertaking evaluations that use internal program staff versus those undertaking evaluations that use external expertise illustrates the evolution of programs in terms of collaborative arrangements and governance mechanisms. As support from WHO develops from successful pilot projects into global projects, programs, and initiatives, the number of stakeholders increases and the governance becomes more complex. In our experience, external evaluations are often associated with collaborative partnership arrangements composed of multiple stakeholders and formalized governance structures, which mandate periodic external evaluations every three or five years.[3]

We also noticed four crucial stages at which participatory approaches can make a difference in boosting ownership of the process and findings of evaluations and, thus, influence their utility. These are developing the annual evaluation work plan, reporting on the evaluation, report dissemination, and following up on implementation of recommendations.

Developing the Annual Evaluation Work Plan

WHO attaches importance to transparency and uses three main criteria to identify priority areas for inclusion in the annual evaluation work plan at the corporate level:

1. Organizational requirement relevant to global, international, or regional commitments; specific agreements with stakeholders, partners, or donors; and requests from governing bodies

2. Organizational significance, relating to priorities of the General Programme of Work and core functions, level of investment, inherent risks, and performance issues and concerns in relation to achievements of expected results

3. Organizational utility, relating to a crosscutting issue, theme, program, or policy question, potential for staff or institutional learning (innovation), and degree of comparative advantage of WHO

Consultation with senior management in the finalization of the evaluation work plan has proven crucial to ensure that evaluations meet their requirements, determine "ownership" of the evaluation, and obtain managers' buy-in. Subsequently, the evaluation's terms of reference and detailed planning mechanisms need to specifically formalize who will be the owner of the evaluation and take the recommendations forward. Failure to identify who are the owners and end users of the evaluation findings, both at the beginning and on completion of the

evaluation report, will threaten the success of an evaluation as well as the implementation of its recommendations (Patton, 1996; Shepherd, 2010). WHO conducted thematic evaluations of its Fellowships Program (WHO, Office of Internal
Oversight Services, 2004) and of its work with collaborating centers (WHO,
Office of Internal Oversight Services, 2007).[4] Both evaluations were carried out
because they were identified by WHO senior management as important and
relevant since both areas absorbed considerable resources and relate strongly to
organizational reputation, performance, and visibility. However, while the evaluation on the work with WHO collaborating centers had an institutional structure
for follow up on the evaluation recommendations, the Fellowships Program
evaluation report fell between several departments, none of which assumed
responsibility for addressing the recommendations. Without an institutional
owner of this evaluation, the usefulness of this evaluation was limited.

Evaluation Reporting

When program managers act as both evaluation commissioner and evalu-
and, they face a common dilemma: the need for a balanced and objective
reporting process and an independent approach that could be perceived as "off
target." The evaluation commissioner's potential concern is that external evaluators may not be fully familiar with the program and the organizational
constraints and, thus, come up with incomplete or inaccurate findings. From
the commissioner's perspective, recognizing the program's context and challenges and proposing appropriate recommendations, even if incremental, may
be more acceptable and effective than a "big-bang approach" that may call into
question the management of the entire program and thereby affect the acceptability of the report (Picciotto, 2003). Having the primary focus on the users'
perspective throughout the evaluation and ensuring that the evaluation demon-
strates a sound understanding of the program's theory and the program's
environment and constraints should address most of the concerns about the
purpose of the evaluation (Balthasar, 2011; Patton, 2008).

The above raises the issue of the quality of reporting. There are attributes
related to the internal validity of the report that are universally accepted. These
include accuracy, completeness, and relevance (institutional and programmatic). Other attributes have a more nuanced understanding because they
address utility issues as well. Quality therefore affects effectiveness from the
perspective of the evaluand, the commissioner, and the evaluator (Patton,
2008). Sometimes, a report, criticizing reduced program achievements or not
achieving expected results on time despite valid reasons, may cause disengagement
from the evaluation process, with reduced acceptance of the final report. This

occurred in IOS's evaluations of the program on Child and Adolescent Health and Development (WHO, Office of Internal Oversight Services, 2006b) and of the headquarters Department of Making Pregnancy Safer (WHO, Office of Internal Oversight Services, 2010) where the departments did not feel they were sufficiently involved in the evaluation process and initially questioned the report findings.

Report Dissemination

Given that dissemination is crucial for the success of the evaluation (Patton, 1996; Weiss, 1998), this aspect needs to be closely considered and planned. Dissemination of the report to management and program staff is the responsibility of the commissioner. In WHO, technical programs share the results of their evaluations through presentations at technical meetings and external publications. However, the dissemination approach of corporate evaluations is limited to briefings, presentations, and annual reports to WHO governing bodies and to WHO senior management. The dissemination of evaluation reports has been identified as an institutional weakness (DFID, 2011) which is being addressed in the revised evaluation policy (WHO, 2011, 2012). However, full details on how the dissemination approach will be implemented are still to be finalized.

Following Up the Evaluation

Having an appropriate management response to an evaluation is considered good practice for enabling evaluation stakeholders to benefit from the exercise (UNEG, 2010; U.S. Agency for International Development [USAID], 2009). The follow-up process is an important aspect of ensuring that there is an appropriate management response and that the recommendations are acted upon. In WHO, the absence of an organization-wide policy on this issue was recognized as an institutional weakness that is addressed in the revised evaluation policy.

Policy to Support Institutionalization of Evaluation Culture and Practice

Evaluation practice and evaluation policy are interrelated and coexist in every organization. Trochim argues that while some organizations have explicit and written evaluation policies, in other organizations, these "are unwritten and implicit, ad hoc principles or norms that have simply evolved over time" (Trochim, 2009, p. 16). However, having explicit evaluation policies is important because in their absence, the potential for organizational learning is reduced. Often standards, theory, or approaches remain as such, unless there is a conscious decision to adopt them or foresee the consequences when failing to do so. In this sense, having an explicit evaluation policy is potentially an efficient mechanism for changing practice and ultimately, for fostering evaluation culture in organizations (Trochim, 2009). At the same time, having an agreed evaluation policy and guidelines that are relevant to the needs of the institution are crucial to ensuring the independence, credibility, and utility of evaluations (Foresti, Archer, O'Neil, & Longhurst, 2007). In other normative and technical assistance organizations that cover a wide range of program areas, there are likely to be programs that have developed a strong evaluation culture at all levels which coexist with others that do not fully understand the benefits of evaluation (Foresti et al., 2007).

The knowledge gained from experience since 2003 signaled a number of shortcomings in WHO's evaluation practices (Box 8.5). These shortcomings have informed the WHO evaluation policy of 2012, as part of an overall WHO reform initiative (WHO, 2011, 2012).

BOX 8.5
SHORTCOMINGS ASSOCIATED WITH THE EVALUATION PRACTICE IN WHO

- Ad hoc approach to evaluation
- Evaluations largely driven by donor requirements rather than organizational and programmatic demand and needs
- Numerous external programmatic evaluations for some specific programs, whereas others remain neglected
- Normative work ill evaluated
- Lack of an organization-wide policy on evaluation (before 2012)
- Insufficient, readily available information within WHO on accepted evaluation methodologies
- Inadequate quality assurance approach to evaluation and follow-up of recommendations
- Insufficient efforts to strengthen the evaluation culture across WHO
- Inadequate knowledge management of the existing evaluation practice
- Inadequate organizational resources to implement the evaluation function at corporate level
- Inadequate dissemination of evaluation findings and reports

---

Sources: Review of the evaluative work at headquarters, WHO, Office of Internal Oversight Services, 2009; and WHO reform working paper (WHO, 2011).

Having a specific institutional framework for evaluation in WHO was found to be crucial for three main reasons. First, with progress in standardization of quality control mechanisms and their global adherence in organizations, there is a need for harmonizing procedures with others; second, institutional quality control of the evaluation work performed by technical programs, including the follow-up of findings and recommendations, can improve achievement of program objectives; and third, to support fostering an evaluation culture and use of evaluations across WHO.

In addition to addressing the identified shortcomings (Box 8.5), the implementation of the evaluation policy will (a) clarify the roles and responsibilities for evaluation in WHO, (b) improve accountability for assessing performance and results, (c) increase organizational learning and inform policy for decision makers, and (d) articulate the role and purpose of corporate and decentralized evaluations. This will foster alignment and harmonization of procedures and decrease the need for other stakeholders to carry out their own independent external evaluations of WHO performance (USAID, 2009).

DISCUSSION

There are multiple and interrelated causes limiting the full implementation of the evaluation function across WHO. These include the institutional arrangements for the evaluation function, lack of clear leadership and institutional "champions," limited ownership by WHO governing bodies, decrease in the available resources (technical and financial), insufficient visibility, and the decentralized nature of WHO. The current evolution of the evaluation function within WHO reflects a policy development process within an organization, with forces playing an enabling or constraining role that varies depending on the circumstances. One of these forces relates to the institutional structure of the unit responsible for corporate evaluations. There is still considerable debate among agencies about the ideal location of these units, with some proposing that maximum independence may not be the ideal situation, since in each setting, there are benefits and drawbacks that evolve over time (Foresti et al., 2007; Shepherd, 2010; USAID, 2009).

In the case of WHO, the location of the evaluation function within IOS affected the evolution of the evaluation function and presented both benefits and drawbacks (Box 8.6). Evaluation remained associated with audit in the organizational chart, and IOS could not establish an "evaluation identity" so as to allow a full implementation of an organization-wide evaluation function. Nevertheless, IOS implemented the corporate evaluation work plan in line with UNEG standards and advised technical units on evaluation methodologies and organizing evaluations. WHO's model was more along the lines of modern audit support to managers, rather than that of a fully-fledged Evaluation Unit (Mayne, 2006). There is no consensus on the role of the office responsible for corporate evaluations in other institutions (USAID, 2009). The setting of the Evaluation Unit within WHO seems to be similar to about 25% of the institutions of the United Nations, with a broad agreement on oversight and contribution to program management, and a less clear role with respect to contribution to learning in real practice (UNEG, 2007).

BOX 8.6
EFFECTS ON EVALUATION IN WHO RELATED TO
THE LOCATION OF THE EVALUATION FUNCTION IN IOS

Benefits

- Independence of corporate evaluations reporting directly to WHO governing bodies
- Access to all documents and personnel within the organization
- Outlook and capacity to systematically approach audit and evaluative work
- Mandate and authority to conduct structured follow-up of recommendations
- Cross exposure of work and methodologies between the auditors and evaluators

Drawbacks

- Some programs perceived the evaluation work as an audit accountability function rather than as an enabling learning function
- No culture of widely disseminating reports
- IOS focused its annual work plan and its work on an audit risk approach, not always fully aligned with a more participatory approach for evaluation
- Absence of a firewall between auditors and evaluators within IOS, affecting its involvement in developing a network of evaluation experts within the organization
- The location of evaluation within IOS, where the predominant focus was on audit work, complicated resource mobilization efforts and made it difficult to receive seconded staff from other departments or use trainees
- Lack of a dedicated budget for evaluation activities

Over time, there was an internal call for the institutionalization of evaluation and for an organization-wide evaluation policy. This call was attributed to multiple reasons, including the recognized need for a mechanism to ensure representativeness, quality, and use of evaluations, and to collect the varied experiences in supporting evaluation processes. The budgetary structure and financial crisis at the macro level, with an increased number of programs being funded with external funding, have also acted as a driving force. However, the budgetary structure and lack of resources had a reverse effect on the evaluation practice for those individual programs that were unable to forecast and/or allocate resources for evaluation at the planning stage. Due to the lack of an independent budgetary mechanism for the evaluation function, securing resources for the corporate evaluation function constituted a challenge as well. In addition, the lack of an effective mechanism for evaluation oversight by WHO governing bodies resulted in an institutional underestimation of evaluation as an effective tool for accountability and learning.

In recent years, there has been an overall trend to develop the evaluation function in institutions to enhance aid effectiveness (USAID, 2009). In the case of WHO, both above internal and external forces were pushing for the strengthening of the evaluation function and the establishment of the evaluation policy. These forces acted at two levels. First, by adhering to the UNEG standards, there was peer pressure to comply with best practice. This includes having a clear policy on evaluation for the organization. Second, stakeholders and the WHO governing bodies exerted pressure on WHO to further develop an evaluation culture and utilization of evaluations and to establish a clear policy on evaluation. The pressure from stakeholders resulted from external evaluations of WHO that looked at governance and adherence to best practices of organizational effectiveness.

The WHO reform process has acted as an overall force to support the development of the evaluation policy. The need for an evaluation policy was included as one of the main aspects among the management reforms. This has resulted in much discussion internally and with WHO's Executive Board on the policy itself and on the implementation details. Overall, the consultative process has contributed to the institutionalization of evaluation in a sustainable manner. The approval of the evaluation policy in 2012 has marked a new era for the evaluation function within WHO.

CONCLUSION

The WHO experience with the development of the evaluation function and an evaluation policy illustrates a complex process of organizational change and policy development. The path toward the institutionalization of a culture of evaluation across the organization is not unique and reflects the need to allow sufficient time for organizational change and secure the support and involvement of all stakeholders.

The interplay between enabling and restraining forces considerably slowed the institutionalization of evaluation within WHO. At the same time, an ongoing process of organizational change is contributing to a sustainable mechanism for addressing the weaknesses identified in the evaluation practice. As part of this process, the organization went through several stages that were necessary, but they were not sufficient to generate the required institutional change. Pressure from external stakeholders, rather than internal demand, accelerated the process of explicit policy formulation.

Having an explicit evaluation policy helps ensure participatory approaches and stakeholder involvement in evaluation. The launching of the evaluation policy increases the institutional momentum, but it will take more than the policy formulation to foster an evaluation culture across an organization. Policy implementation will need to proactively promote a culture of evaluation, with greater focus on organizational learning, participatory approaches and enhanced institutional networking, and establishment of a clear institutional identity for the corporate Evaluation Unit.

The evaluation policy will provide greater visibility for evaluation and increase the awareness of technical programs. However, improving the quality and utilization of evaluation work will need continuous attention and sufficient funding to ensure the implementation of a well-resourced evaluation agenda that responds to the expectations of stakeholders and organizational needs.

DISCUSSION QUESTIONS

1. Is a participative approach to evaluation always appropriate when evaluating publicly funded programs. Why or why not?

2. How, if at all, might the evaluation policy of a small to medium-sized nongovernmental organization differ from that of an international or government agency?

3. Often, there is a distinction made between the nature of evaluations designed for accountability and those designed to provide lessons on what can be improved or changed in the future. Does one always necessarily exclude the other?

4. What are the advantages and disadvantages of systematically using external consultants for conducting commissioned evaluations?

NOTES

1. The WHO Constitution Article 28(g) requires that the WHO Executive Board submit to the Health Assembly for consideration and approval a General Programme of Work for a specific period.

2. UNEG defines *evaluation* as the systematic and impartial assessment of an activity, project, program, strategy, policy, topic, theme, sector, operational area, or institutional performance. It focuses on expected and achieved accomplishments, examining the results chain, processes, contextual factors, and causality, to understand achievements or the lack thereof. An evaluation should provide evidence-based information which is credible, reliable, and useful, enabling the timely incorporation of findings, recommendations, and lessons learned in the decision-making processes of the organization.

3. Examples of such collaborative partnerships include (a) the Special Programme for Research and Training in Tropical Disease Research (TDR), which is formed by UN Children's Fund (UNICEF), the UN Development Programme (UNDP), the World Bank, and WHO; and (b) the Special Programme of Research, Development and Research Training in Human Reproduction (HRP), which is formed by UNDP, UN Population Fund (UNFPA), the World Bank, and WHO.

4. WHO collaborating centers are part of the networks of expert institutions around the world, with which WHO relates for specific technical work. However, in some cases, it is not clear how these collaborating centers contribute to the overall work of WHO and to the achievement of WHO objectives and goals.

REFERENCES

Balthasar, A. (2011). Critical friend approach: Policy evaluation between methodological soundness, practical relevance, and transparency of the evaluation process. *German Policy Studies, 7*(3), 187–231. Retrieved January 3, 2012, from http://www.spaef.com/file.php?id=1321

Bryce, J., Victora, C. G., Habicht, J. P., Vaughan, J. P., & Black, R. E. (2004). The multi-country evaluation of the integrated management of childhood illness strategy: Lessons for the evaluation of public health interventions. *American Journal Public Health, 94*(3), 406–415.

Canadian International Development Agency (CIDA). (2009, March). *Review of the effectiveness of CIDA's multilateral delivery channel.* Retrieved November 30, 2011, from http://www.acdi-cida .gc.ca/INET/IMAGES.NSF/vLUImages/Evaluations/$file/REVIEW_OF_THE_EFFECTIVENESS_ OF_CIDA.pdf

Coryn, C. L., Noakes, L. A., Westine, C. D., & Schroter, D. C. (2011). A systematic review of theory-driven evaluation practice from 1990 to 2009. *American Journal of Evaluation, 32*(2), 199–226. Retrieved March 13, 2012, from http://www.wmich.edu/evalphd/wp-content/ uploads/2010/05/A-Systematic-Review-of-Theory-Driven-Evaluation-Practice-from-1990- to-2009.pdf

Department for International Development (DFID). (2011, March). *Multilateral aid review: Ensuring maximum value for money for UK aid through multilateral organizations.* Retrieved November 30, 2011, from http://www.dfid.gov.uk/About-DFID/Who-we-work-with/Multilateral- agencies/Multilateral-Aid-Review/

Fleischer, D. N., & Christie, C.A. (2009). Evaluation use: Results from a survey of U.S. American Evaluation Association Members. *American Journal of Evaluation, 30*(2), 158–175.

Foresti, M., Archer, C., O'Neil, T., & Longhurst, R. (2007). *A comparative study of evaluation policies and practices in development agencies.* Paris, France: French Agency for Development. Retrieved January 2, 2012, from http://www.odi.org.uk/resources/docs/4343.pdf

Hatch, M. J., & Cunliffe, A. (2006). *Organization theory: Modern, symbolic, and postmodern perspectives* (2nd ed., pp. 295–325). Oxford, UK: Oxford University Press.

The Lancet. (2010, February 13). Evaluation: The top priority for global health. *Lancet, 375*(9714), 526. Retrieved November 30, 2011, from http://www.thelancet.com/journals/lancet/article/PIIS0140–6736(10)60056–6/fulltext

March, J. G. (1991). Exploration and exploitation in organizational learning. *Organization Science, 2*(1), 71–87. Retrieved March 10, 2012, from http://www.cor.web.uci.edu/sites/www.cor.web.uci.edu/files/u3/March%20(1991).pdf

Mayne, J. (2001). Addressing attribution through contribution analysis: Using performance measures sensibly. *Canadian Journal of Program Evaluation, 16*(1), 1–24. Retrieved November 30, 2011, from http://dsp-psd.pwgsc.gc.ca/Collection/FA3–31–1999E.pdf

Mayne, J. (2006). Audit and evaluation in public management: Challenges, reforms, and different roles. *Canadian Journal of Program Evaluation, 21*(1), 11–45.

Multilateral Organizations Performance Assessment Network (MOPAN). (2011, January). *MOPAN common approach: World Health Organization 2010.* Retrieved November 30, 2011, from http://static.mopanonline.org/brand/upload/documents/WHO_Final-Vol-I_January_17_Issued1_1.pdf

Patton, M. Q. (1996). *Utilization focused evaluation: The new century text* (3rd ed.). Thousand Oaks, CA: Sage.

Patton, M. Q. (2008). *Utilization-focused evaluation.* Thousand Oaks, CA: Sage.

Picciotto, R. (2003). International trends and development evaluation: The need for new ideas. *American Journal of Evaluation, 24*(2), 227–234.

Rogers, P. J. (2008). Using programme theory to evaluate complicated and complex aspects of interventions. *Evaluation, 14*(1), 29.

Rossi, P. H., Freeman, H., & Lipsey, M. W. (1999). *Evaluation: A systematic approach* (6th ed.). London, UK: Sage.

Russ-Eft, D., & Preskill, H. (2009). *Evaluation in organizations: A systematic approach to enhancing learning, performance and change* (2nd ed.). Cambridge, MA: Perseus.

Shepherd, R. P. (2010, April 7–9). In search of a balanced evaluation function: The state of federal programme evaluation in Canada. In *International Research Symposium on Public Management.* Symposium conducted in Berne, Switzerland. Retrieved January 3, 2012, from http://www.irspm2010.com/workshops/papers/E_insearchofa.pdf

Sridharan S., & Nakaima, A. (2011). Ten steps to making evaluation matter. *Evaluation and Program Planning, 34*(2), 135–146. Retrieved November 30, 2011, from http://torontoevaluation.ca/solutions/_downloads/pdf/A_epp%20ten%20steps.pdf

Trochim, W. M. (2009). Evaluation policy and evaluation practice [Special issue]. W. M. Trochim, M. M. Mark, & L. J. Cooksy (Eds.), *New Directions for Evaluation: Evaluation Policy and Evaluation Practice, 123,* 13–32. Retrieved November 30, 2011, from http://www.ecommons.cornell.edu/bitstream/1813/15124/2/Trochim%2009%20pub%2006.pdf

UN Evaluation Group (UNEG). (2005a). *Norms for evaluation in the UN system.* [An update of 2011]. Retrieved November 10, 2011, from http://www.uneval.org/papersandpubs/documentdetail.jsp?doc_id=21

UN Evaluation Group (UNEG). (2005b). *Standards for evaluation in the UN system.* Retrieved November 10, 2011, from http://www.uneval.org/papersandpubs/documentdetail.jsp?doc_id=22

UN Evaluation Group (UNEG). (2007). *Oversight and evaluation in the UN system.* Retrieved June 21, 2012, from http://www.uneval.org/papersandpubs/documentdetail.jsp?doc_id=88

UN Evaluation Group (UNEG). (2010). *UNEG good practice guidelines for follow-up to evaluations.* Retrieved June 21, 2012, from http://www.uneval.org/papersandpubs/documentdetail.jsp?doc_id=610

UN Evaluation Group (UNEG). (2011, March 23–25). *Summary of outcomes from the UNEG AGM 2011: Decisions taken and provisional Programme of Work 2011/2012.* Paper presented at the Annual General Meeting, Paris, France. Retrieved June 21, 2012, from http://www.unevaluation.org/unegcalendar/eventagenda.jsp?event_id=270

U.S. Agency for International Development (USAID). (2009, August 17). *Trends in international development evaluation theory, policies and practices.* Retrieved November 30, 2011, from http://pdf.usaid.gov/pdf_docs/PNADQ464.pdf

Weber, M. (1968). *On charisma and institutional building.* Chicago, IL: University of Chicago Press.

Weiss, C. (1979). The many meanings of research utilization. *Public Administration Review, 39*(5), 426–431. Retrieved January 2, 2012, from http://www.g-rap.org/docs/Mixed/Weiss%20 1979%20The%20Many%20Meanings%20of%20Research%20Utilisations.pdf

Weiss, C. (1998). *Evaluation* (2nd ed.). Upper Saddle River, NJ: Prentice Hall.

World Health Organization (WHO). (1946). *Constitution of the World Health Organization.* New York, NY: United Nations.

World Health Organization (WHO). (2002a). *Programme management in WHO: Monitoring, evaluation and reporting: Guidance for 2002–2003* [Report No. WHO/PME/02.5, October 2002]. Geneva, Switzerland: Author.

World Health Organization (WHO). (2002b). *Programme management in WHO: Operational planning, guidance for 2004–2005* [Report No. WHO/PME/02.6, December 2002]. Geneva, Switzerland: Author.

World Health Organization (WHO). (2003). *Multi-country evaluation of the Integrated Management of Childhood Illnesses (IMCI): Effectiveness, cost and impact (MCE): Progress report: May 2002—April 2003.* Retrieved November 30, 2011, from http://www.who.int/imci-mce/ Publications/WHO_FCH_CAH_03.5.pdf

World Health Organization (WHO). (2006, January). *WHO accountability framework: A policy paper.* Geneva, Switzerland: Author.

World Health Organization (WHO). (2011). *WHO reforms for a healthy future: Report by the Director General* [Report No. EBSS/2/2, October 15, 2011]. Retrieved July 20, 2012, from http://apps.who.int/gb/ebwha/pdf_files/EBSS/EBSS2_2-en.pdf

World Health Organization (WHO). (2012, May). *WHO reform: Draft formal evaluation policy* [No. EB131/3]. Retrieved June 21, 2012, from http://apps.who.int/gb/e/e_eb131.html

World Health Organization (WHO), Office of Internal Oversight Services. (2004, November). *Thematic evaluation of WHO Fellowship Programme.* Geneva, Switzerland: Author.

World Health Organization (WHO), Office of Internal Oversight Services. (2006a, March). *Evaluation guidelines.* Geneva, Switzerland: Author.

World Health Organization (WHO), Office of Internal Oversight Services. (2006b, March). *Programmatic evaluation of Child and Adolescent Health and Development.* Geneva, Switzerland: Author.

World Health Organization (WHO), Office of Internal Oversight Services. (2007, June). *Thematic evaluation of WHO's work with collaborating centres*. Geneva, Switzerland: Author.

World Health Organization (WHO), Office of Internal Oversight Services. (2009, July). *Review of evaluative work at headquarters* [Internal Working Document No. 08/781]. Geneva, Switzerland: Author.

World Health Organization (WHO), Office of Internal Oversight Services. (2010, June). *Evaluation of the WHO's headquarters Department of Making Pregnancy Safer* [Report No. IOS/09/815]. Geneva, Switzerland: Author.

CHAPTER 9

BUILDING FOR UTILIZATION

The Case of the International Labour Organization (ILO)

Janet Neubecker, Matthew Ripley,
and Craig Russon

CHAPTER TOPICS

- Developing a model for optimal evaluation utilization (utilization maturity model)
- Using systems theory to identify helpful "leverages"
- Challenges faced along the way

This chapter presents a model to optimize evaluation utilization in an organization and its application to our work in the International Labour Organization (ILO). It was developed through our individual expertise in project design and appraisal, information management, and evaluation of development projects. We begin with a brief description of the ILO context and then a summary of its evaluation mandate and policy. The overarching aim of the ILO is to reach a level of quality evaluation that achieves a harmonious balance between accountability to donors and management and fostering optimum utilization of evaluation findings to improve project and program design and organizational learning.

The *utilization maturity model* depicts five hypothetical maturity steps that could lead to optimum use of evaluation findings. In our own efforts to improve utilization, we reviewed organizational cycles beyond evaluation. We looked for leverage points where more profound understanding of the knowledge benefits that evaluation can contribute to organizational learning could be nurtured. To review organizational cycles, we used systems thinking to map out the critical intersections that involve evaluation. We identified five: *vision and strategy, project design and appraisal, implementation, evaluation of results,* and *using evaluation findings.*

ILO is not yet at Level 5 in the maturity model (optimized use) but sits between Levels 3 and 4 in the utilization maturity model. Examples of how this can be improved are examined for each phase of the organizational cycle by identifying potential leverage points that could be initiated or strengthened. This analysis is then matched to a matrix, depicting various challenges and how they might be addressed. Each subsection concludes with some specific ILO experience relevant to the organizational cycle.

With regard to the evaluation management cycle, we present some detailed treatment of three areas where ILO has developed some specific strengths: its information system and database, procedures and exercises for management response, and establishing an evaluation culture through active networks. A separate section deals with the very important area of knowledge utilization and "closing the loop." The chapter concludes with a look at our major achievements and upcoming challenges in our search for optimizing evaluation utilization.

EVALUATION AND ILO

The ILO is a specialized agency of the United Nations (UN) responsible for drawing up and overseeing international labor standards. It is the only UN agency that actively uses tripartite partnerships with governments, employers, and workers to jointly promote its Decent Work Agenda founded on fundamental principles and rights at work. This unique tripartism is the basis of ILO's comparative advantage in generating real-world knowledge about employment and working conditions.

ILO evaluation policy follows the principles laid out by the Organisation for Economic Co-operation and Development, Development Assistance Committee (OECD-DAC, 2001, 2010b), as well as the norms and standards set out by the UN Evaluation Group (UNEG, 2005a, 2005b, 2010b). The ILO Evaluation Unit released a new set of guidelines in 2012 titled *ILO Policy Guidelines for Results-Based Evaluation: Principles, Rationale, Planning and Managing for Evaluations* (International Labour Office [ILO], 2012), which serves as ILO governance on evaluation.

The ILO Evaluation Unit is an independent entity, reporting directly to the Director-General, the head of the organization. An Evaluation Advisory Committee (EAC), comprising key representatives from senior management who sit on a rotational basis, was established to promote institutional follow-up on organizational-level evaluation findings and to provide pertinent information and advice to the Director-General on progress made by the ILO on management follow-up in this regard. Figure 9.1 depicts the reporting structure of evaluation in the ILO.

The ILO Evaluation Unit (EVAL) consists of a director, three senior evaluation officers, a knowledge official, and a secretary. In addition, the Evaluation Unit works with five regional evaluation officers who coordinate the evaluation work in the regions. These five officers provide guidance and support for the country evaluation work within their regions.

This central Evaluation Unit (EVAL) is responsible for conducting three governance or high-level evaluations per year: one country program and two strategy evaluations. The EVAL is further responsible for providing advisory support and approval of approximately 70 to 80 decentralized independent

Figure 9.1 Structure of Reporting on Evaluation in the ILO

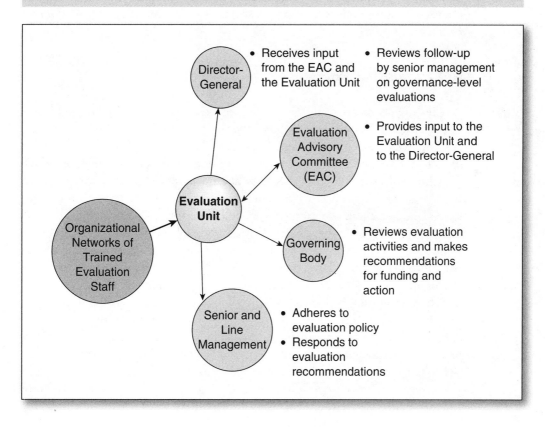

project evaluations per year (with project budgets over US$1 million). Budgets for conducting independent project evaluations come from a mandated 2% set aside from the overall project budget, which is dedicated to monitoring and evaluation requirements, usually 5%. Independent evaluations are managed by staff outside the central unit and conducted by external consultants, with the final approval given by the central Evaluation Unit. The various technical departments and regional offices are responsible for managing and conducting internal evaluations for all projects under that budget threshold, usually amounting to approximately 30 to 40 internal evaluations per year. All evaluations conducted in the ILO are included in the central evaluation database.

Independent evaluations require formal management response and follow-up to recommendations. High-level evaluation follow-up is conducted by senior management and reported through the Evaluation Advisory Committee and its Governing Body. Independent project evaluation follow-up is initiated by EVAL, using specific modules in its database to generate templates for managers to record their responses. The adequacy and quality of follow-up is reported by the Evaluation Unit to the ILO Governing Body in its *Annual Evaluation Report.*

ILO Evaluation Policy

The ILO considers evaluation a tool of both accountability and organizational learning. To this end, it follows the rigorous standards set by the OECD-DAC and UNEG to ensure independence, validity, and reliability in the conduct of its high-level and project independent evaluations. The ILO evaluation policy guidelines (ILO, 2012) comprise a policy document supported by guidance notes and checklists on how to conduct evaluation. With respect to organizational learning, the Evaluation Unit, in collaboration with all technical departments, works on disseminating evaluation findings and ensuring that these are acknowledged and followed up by management and thereby mainstreamed back into the realm of project planning and design. The aim here is to "close the learning loop," ensuring that no evaluation goes unread or unused.

While examining processes to improve organizational learning in the ILO, we came across excellent sources in the literature that guided us to our goal concept of utilization maturity.[1] Using models from information technology and project management, we put together our own version of a maturity model that would lay out key steps to optimized utilization. We applied this model to processes in our own organization by applying a systems approach to identify leverage points within the organization where there was contribution value for evaluation or an opportunity for evaluation to build some additional partnership or knowledge. What we experienced was a melding of organizational culture and cycles with evaluation activities that put our model in perspective and continues to help us strengthen utilization.

THE UTILIZATION MATURITY MODEL

Evaluation should play an active part in informing many aspects of the policy cycle, and a high-performing evaluation function can contribute independently validated knowledge to organizational learning. Our model, as shown in Table 9.1, maps the evolution of organizational behavior as it moves closer to a goal of optimized use.

Table 9.1   Utilization Maturity Model

Maturity Level	Description
1. Unreliable use	Sporadic use of evaluation knowledge. Formal policies and procedures are lacking. No organizational support to capture and disseminate evaluation knowledge.
2. Informal use	Evaluation knowledge is being used informally, mostly in a few larger projects or units. There may be a formally approved evaluation policy or procedure, but it is either not adhered to or there is limited knowledge among staff. Management attitudes toward evaluation are mixed and there is limited organizational support for evaluation knowledge.
3. Standardized use	Staff members are aware of the existence of evaluation knowledge, and there is a formal evaluation policy or procedure in place. Management sees learning from evaluations as a routine requirement, and there is organizational support to manage evaluation knowledge, such as a knowledge-sharing platform or database.
4. Monitored use	Staff members accept the use of evaluation, and evaluation knowledge is integrated into the policy, program, and project cycle. Application of the use of evaluation knowledge is systematically monitored across the organization. Management encourages the use of evaluation findings, and knowledge is being shared across the organization.

(Continued)

Table 9.1 (Continued)

Maturity Level	Description
5. Optimized use	Staff members actively use evaluation knowledge to inform all aspects of the policy, program, and project cycle. There is need only for periodic oversight of the use of evaluation knowledge. Management focuses on continuous improvement through the use of evaluation findings and knowledge is being transferred to enhance organizational performance.

It is based on the premise that organizations that are serious about developing evaluative thinking strive to reach an optimal level of use: one where evaluations are actively and continuously used to produce a positive effect on performance. Box 9.1 provides definitions for some of the terms used in the utilization maturity model and the challenge matrices for the different levels of the organizational cycles.

BOX 9.1
DEFINITIONS FOR TERMS USED IN THE
UTILIZATION MATURITY TABLES

- *Evaluation policy* governs requirements for evaluation within the organization.
- The *Evaluation Unit* means a specific unit responsible for the evaluation function.
- The *approval team* comprises officials that deal with internal and external funding, appraisal, approval, and project budgets. They ensure evaluation requirements are reflected in the approval documents.
- *Evaluation focal points* are staff members outside the central Evaluation Unit who are trained in evaluation procedures. They can act as evaluation managers or provide evaluation guidance and support to staff.
- *EDB* is a centralized evaluation database.
- *Evaluability* means the extent to which an activity or an intervention can be evaluated in a reliable and credible manner, usually associated with an *evaluability assessment* and undertaken as an early review of a proposed activity in order to ascertain if its objectives are adequately defined and its results verifiable.[2]

DEVELOPING THE MODEL IN CONTEXT

Linking the Model to an Organizational Cycle

Figure 9.2 shows the basic cycle of an organization: vision and strategy, designing and approving projects to reflect the vision and strategy, implementation of projects, evaluation of projects, and using evaluation to feed vision and strategy. This simple causal loop diagram (CLD) shows a closed and holistic learning loop: vision feeds action, action is evaluated, and evaluation findings feed innovation and redesign for the vision and strategy.

Figure 9.2 The Basic Organizational CLD

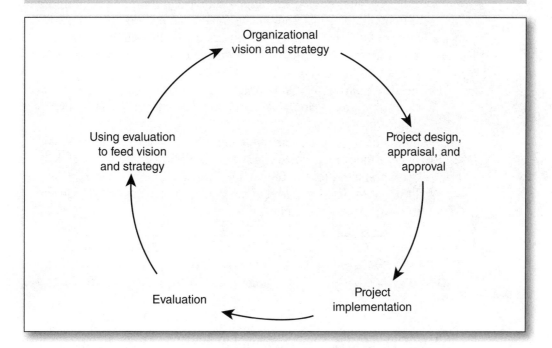

We linked the goals in our utilization maturity model to our basic organizational cycles and applied systems thinking to discover important leverage points of collaboration with internal partners. This collaboration was found to be mutually beneficial and broadened the understanding of evaluation in a cooperative way. In addition, we were able to streamline bureaucratic processes while ensuring evaluation findings were being recycled back into program design and were made available for the strategic cycle of improving vision and programming.

BOX 9.2
ILO EXPERIENCE: FIRST STEPS TO DEVELOPING
UTILIZATION MATURITY IN THE ILO

In 2011, the ILO's Governing Body revised its evaluation policy and strategy of 2005. The following are some of the key factors that have been instrumental in moving the ILO from *informal* to *standardized use* in the maturity model:

- Establishment of a systematic approach to collecting, compiling, and sharing evaluation findings through a central knowledge system, enabling key lessons learned and good practices to be filtered, searched, and categorized for easy access
- Decentralization of responsibility for evaluation oversight to a network of field-based evaluation experts that allows dedicated evaluation officers based in the ILO's regional offices to provide more evaluation support to regional and national staff
- Institutionalization of formal requirements to incorporate evaluation into project appraisal, with appropriate funds set aside at approval
- Strong political leadership, promoting the use and benefits of evaluation; establishing binding directives to clarify roles, responsibilities, and accountabilities for the conduct of evaluation and its follow-up; and linking it as part-and-parcel of the result-based management agenda and organizational culture

Source: Adapted from the independent evaluation of the ILO evaluation function, ILO (2010a, 2010b).

Organizational culture can be viewed as a system, a collective personality reflecting vision and values through analysis and action (Russon & Russon, 2005). The systems drawings, found in this chapter, map out those leverage points in our organization that have contribution value for evaluation. We use a modified version of the CLD systems tool to chart where evaluation works with other key parts of the ILO.[3] CLDs are useful to model complex feedback processes in a manner that can reveal the context and links of certain activities, allowing analysis on many levels (Burke, 2006).

Systems Thinking, Organizational Cycles, Leverage Points

Systems thinking has evolved over the last 50 years and offers a wide range of approaches and theories.[4] Common to all approaches are three areas that make a systems approach particularly interesting to our goal of finding ways to mainstream and integrate the evaluation contribution into everyday processes and organizational culture. Williams and Hummelbrunner (2011, p. 3) define these three as understanding of interrelationships, commitment to multiple perspectives, and awareness of boundaries.

In the following section, we present diagrams, depicting intersections in organizational cycles where there is an opportunity to improve the understanding, value, and benefit of evaluation work, particularly in project design, appraisal, and approval; project implementation; evaluation; and the process by which findings move upstream into vision and strategy innovation. Each diagram is briefly discussed, highlighting the key leverage points. A challenges and actions table follows where utilization maturity is applied. Examples of ILO experience conclude each of the subsections.

APPLYING OUR MODEL AT EACH STAGE OF THE ORGANIZATIONAL CYCLE

During Design, Appraisal, and Approval

During a project's design, appraisal, and approval a special team of experts in the ILO works with the project designers to ensure that a range of quality components are included. Adherence to organizational policies is checked, including evaluation requirements. For very large budget projects, effective ex ante evaluations[5] can also be used to check on evaluability of new initiatives, that is to say, the project design allows for appropriate evaluation further down the road.[6]

The systems map for this stage of the organizational cycle is shown in Figure 9.3.

From the outset of project formulation, it is important to identify what types of knowledge will be generated and to front-load thinking about how evaluations will be used. During appraisal, decisions are made on the kind of evaluation(s) that will take place. At that stage, especially for large budget projects, a communications strategy is drafted as part of the monitoring and evaluation (M&E) plan, identifying initial target users as well as setting aside

Figure 9.3 Project Design, Appraisal, and Approval

Project idea is
proposed

Check if similar projects
have been reviewed and
evaluation findings considered
in project design

Project
implementation

Appraisal team checks the
proposal for good design
prior to approval

Does it need an
evaluability exercise

Project is approved
with evaluation
components

Is an adequate monitoring
and evaluation plan a part
of project design

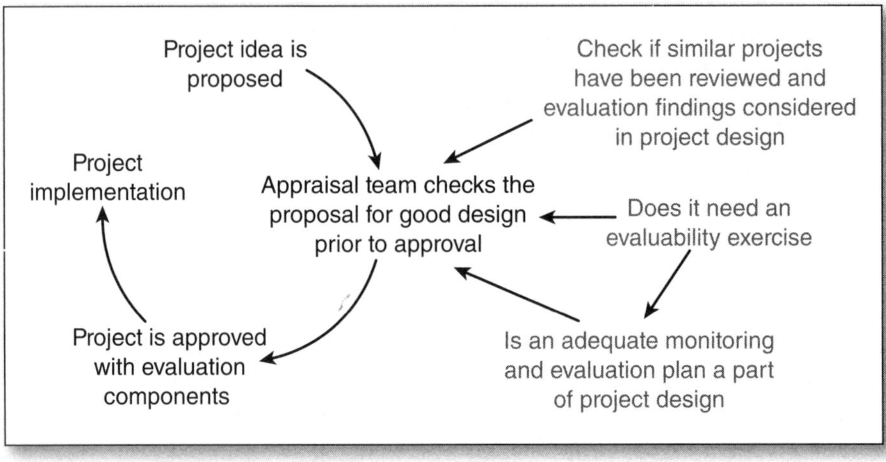

adequate resources for the final stakeholder workshop and report dissemination. We have found that when evaluation is considered and planned at the design stage, chances are higher that evaluation findings are fed back into the policy cycle through higher participation of actors, more interest in reading the final evaluation report, and higher quality management response to recommendations.

Key leverage points for this organizational process are shown in Figure 9.4.

Figures 9.3 and 9.4 demonstrate where evaluation can support the design and approval stages by providing an easily accessible source of information on the relevant evaluations already conducted. Since 2009, ILO policy now requires that new project proposals include some citation that previous ILO experience has been reviewed, particularly evaluations of similar projects, and that relevant application of any lessons learned or good practices have been included in the project proposal. The database was set up in 2009 to provide project drafters with quick web-based access to previously conducted evaluations, and separate data sets on related recommendations, lessons learned, and good practices.

During the appraisal and approval stages, especially for large projects, project staff continues to rely on the Evaluation Unit to provide input and guidance on appropriate monitoring and evaluation plans for larger projects. This is a participatory process that must also include the primary stakeholders of the ILO: employers' and workers' organizations, as well as specific government ministries.

Figure 9.4 Leverage Points for Program Design, Appraisal, and Approval

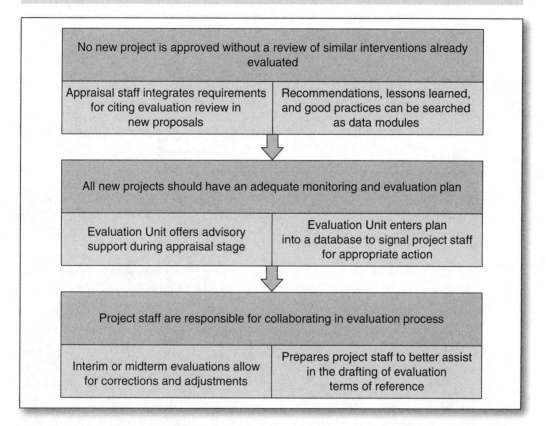

No new project is approved without a review of similar interventions already evaluated

| Appraisal staff integrates requirements for citing evaluation review in new proposals | Recommendations, lessons learned, and good practices can be searched as data modules |

All new projects should have an adequate monitoring and evaluation plan

| Evaluation Unit offers advisory support during appraisal stage | Evaluation Unit enters plan into a database to signal project staff for appropriate action |

Project staff are responsible for collaborating in evaluation process

| Interim or midterm evaluations allow for corrections and adjustments | Prepares project staff to better assist in the drafting of evaluation terms of reference |

Table 9.2 Utilization Maturity: Challenges and Actions at the Project Appraisal and Approval Stage

Challenge	Action at Informal Maturity Level	Action at Standardized Maturity Level	Action at Monitored Maturity Level
Some projects receive neither an evaluation budget nor an M&E plan.	The Evaluation Unit sets criteria for which projects require evaluations.	Evaluation Unit ensures that requirements for the different kinds of evaluation mandated—independent, self-, internal, external, and so on—are followed.	Routine meetings between the Evaluation Unit and approval team take place to update policy and process issues and to reconcile policy with practice.

(Continued)

Table 9.2 (Continued)

Challenge	Action at Informal Maturity Level	Action at Standardized Maturity Level	Action at Monitored Maturity Level
The organization needs to show evidence of use of evaluation findings.	EDB captures data on recommendations, lessons learned, and good practices, as well as samples of management response.	Approval team and Evaluation Unit ensure that new proposals cite evaluation findings, when appropriate.	The EDB tracks use of its modules and provides quantitative reporting on utilization of evaluation findings.
New proposals are not evaluable.	Evaluation Unit and approval team offer training materials on evaluability and quality M&E plans for proposal drafters.	Evaluation Unit and approval team provide checklists on controlling the quality of M&E plans.	Evaluation Unit and approval team routinely update guidelines and training materials.

BOX 9.3
ILO EXAMPLE OF EVALUATIVE THINKING AT THE PROJECT APPRAISAL STAGE

During ex ante evaluation processes, such as appraisal, two checks can be made on the use of evaluation knowledge. First, the new project, program, or policy should contain evidence that it has learned from previous interventions in the same geographic or subject area. Evaluations will form a primary body of evidence for learning from past experiences. Second, appraisers can check for the existence of a sound evaluation plan for the new intervention. For large projects, this would also include a dissemination plan.

In the ILO, clear quality standards for project and program proposals have helped improve both the generation and integration of evaluation knowledge into the project and program cycle. While appraisal takes place at the end of project and program formulation to check the use of evaluation knowledge against quality standards, all program designers are required to carry out a self-appraisal and answer questions about how they have taken on board evaluation findings during design.

During Project Implementation

Figures 9.5 and 9.6 show the organizational cycle and key leverage points during project implementation. This critical leverage point is where support by the Evaluation Unit will affect the success and quality of evaluation reports later and further down the organizational cycle. During implementation, regional focal points who work as evaluation support often must deal with project changes and delays that affect the evaluability of the project. Having a strong understanding of evaluation is important with regard to the planning and execution of evaluability assessments and conducting midterm evaluations—especially when these are either internal or self-evaluations conducted by project staff.

Figure 9.5 Project Implementation

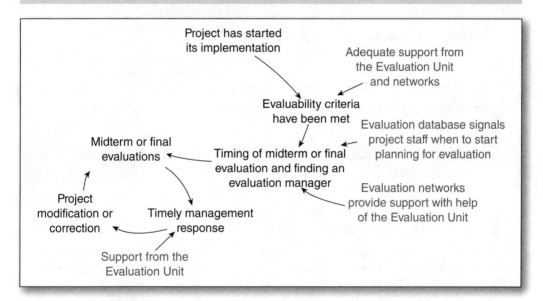

Some of the key aspects we picked up at the implementation stage involved timing and capacity of project staff to understand evaluation requirements. But more importantly, this was the part of an organizational cycle that primarily dealt with the action of project staff and support from the Evaluation Unit.

Box 9.4 summarizes components of ILO's requirements to make certain that once a large project mandated for evaluation starts implementation, it must have an evaluability assessment after one year to ensure that key components are in place to ensure evaluation quality later. These are evaluations over US$5 million that require a midterm and final independent evaluation.

Figure 9.6 Leverage Points for Project Implementation and Monitoring

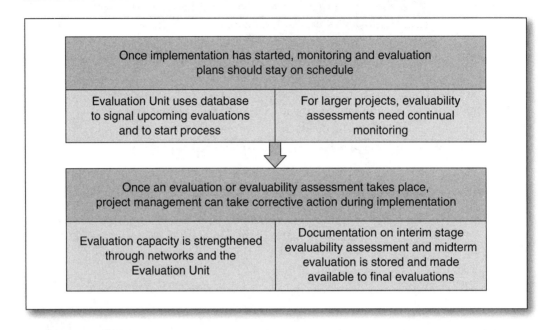

Table 9.3 Utilization Maturity: Challenges and Actions for Implementation and Monitoring

Challenge	Action at Informal Maturity Level	Action at Standardized Maturity Level	Action at Monitored Maturity Level
Project staff identifies problems with evaluability.	Project staff identifies an evaluation focal point to liaise with the Evaluation Unit.	Continuous collaboration between project staff and the Evaluation Unit takes place and resets evaluation priorities if necessary.	The approval team reports problems to donors or management; and the Evaluation Unit proposes M&E plan modifications.
Project staff are not aware of scheduled evaluations and preparations are skipped or delayed too late to undertake the evaluation.	The EDB provides a schedule of planned evaluations, which is available to all evaluation focal points or managers.	Preparation for evaluations begin at least 3 months in advance of the starting date and are signaled on a routine basis to project staff.	Planning schedules are routinely reviewed with evaluation or focal point staff. Process documents are kept in a centralized repository.

Challenge	Action at Informal Maturity Level	Action at Standardized Maturity Level	Action at Monitored Maturity Level
Project staff cannot identify an adequately trained evaluation manager for independent evaluations.	Line management identifies staff as potential evaluation managers.	The Evaluation Unit provides training materials and events to support the creation of a wide pool of internal evaluation managers.	The Evaluation Unit and evaluation focal points provide direct assistance to approve draft ToRs and prepare contracts.
Self- and internal evaluations get lost in the system.	The EDB encourages staff to send all evaluations for inclusion in the central database.	Self- and internal evaluation guidelines are provided by the Evaluation Unit.	The Evaluation Unit conducts training on self- and internal evaluation to encourage participation in the evaluation process.

BOX 9.4
EVALUABILITY ASSESSMENTS AT THE ILO

The capacity to manage for results depends to a great extent on having projects that feature the minimum characteristics needed in order for outcomes to be measured. This can be determined by a set of design-specific aspects that allows these projects to be evaluated and that is therefore defined as *evaluability*.

Evaluability assessments are an established means for evaluators to review project coherence and logic, as well as ensure adequate data availability and reliability. Criteria for an evaluability assessment can be

- clarity of project intent (relevance and design of expected outcomes and result matrices);
- quality of project design for the achievement of results (e.g., the existence of clear and measurable indicators, establishment of baselines, and milestones for reliable analysis);
- overall quality of monitoring systems;
- initial appraisal of processes for optimal involvement of the relevant national and international stakeholders; and
- external factors that have influenced or would be expected to influence the realization of the expected outcomes.

OUR MODEL IN RELATION TO THE EVALUATION MANAGEMENT CYCLE

Setting the Scene: Some General Challenges

Evaluation demand has grown across the UN community, and budgets for this function may be unable to keep pace with demand as demonstrated in the OECD-DAC study of members' evaluation capacity (2010a, pp. 27–29). Evaluation capacity needs to be continually monitored against rising demand to ensure that the Evaluation Unit can cope with workload at a professional standard. We deal with evaluation capacity issues in this chapter insofar as they are directly connected to the processes and achievement of utilization in the ILO.

Requirements of independence in the ILO stipulate that independent evaluations must be managed by staff, albeit not by project management staff. The central Evaluation Unit merely provides the policy environment, guidance, and approval. Not only does this give hands-on experience to a number of staff members on evaluation principles, ethics, and methods, but this arrangement will also strengthen evaluative thinking among the staff members in general. Figure 9.7 depicts some of the areas where the central evaluation is active (in boxes), and most others are performed by regular staff members outside of the Evaluation Unit.

Figure 9.7 Evaluation Management Cycle

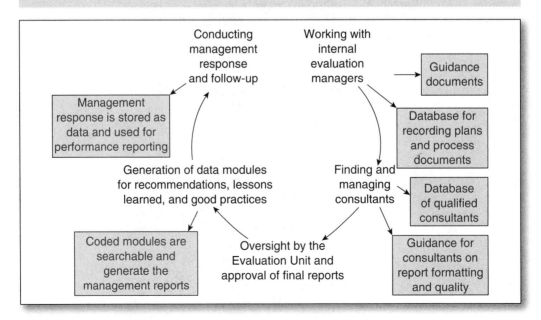

There are three particular leverage points mentioned in Figure 9.8, for which we will give some detailed treatment, as ILO has developed some tools and experience with these: development of a centralized evaluation database (EDB), facilitation of meaningful management response to evaluation findings, and establishment of networks of staff collaborating on evaluation work.

Finding consultants is a problem for most UN agencies. The difficulty of finding 50 to 70 consultants per year familiar enough with ILO to have sensitivity to our technical subjects but not too familiar to endanger their independence is a conundrum and requires very good record keeping, preparing guidance for consultants, and finally keeping track of the work that they do. In a small unit like ours, this could not be done with our limited manpower without a database.

Figure 9.8 Key Leverage Points for the Evaluation Management Cycle

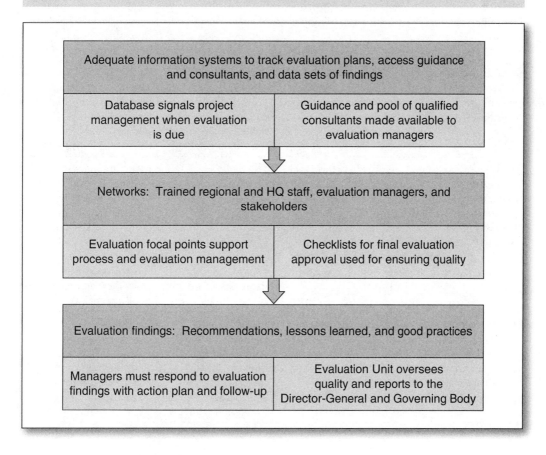

The networks of trained regional staff involve national counterparts and national evaluation societies and organizations. We encourage this networking and try to facilitate as much training as possible to ensure evaluation management is adequately covered by knowledgeable staff.

Table 9.4 Utilization Maturity: Challenge and Actions Table for Evaluation Management Cycle

Challenge	Action at Informal Maturity Level	Action at Standardized Maturity Level	Action at Monitored Maturity Level
Evaluation needs are increasing, but the Evaluation Unit is understaffed to meet evaluation workload and organizational needs.	A logistical reconciliation is undertaken periodically to determine an adequate match of workload to manpower.	A network of evaluation focal points provides support and helps broaden awareness of evaluation value.	An evaluation database coordinates the high volume of work, and provision of training materials helps build necessary skills needed by evaluation focal points supporting the Evaluation Unit.
It is difficult to identify qualified consultants.	The EDB records information on all hired and potential consultants, with metadata for expertise.	Evaluation focal points collaborate with national staff to build up a potential consultant pool.	The Evaluation Unit provides access to ratings and work samples for previously contracted consultants.
There are more than a hundred evaluations in the pipeline and another hundred being finalized. Technical departments cannot keep track of all the evaluations which are to be done.	The EDB performs the centralized planning and document coordination for all evaluations in headquarters and the field offices. It is web based and accessible by all staff.	The EDB administrator works with the evaluation focal points to ensure work plans, and completed evaluations are reconciled with database records.	Metadata allows searches on evaluations by a range of criteria. The EDB serves as a permanent data and document silo and provides modular data sets to support analysis of lessons learned and good practices.
Reports do not produce actionable recommendations, clear identification of lessons learned, or good practices.	The Evaluation Unit requires consultants to follow concise formatting and content guidelines for the presentation of key evaluation findings.	Presentation of the draft report is a checkpoint for quality, and this is undertaken by key stakeholders and the evaluation manager.	Consultants are contracted to follow guidelines, and payment is withheld until the report conforms to UN standards.

Challenge	Action at Informal Maturity Level	Action at Standardized Maturity Level	Action at Monitored Maturity Level
The evaluation is over, and the report is shelved. Nothing happens.	Dissemination plans are set in the M&E plan and supported by the evaluation budget.	Management response is solicited with data sets generated by the EDB. In response, line managers report on action plans and timelines. This is followed up and updates are recorded in the EDB.	Data on management response is included in annual performance reporting. Evaluation findings on lessons learned and good practices are used for performance analysis.

Evaluation Database

ILO tracks a large volume of project evaluations, with pipeline evaluations usually totaling 250 to 300 planning records. About 75% of our project evaluations take place in the regions, so we found it was imperative to have a database that could support a centralized silo to manage the initial planning and process stages, which are initiated in headquarters and provide adequate support to field staff for storage of process and draft documentation. The database also facilitates the convenient extraction of data sets on recommendations for inclusion in management response templates, as well as separate coded data sets on lessons learned and identified good practices.

Planning Module. This module contains details of planned project evaluations, the aim being to avoid poor timing of evaluations or, worse, evaluations being overlooked and not done at all. This module signals staff to start selecting evaluation managers, finding and engaging consultants, and so on. During the evaluation process, the database record stores draft documents, which are accessible to all regional and headquarter teams. Once the evaluation report is completed and approved, recommendations, lessons learned, and good practices are entered as submodules in each record. These are coded by metadata and can be searched by a range of criteria to create management reports. Additionally, this module enables the Evaluation Unit to keep track of what is mandated to be evaluated and what is actually carried out, providing a reliable oversight mechanism for evaluation performance.

Reports Module. This module stores and disseminates the finalized evaluation reports and evaluation summaries. It is linked to the evaluation planning module as the storage component for completed evaluations.

Figure 9.9 Modeling of the ILO Evaluation Database

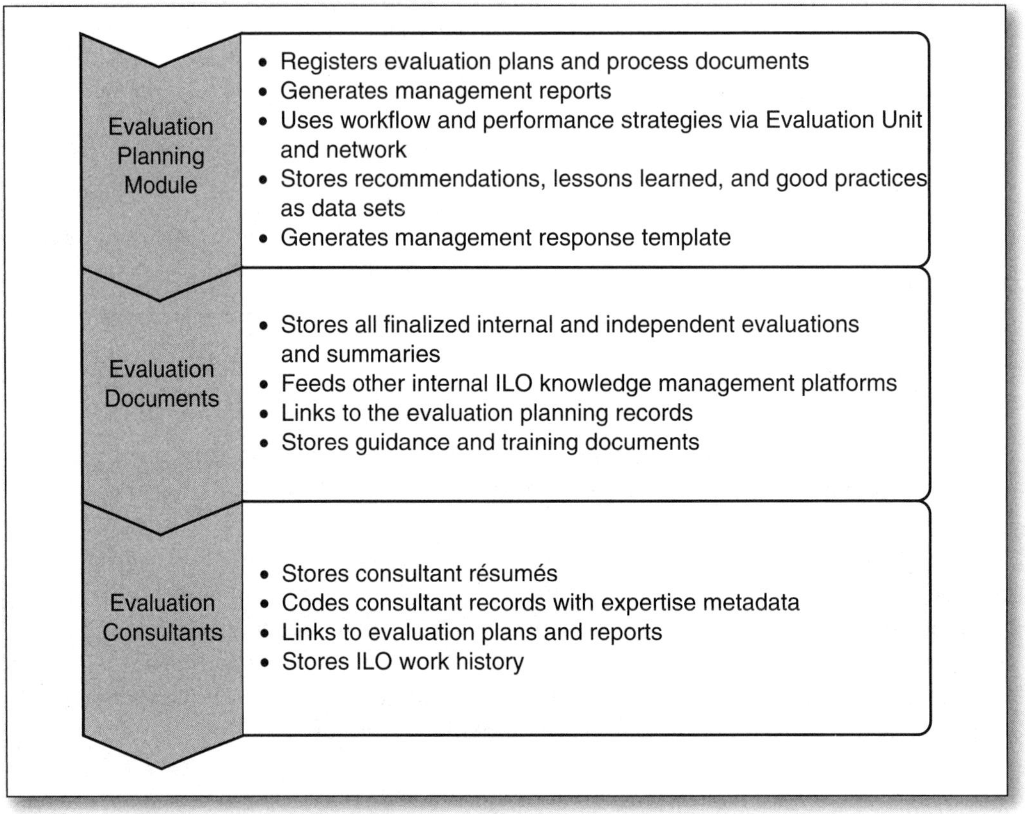

Evaluation Planning Module	• Registers evaluation plans and process documents • Generates management reports • Uses workflow and performance strategies via Evaluation Unit and network • Stores recommendations, lessons learned, and good practices as data sets • Generates management response template
Evaluation Documents	• Stores all finalized internal and independent evaluations and summaries • Feeds other internal ILO knowledge management platforms • Links to the evaluation planning records • Stores guidance and training documents
Evaluation Consultants	• Stores consultant résumés • Codes consultant records with expertise metadata • Links to evaluation plans and reports • Stores ILO work history

Consultants Module. This module provides full contact details and résumés on consultants who have worked for the ILO and those who are potential consultants. It has metadata to cover language, expertise, and geographical experience. Consultant records link to the evaluation manager's rating of work performed and the reports they have conducted.

Engaging high-quality consultants in an atmosphere of rising demand creates lively competition among the institutions competing for them, and this can be a severe hindrance to the smooth running of an evaluation function. It is our experience that not all problems related to the quality of reports have to do with inferior consultants but also with organizational preparation. It is well known, for instance, that consultants experience problems with time constraints, as well as obtaining adequate documentation and access to potential interviewees. Better timing and planning by the organization can correct this problem substantially and is further discussed in our section on databases below. We also offer some suggestions on guidance for consultants so that reports will conform to organizational requirements of quality.

ILO evaluation consultants are provided with criteria for formatting reports and additional specific guidelines for drafting recommendations, lessons learned, and good practices. Internal complaints about evaluation quality often have to do with recommendations not being actionable[7] and lessons learned and good practices not meeting professional standards—making the findings practically useless. The ILO requires that the evaluation consultant be provided with guidance on these issues as an annex to the terms of reference and held responsible for adherence to them as part of their contract. We found it better to be contractually specific about what constitutes a recommendation, lessons learned, or good practice to ensure quality of these critical elements in our evaluation reports.

Box 9.5 presents a sample of such requirements, drawn from ILO's internal guidance. In this way, the consultant is informed before writing begins, avoiding confusion and rewriting at later stages of the process. This helps to ensure that recommendations and lessons learned adhere to a protocol format as data sets, which is important to their reliability, validity, and access through a database.

BOX 9.5
CONSULTANT GUIDANCE ON PRESENTING FINDINGS
(ADAPTED FROM ILO GUIDELINES)

Recommendations: The consultant is expected to follow the criteria below in drafting recommendations, which should

- be numbered in the report and limited—ideally not more than 12;
- be formulated in a clear and concise manner;
- be relevant and useful;
- be supported by evidence and follow logically from findings and conclusions;
- link to the program indicators when feasible;
- not be too general but specific to the strategy or country whose program is evaluated;
- specify who is called upon to act;
- specify action needed to remedy the situation;
- distinguish priority or importance (high, medium, low);
- specify the recommended time frame for follow-up; and
- acknowledge whether there are resource implications.

Lessons Learned: ILO defines a lesson learned as an observation from project or program experience that can be translated into relevant, beneficial knowledge by establishing clear causal factors and effects. It focuses on a specific design, activity, process, or decision and may provide either positive or negative insights on operational effectiveness and efficiency, impact on the achievement of outcomes, or influence on sustainability. The lesson should indicate, where possible, how it contributes to (a) reducing or eliminating deficiencies or (b) building successful and sustainable practice and performance. The format for presenting lessons learned should be a concise statement of one or two sentences, which is followed by explanatory text. The concise statements are used for the evaluation summary and the database module on lessons learned. In the explanatory text, the consultant should list any positive or negative insights gained through the life of the project that had substantial impact on operations, achievement of outcomes, or impact on sustainability. These can be aimed at the administrative aspects of the project or the technical context of the intervention, but they should not be general statements of success or lack of success.

Good Practices: Here, the evaluator is requested to list emerging good practices that have all of the qualities of a lesson learned but additionally show potential for replication and application to future projects and point to organizational learning in a broader context. These should be expressed in a concise statement of one or two sentences. The concise statements are used for the evaluation summary and the database module on good practices.

Management Response to Evaluation Recommendations

OECD-DAC has reported that the "lack of attention to and use of evaluation findings is perhaps the primary area of weakness within the evaluation process today" (2010a, p. 36). The aim of management response to evaluation recommendations is to provide a formal process by which the externally validated evaluation findings are addressed by management. The initial response should indicate an action plan to deal with accepted recommendations, and later, to ensure adequate follow-up to this action is carried out, reported to the Evaluation Unit, and reported to our Governing Body (UNEG 2010a). What tends to make this an ineffective exercise in many organizations is that it comes late in the project cycle, usually when the project is finishing, and is considered just additional duties on top of a burgeoning workload.

The ILO has been recording management response for many years for its high-level evaluations on strategy or country programs. For projects, however, the ILO introduced the management response exercise only in 2009, and this presented a large volume of new information to classify, circulate, record responses for, and report on performance. Challenges we have found in the first years had to do with the quality, coherence, and relevance of the recommendations.

Without a database, we would not have had the manpower to conduct this important oversight exercise of our project portfolio. ILO has streamlined the process through the use of its database so that templates for response can be generated easily and in a timely manner. These data sets also allow for compilation and analysis of all recommendations being followed up in a specific technical area or in a reporting period.

Line management receives the EDB-generated template that contains all the recommendations within a week of receipt of the finalized and approved evaluation report. Line management is required to respond with an action plan to address the recommendations where appropriate. After 6 months, a further follow-up exercise is conducted to ensure that relevant action has been started, if not concluded, in response to recommendations. An example of the ILO template is shown in Figure 9.10.

Figure 9.10 The Management Response Template of the ILO Evaluation Unit

Sample of database-generated ILO management response template

This template is automatically generated by the database of the Evaluation Unit. The evaluation title and the first four columns are filled in, including the verbatim texts of recommendations extracted from the evaluation report. The template is then sent to line management, the individuals responsible for filling in the remaining columns with their responses and returning the completed template to the Evaluation Unit.

Title of evaluation and name of project

Project code	Recommendation number	Text	Date	Status	Action taken	Addressed to	Comments

As stated earlier, for this to be a meaningful exercise and ensure good response, the quality of the recommendations themselves must be good. ILO requires consultants to follow certain criteria, and the managers must also follow certain criteria in their response; see Table 9.5 below, which is a compilation of UNEG, UN Development Programme (UNDP), and ILO guidance on management response.

Building Evaluation Networks

We found the best way to approach the establishment of a culture of inquiry, an evaluation culture, was to activate the broadest participation of

Table 9.5 Quality Criteria for Recommendations and Management Response

Recommendation Quality Criteria	Management Response Quality Criteria
To ensure quality in reports, recommendations should have	*To ensure effective response and follow-up, recommendation responses should have*
Compliance: Be numbered and not more than 12.	*Compliance:* Indicate compliance. If there is no compliance, explain. *Completion:* All recommendations for which the line managers take responsibility must be completed and, if not, adequate explanation given in the comments field.
Relevance: Be clear and concise. Relevance requires that recommendations <ul><li>be specific,</li><li>follow logically from findings,</li><li>specify who is called upon to act,</li><li>link to indicators when possible,</li><li>specify action to be taken,</li><li>specify time frame for follow-up,</li><li>acknowledge resource implications.</li></ul>	*Relevance:* Be clear and concise and linked to the project and/or country. Relevance requires that the management response must <ul><li>contain language that is clear and concise,</li><li>be relevant to the recommendation and linked to the requested action,</li><li>indicate who has taken action,</li><li>clearly indicate timelines for follow-up,</li><li>indicate any resource implications.</li></ul>
Coherence: Be firmly based on evidence and analysis, be relevant, and realistic. Make priorities clear. Recommendations should not contradict one another.	*Coherence:* Respond to the action and priorities recommended, being coherent in their totality and expressing priorities. Management responses should be coherent as a group response and not contradictory.

relevant organizational units and staff members to participate in, produce, and benefit from evaluative work. The Evaluation Unit oversees the core work of evaluation, but it is essentially done by a range of actors, internal and external, and our Evaluation Unit attempts to support and encourage every kind of evaluative work that is taking place out of our immediate responsibility and purview.

Mayne and Rist (2006, p. 98) call this "facilitating evaluative activities," which involves assisting in the design of services and policies to achieve results across the organization. This includes building results-based management capacity and contributions to evaluative knowledge platforms and systems, as well as the core function of providing guidance for evaluation relevance, quality, and oversight. The evaluation database routinely gets upgrades to its metadata coding to align with results-based management objectives and any other relevant management trend that affects use of evaluation findings.

These internal networks have core members but are also seen as a source of "flexible and non-hierarchical means of exchange and interaction that is also more innovative, responsive and dynamic, while overcoming spatial separation" (Rodriguez-Bilella, 2008, p. 5). The ILO evaluation networks involve all actors who seek or benefit from evaluation information. Throughout this chapter, we refer to *evaluation focal points* (EFPs) which we identify as specially appointed staff trained in evaluation but working outside the Evaluation Unit to support their particular technical areas or regions. Table 9.6 summarizes potential actors, activities, and benefits in the ILO evaluation framework. Evaluation focal points play the role of occasional evaluation manager, as well as advocates for evaluation and utilization (Dibella, 1990). The EFPs are capable, with occasional support from the central Evaluation Unit, of understanding the importance of the terms of reference and ensuring that these appropriately guide the evaluation. They are also capable of reviewing and approving the selected data collection methodology, evaluation questions, and assessment of consultants and of managing the general evaluation process. Another key role of an EFP is to create a bridge between stakeholders and the evaluation process, to allow stakeholders to participate without influencing the independence of evaluations. Dibella (1990) warns that "when you open up the evaluation process to stakeholders, you unfortunately open up the possibilities for having the process co-opted and manipulated" (p. 117).

Evaluation management training is important for all staff. This applies equally to self- or internal evaluation and independent evaluations with higher budgets. ILO has conducted many training sessions to build this capacity and

Table 9.6 The ILO Evaluation Network Matrix

Organizational Cycle	Actors and Timing	Networking Activity	Networking Benefit
Appraisal and approval	Line managers, approval team, project staff, EDB support team, evaluation focal points (EFPs); *Project design stage*	Fruitful access to lessons learned and good practice data to aid in project or project design	Setting the corner stone for evaluation utilization in future projects
	Evaluation Unit, EFPs; *Project appraisal stage*	Guidelines and advice on evaluable M&E plans	Higher quality and relevance of evaluations
Implementation	Project staff, EFPs, Evaluation Unit; *Onset of project*	Reviewing evaluability during the project	Identifying problems early so that correction can be taken
	Project staff, EFPs, Evaluation Unit, EDB; *Self- or internal evaluations*	Providing guidance and support for the conduct of useful self- or internal evaluations	Ensuring that these internal reports are included in the organizational knowledge base and used to guide further planning
Conducting evaluations	EFPs, Evaluation Unit, line managers; *Ongoing*	Evaluation scheduling and portfolio	Improved timing and execution
	EFPs, EDB; *Ongoing*	Consultant database with metadata	Improved access to qualified consultants
	Stakeholders, line managers, EFPs, Evaluation Unit; *Onset and drafting stages*	Evaluation processes, evaluation questions, ToRs, approval of draft	Organizational learning strengthened, high standard evaluations
Disseminating findings and feeding knowledge systems	Selected target audiences, approval team (donor reporting), project staff, EFPs and managers; *Ongoing, learning events*	Present report, discussing findings and recording stakeholder input	Increases knowledge, provides input for organizational performance reporting

Organizational Cycle	Actors and Timing	Networking Activity	Networking Benefit
	Evaluation Unit, line managers and EFPs (see Table 9.8), EDB; *Ongoing, learning events*	Management Response, building modules on lessons learned and good practices	Ensuring management follow-up of recommendations; capturing critical findings in retrievable data sets
Organizational vision and strategy	Top management, line managers, Evaluation Unit, approval team; *Bi-annual*	Looks at high-level performance in administrative processes, technical issues, and evaluation capacity	Increases relevance and accountability; provides input to future strategy; provides input for high-level evaluations such as meta or strategy evaluations

is now looking into a "job-enrichment" strategy that will allow certification of qualified staff. Specific guidance for evaluation managers is covered in its policy guidelines (ILO, 2012). Self-evaluations are usually carried out by project staff, while internal and independent evaluations require managers external to project management. All evaluations have organizational learning value, and for this reason, we are concerned that the quality of these reports needs to conform to a professional standard and be made available for future project designers through the EDB.[8]

USING EVALUATION KNOWLEDGE TO FEED VISION AND STRATEGY: CLOSING THE LEARNING LOOP

This final section briefly surveys the end stages of evaluation work: dissemination of findings and avenues of feedback, use of and access to evaluation products, and organizational-level performance reporting. For independent ILO evaluations, the dissemination of findings marks the end of the process of evaluation and the beginning of knowledge generation and regeneration. Because there is widespread pressure on developing agencies to prove impact, to show accountability, and to identify lessons learned and good practices, knowledge generation must have an iterative and established process.

Figure 9.11 includes more detail on how the ILO Evaluation Unit provides input to technical department reporting and eventual input to reporting on organizational performance, which represents the final stages of our mapping to utilization maturity.

Figure 9.11 Using Evaluation Findings to Feed Vision and Strategy

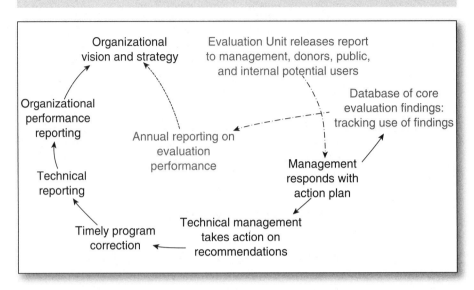

Promoting Evaluation Knowledge as a Part of Organizational Learning

Mayne and others have argued convincingly for the need for structured organizational mechanisms to foster learning within an organization (Mayne & Rist, 2006). Evaluators, commissioners, and the evaluand all have a vital role to play in making sure that learning events are informed by a sound evidence base. For instance, in select, large project evaluations, we encourage evaluators to play a role in presenting evaluation findings, since in our experience busy project staff members are more likely to respond positively to and retain more from verbally communicated information than reading long evaluation reports.

In this light, ILO's approval teams or project staff organize and facilitate learning events to encourage a frank and open discussion. The ILO Evaluation Unit conducts its own discussion groups with technical department staffs. In the case of an approval team organizing a discussion, we feel that it is important to have an alternative forum where evaluation plays a participating and not a lead role. Consideration should be given to ownership of knowledge events since in our experience, it offers an alternative and produces different results when actual project or policy implementers take a lead. The idea of these events is to leave

Figure 9.12 Using Evaluation Knowledge to Improve Vision

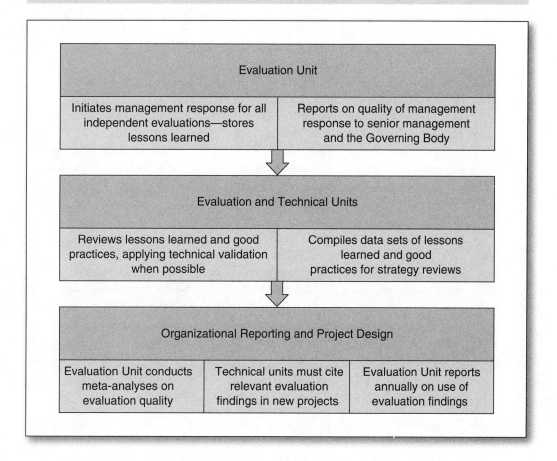

hierarchies outside the door and speak under Chatham House rules.[9] While both formal and informal structures can be used, too much formality risks politicizing the event and stifling open discussion. Ultimately, however, the ILO does not see these as one-off events but part of a structured learning program, which fosters interest and participation in a growing knowledge community.

The ILO Evaluation Unit has a quarterly newsletter that circulates information on newly completed projects, high-level evaluations, and evaluation studies and provides links to developments in the evaluation profession and in the UN community. Additionally, it provides links to evaluation networks in the international community.

Table 9.7 fleshes out an array of challenges that deal with knowledge generation. One of the biggest impediments to learning in many organizations is the intolerance of failure (Mayne, 2008; Toulemonde, 2000). This is particularly acute in public organizations where a range of pressures and incentive structures mean that failures are traditionally seen as being "bad" and therefore tend not to be discussed. Evaluation knowledge inevitably reveals what did not work as well as what did work, and organizations certainly can benefit from knowledge on how projects fail just as much as from success.

There is also a challenge mentioned in Table 9.8 on the need for more impact evaluation. In the ILO, we are still at the standardized maturity level at this stage of the evaluation management cycle. The lack of funding and manpower to undertake impact evaluation are challenges we face as a centralized Evaluation Unit. Technical departments are, however, working in this area, and we support them through guidance on methodologies and standards for conducting them. Learning and knowledge networks are often established to promote sharing among staff, such as the World Bank's Communities of Practice (www.worldbank.org/wbi). While both knowledge platforms and networks often address thematic or programmatic issues, few explicitly address failure. Since evaluation findings dealing with failure or points of policy weakness are more prone to being misused than those dealing with success, organizations can consider using positive discrimination to create knowledge structures which are dedicated to learning from past mistakes. For instance, the Canadian NGO Engineers Without Borders set up the website Admittingfailure.com to share lessons learned from its failures and encourage others to do the same.

Table 9.7 Utilization Maturity: Challenges and Action for Knowledge Generation

Challenge	Action at Informal Maturity Level	Action at Standardized Maturity Level	Action at Monitored Maturity Level
How can evaluation reports and findings benefit technical departments and overall organizational performance reporting?	Technical reports can utilize evaluation data, results of management response exercises, and other inputs from the EDB to strengthen their own accountability and performance reporting.	Independent evaluation data and analysis contribute to organizational performance reporting. Data collection methods and terminology are harmonized with RBM reporting.	Knowledge platforms include access to the EDB as part of the organizational knowledge base. Knowledge events encourage technical discussion.

Challenge	Action at Informal Maturity Level	Action at Standardized Maturity Level	Action at Monitored Maturity Level
It is difficult to find lessons learned (LLs) and good practices (GPs) for future project design without going through a mountain of paperwork.	The EDB contains easily accessed data modules extracted from the full reports.	The Evaluation Unit works with technical departments for further validation of these.	The Evaluation Unit provides information "packets" on LLs and GPs on their website.
Technical departments want more information on program or policy impact and less on project evaluation.	The Evaluation Unit conducts evaluations on strategies and provides guidance on impact evaluation.	The Evaluation Unit works with technical departments to manage impact evaluations, secured by broader budgetary funding.	Impact evaluation is routinely funded from a combination of organizational, technical department, and evaluation budgets to cover long-term impacts of strategies or program outcomes.
Addressing failures is contradictory to how the ILO wants to represent itself and its work. What if the evaluation signals big failure?	Problems and even failures can be addressed frankly in the final workshop with stakeholders, and they should use this opportunity to propose project changes.	Line managers and the Evaluation Unit ensure internal discussions can take place on performance in order to respond to recommendations.	Technical units are supported by the Evaluation Unit to generate studies of interventions that do and don't work.

BOX 9.6
ILO BROWN BAG LUNCHES AND ONLINE DISCUSSION GROUPS[10]

- Informal working lunches can be used as a means of networking and knowledge dissemination. These might include a range of brainstorming activities. The informal exchange of information and discussion on evaluation findings is based on the premise that large bureaucracies often contain siloed knowledge within individuals or units and that other colleagues would be able to extract valuable learning from such knowledge.

(Continued)

(Continued)

- ILO is now incorporating online knowledge-exchange groups to discuss lessons learned with technical units and benefit from this joint collaboration to strengthen the evaluation products that are emerging from the lessons learned and good practices that are identified in evaluations. Collaboration with technical experts will help refine these findings and help to create a refined collection of lessons learned and even the identification of good practices when possible.
- In the ILO, the project approval team organized brown bag lunches on a series of thematic areas. These lunches were aimed not at generating new knowledge but at sharing experiences and approaches to operational work. This provided staff with not only the opportunity but also the learning space, which may not have otherwise been available in the office environment.

Knowledge Generation

At the end of the evaluation process, there is a workshop where all key stakeholders and evaluation actors get together to discuss the consultant's findings and conclusions. In addition, later on, technical departments arrange discussions on evaluation findings related to specific interventions in the project, such as advocacy or media campaigns, to share experience. The Evaluation Unit, the evaluation network, and the appraisal team all organize brown bag lunch meetings to encourage informal discussion on various reports and evaluation findings, working toward strengthening impacts that are aligned with our official outcomes.

We have found that the most important element in our efforts to improve knowledge generation and utilization is *collaboration*. When something falls through the proverbial evaluation cracks, we have meetings with the appropriate member of the evaluation network and find ways to work together to solve the problem. It was only through congenial and routine collaboration with all internal partners that we found ways to stimulate participation and create our own evaluation culture. It became clear once we began our newly structured unit in 2005 that it was to everyone's benefit to improve the evaluability of projects and programs, to correct situations during project implementation that hinder the quality of evaluation, to meet evaluation information needs of technical departments and constituents, and to achieve the broadest possible exchange and use of evaluation findings.

Using the key leverage points we identified in our systems diagrams and incorporating the evaluation network and evaluation capacity of our unit, we can show the full integration of evaluative work in Figure 9.13 and Table 9.8. Figure 9.13 is the full map of the different aspects of organizational activity that involve evaluation, which depicts how a broad collaboration can result in a comprehensive reach for fostering an evaluation culture. Table 9.8 summarizes how activating the skills and knowledge of a wide range of staff members is not only a natural part of an organizational culture, but also it provides the human resource underpinning of an evaluation culture that can lead to optimized utilization. Here, we use tables and systems mapping to show how collaboration across teams in project design, approval, and appraisal; project implementation and the technical departments; and evaluation help meet the growing challenges with a relatively small central Evaluation Unit.

Table 9.8 Partners in Utilization Maturity

Actor	Leverage Point	Action
Program staff	Appraisal and approval	Reviews evaluation findings and incorporates relevant lessons learned and good practices into new projects. Drafts M&E plans and sets communication strategy used for dissemination.
	Implementation	Works with evaluability throughout the project and Evaluation Unit if necessary.
	Evaluation	Identifies evaluation manager. Updates the communication strategy, holds draft report workshop.
	Dissemination	Ensures the evaluation manager initiates an adequate communications strategy for dissemination of the report. Works with Evaluation Unit for optimal dissemination. Participates in management response.
	Knowledge generation	Benefits from the centralized evaluation database (EDB) to feed new project design.
Line managers	Appraisal and approval	Reviews organizational knowledge base for input into new design and supports project staff in the identification of appropriate evaluation findings to be used in new project design.

(Continued)

Figure 9.8 (Continued)

Actor	Leverage Point	Action
	Implementation	Oversees the implementation process, receiving regular reports on progress to ensure that evaluations can be conducted on schedule and under appropriate circumstances.
	Evaluation	Works with the EFPs to enable the evaluation process and appropriate interview processes and workshops. Gives input to draft evaluation report and ensures stakeholder participation.
	Dissemination	Responds to recommendations with time-bound action plans and continues follow up until completed.
	Knowledge generation	Makes sure the report is adequately linked to departmental knowledge platforms. Uses evaluation reports and data modules to enhance technical performance reporting and identify trends.
Appraisal and approval team	Appraisal and approval	Ensures evaluation policy is followed and that findings from evaluations are considered and cited.
	Implementation	Flags the Evaluation Unit if there are problems with evaluability or planning.
	Dissemination	Liaises with project staff and donors for discussion and exchange on evaluation findings.
	Knowledge generation	Uses EDB to provide lessons learned and good practices from evaluation findings to donors.
Evaluation focal point (EFP)	Appraisal and approval	Assists technical staff in using the EDB for input to new project design, reviews M&E plans.
	Implementation	Assists the technical unit to coordinate evaluation planning schedules and provides support to evaluation managers, using training and guidance materials.
	Evaluation	Ensures evaluation manager follows policy. Liaises between Evaluation Unit and evaluation manager. Ensures report follows organizational standards before submitting to Evaluation Unit for final approval.
	Dissemination	Ensures that the communication strategy for dissemination is adequately carried out in the technical departments or field offices.
	Knowledge generation	Uses the EDB and other knowledge platforms to provide evaluation research and findings to technical staff, national or external stakeholders, and intradepartmental knowledge groups.

Figure 9.13 Utilization Maturity: Optimized Use

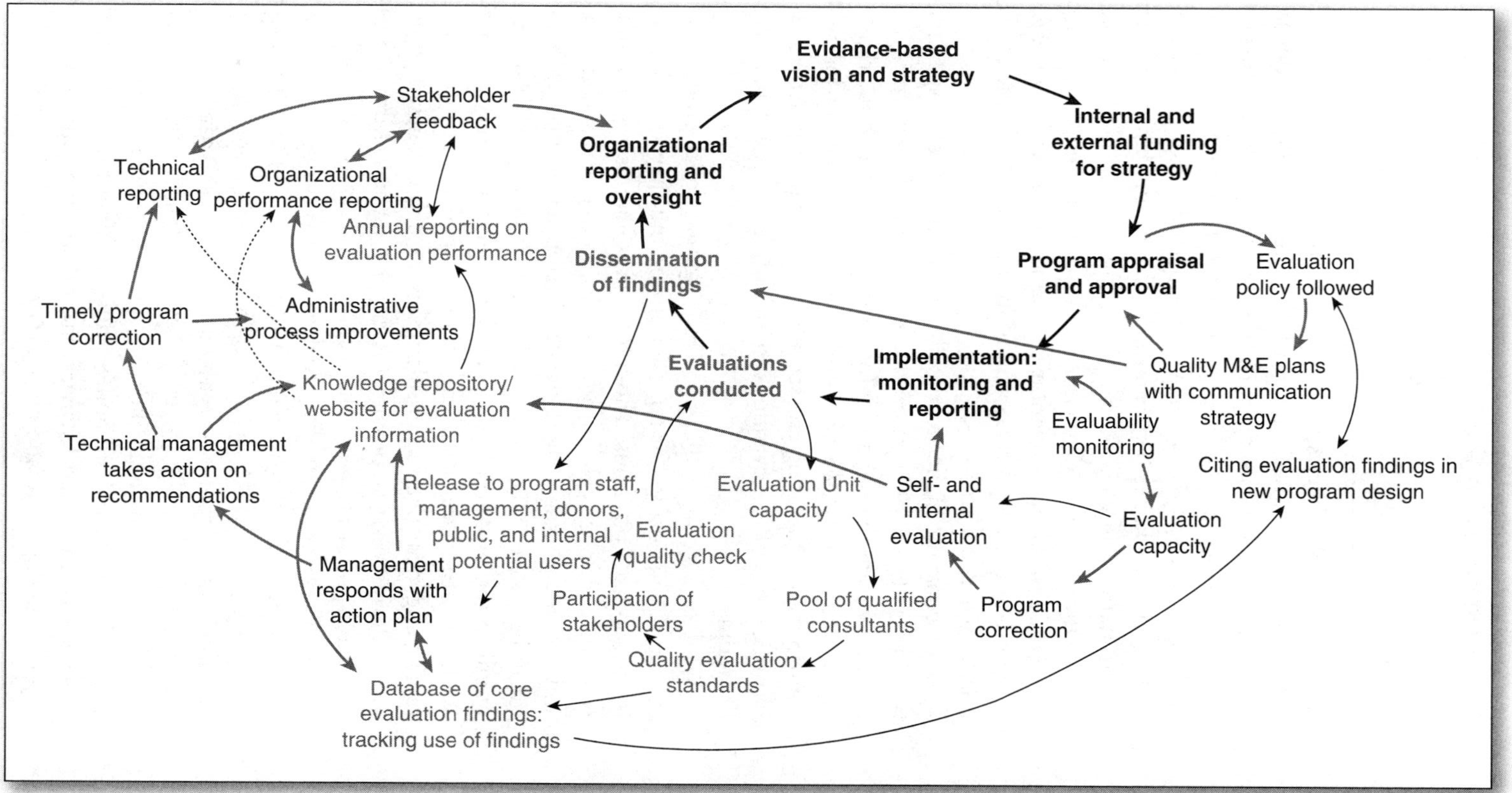

CONCLUSION

As in many UN agencies with central Evaluation Units, the ILO has been fortunate to establish strong support for evaluation culture from strategic and line management. With this support, we have been able to consolidate evaluation work and build internal networks in the ILO, improving our processes and guidelines as we go. Depending on the part of the organizational cycle that we look at, ILO vacillates between the levels of "standardized and monitored use" of our maturity model. We are continually concerned with capacity building of staff members to provide them with an adequate understanding of exactly what is required of them in relation to evaluation, as well as encouraging staff to make use of the broad collection of information available through our evaluation knowledge systems.

It is a constant challenge to collaborate on high-quality evaluation products, provide evidence for organizational performance reporting, and ensure effective knowledge sharing and information that flows to the right users to impact vision and strategy. We are hopeful that this collaboration will continue and contribute to generating crosscutting knowledge of practices, innovations, and identification of interventions that are ready for replication and possible "branding."

We face several challenges. Our regional focal points perform high-level evaluation support to our regional offices, but they are still not incorporated in long-term staff positions. Though we have had very good improvements each year, we continue with our efforts to improve management response. We are still not at the point where we can verify that follow-up is as adequate as it might be, so we will continue to work with management to make follow-up as useful to the organization as possible, and not merely a box-ticking exercise. We have already seen a substantial improvement in the quality of recommendations being identified by consultants as a result of revised guidance. Finally, we are exploring ways to provide better tracking and citing of evaluation findings in project proposals.

ILO is also exploring ways to develop cross-organizational learning through participation in the growing area of joint evaluations that are taking place in the UN community. In addition, we are placing high priority on expanding research and collaboration with our technical departments to produce relevant, timely, and technically oriented lessons learned, using evaluation findings to upscale. The Evaluation Unit's vision is to strengthen the networks and leverage points that we have built and continue to plant the seed of evaluative thinking wherever we find a fertile environment through partnership and training, something occurring more and more every year.

QUESTIONS FOR DISCUSSION

1. What are the benefits in devising a model of "utilization evaluation maturity"?

2. How does "evaluative thinking" in an organization or institution contribute to better evaluation quality?

3. Several figures have been used in this chapter to illustrate cycles within an organization that link to evaluation processes. Which departments, outside of the centralized Evaluation Unit, are potential collaborators in evaluation? How does collaboration strengthen or create evaluative thinking?

4. A number of events and collaborative measures have been presented in this chapter, aimed at improving the usefulness and relevance of evaluation reports. How and why do you think they help to improve utilization? Have you any other suggestions?

NOTES

1. This model is based on the five-point Pricewaterhouse Coopers maturity model, used to assess the project management competency of an organization (Nieto-Rodriguez & Evrard, 2004). Further inspiration was taken from Bamberger (Bamberger, Rugh, & Mabry, 2006), Mayne (2008), Patton (2012), and UN Development Programme (UNDP, 2009).

2. This definition is adapted from the OECD-DAC glossary (2002) and the UNDP evaluation manual (2009).

3. For these purposes, we did not use the usual feedback arrows that are used to indicate dynamics in a system. Once an organization does set a system map for integrating evaluation, the next step would be to go further into this kind of analysis and denote the causal influences among the variables in the system, adding positive and negative influences and addressing these according to an organization-specific CLD.

4. For more information on systems, see Meadows (2009), Midgley (2006), and Williams and Hummelbrunner (2011).

5. The definition of ex ante evaluation is provided by John Mayne in Chapter 1 of this book: "Evaluation can also be *ex ante*, an assessment undertaken of a planned project, program, or policy to determine if it is reasonable to expect that the intervention will achieve its intended aims."

6. For an example of evaluability assessment material, see the European Commission (2010) at http://ec.europa.eu/regional_policy/index_fr.cfm and the Inter-American Development Bank at http://www.iadb.org/, as well as the *ILO policy guidelines for results-based evaluation* (ILO, 2012).

7. *Actionable* in this context means that all recommendation should be clearly formulated as an action that can be taken by the organization. Actions to be taken by people outside the organization are not to be included in the recommendations section of the evaluation, but it can be included in the general text.

8. For more information on internal evaluation, see Love (1991), Rodriguez-Garcia and White (2005), and Sharp (2006).

9. At these meetings, participants are encouraged to exchange and freely use information received, but neither the identity nor the affiliation of the speaker, nor that of any other participant, may be revealed.

10. We would like to express our thanks to our colleague at the ILO, Oliver Liang, for prompting us to discuss the idea of providing organizational space to learn from mistakes.

REFERENCES

Bamberger, M., Rugh, J., & Mabry, L. (2006). *Real world evaluation: Working under budget, time, data and political constraints.* Thousand Oaks, CA: Sage.

Burke, D. (2006). System dynamics-based computer simulations and evaluation. In I. Imam, A. LaGoy, & B. Williams (Eds.), *Systems concepts in evaluation: An expert anthology* (pp. 47–59). Point Reyes, CA: American Evaluation Association.

Dibella, A. (1990). The research manager's role in encouraging evaluation use. *American Journal of Evaluation, 11,* 115–119.

European Commission. (2010). *Evalsed: The guide.* Brussels, Belgium: Author. Retrieved December 5, 2011, from http://ec.europa.eu/regional_policy/sources/docgener/evaluation/evalsed/index_en.htm

International Labour Office (ILO). (2010a). *Evaluations: Independent external evaluation of the ILO's evaluation function* (Governing Body document No. GB.309/PFA/5.5). Geneva, Switzerland: Author. Retrieved April 7, 2011, from http://www.ilo.org/wcmsp5/groups/public/@ed_norm/@relconf/documents/meetingdocument/wcms_145637.pdf

International Labour Office (ILO). (2010b). *Independent external evaluation of the International Labour Office evaluation function.* Geneva, Switzerland: Author. Retrieved March 7, 2011, from http://www.ilo.org/wcmsp5/groups/public/@ed_norm/@relconf/documents/meetingdocument/wcms_145748.pdf

International Labour Office (ILO). (2012). *ILO policy guidelines for results-based evaluation: Principles, rationale, planning and managing for evaluations.* Geneva, Switzerland: Author. Retrieved May 22, 2012, from http://www.ilo.org/eval/Evaluationguidance/WCMS_168289/lang–en/index.htm

Love, A. J. (1991). *Internal evaluation: Building organizations from within: Vol. 24. Applied Social Research Methods Series.* Newbury Park, CA: Sage.

Mayne, J. (2008). *Building an evaluative culture for effective evaluation and results management* (ILAC Working Paper No. 8). Rome, Italy: Institutional Learning and Change (ILAC) Initiative.

Mayne, J., & Rist, R. C. (2006). Studies are not enough: The necessary transformation of evaluation. *Canadian Journal of Program Evaluation, 21*(3), 93–120.

Meadows, D. H. (2009). *Thinking in systems: A primer.* London, UK: Earthscan.

Midgley, G. (2006). Systems thinking for evaluation. In I. Imam, A. LaGoy, & B. Williams (Eds.), *Systems concepts in evaluation: An expert anthology* (pp. 11–34). Point Reyes, CA: American Evaluation Association.

Nieto-Rodriguez, A., & Evrard, D. (2004). *Boosting business performance through programme and project management.* PriceWaterhouseCoopers. Retrieved from http://www.pwc.com/us/en/operations-management/assets/pwc-global-project-management-survey-first-survey-2004.pdf

Organisation for Economic Co-operation and Development, Development Assistance Committee (OECD-DAC). (2001). *Evaluation feedback for effective learning and accountability: Vol. 5. Evaluation and effectiveness.* Paris, France: Author.

Organisation for Economic Co-operation and Development, Development Assistance Committee (OECD-DAC). (2002). *Glossary of key terms in evaluation and results-based management.* Paris, France: Author.

Organisation for Economic Co-operation and Development, Development Assistance Committee (OECD-DAC). (2010a). *Evaluation in development agencies: Better aid.* Paris, France: Author.

Organisation for Economic Co-operation and Development, Development Assistance Committee (OECD-DAC). (2010b). *Quality standards for development evaluation.* Paris, France: Author.

Patton, M. Q. (2012). *Essentials of utilization-focused evaluation.* Thousand Oaks, CA: Sage.

Rodriguez-Bilella, P. (2008, March). *Evaluation networks and governance: The case of the ReLAC (Latin American Network of Evaluation, Systematization and Monitoring).* Paper presented at Easy-Eco Conference, Vienna, Austria. Retrieved September 12, 2011, from http://www.wu .ac.at/inst/fsnu/vienna/papers/rodriguez-bilella.pdf

Rodriguez-Garcia, R., & White, E. M. (2005). *Self-assessment in managing for results: Conducting self-assessment for development practitioners* (World Bank Working Paper No. 4). Washington, DC: World Bank.

Russon, K., & Russon, C. (2005). *Evaluation Capacity Development Group toolkit.* Mattawan, MI: Evaluation Capacity Development Group.

Sharp, C. A. (2006, March). *Internalized self-evaluation: An effective and sustainable approach to managing for results.* Paper presented at the Malaysian Evaluation Society Conference, Kuala Lumpur, Malaysia. Retrieved March 15, 2011, from http://papers.ssrn.com/sol3/papers.cfm? abstract_id=897043

Toulemonde, J. (2000). Evaluation culture(s) in Europe: Differences and convergence between national practices. *No. 69, 3/2000 Vierteljahshefte zur Wirtschaftsforschung.* Retrieved November 3, 2011, from http://www.atypon-link.com/DH/doi/pdf/10.3790/vjh.69.3.350?cookieSet=1

UN Development Programme (UNDP). (2009). *Handbook on planning, monitoring and evaluating for development results.* New York, NY: UNDP.

UN Evaluation Group (UNEG). (2005a). *Norms for evaluation in the UN system.* New York, NY: Author. Retrieved March 15, 2011, from http://www.uneval.org/normsandstandards/index.jsp

UN Evaluation Group (UNEG). (2005b). *Standards for evaluation in the UN system.* New York, NY: Author. Retrieved March 15, 2011, from http://www.uneval.org/normsandstandards/index.jsp

UN Evaluation Group (UNEG). (2010a). *Good practice guidelines for follow up to evaluations* (No. UNEG/G[2020] Guidance Document). New York, NY: Author. Retrieved March 15, 2011, from http://www.uneval.org/papersandpubs/documentdetail.jsp?doc_id=610

UN Evaluation Group (UNEG). (2010b). *UNEG quality checklist for evaluation reports.* New York, NY: Author. Retrieved March 15, 2011, from http://www.uneval.org/papersandpubs/document detail.jsp?doc_id=607

Williams, B., & Hummelbrunner, R. (2011). *Systems concepts in action: A practitioner's toolkit.* Stanford, CA: Stanford University Press.

CHAPTER 10

WHAT CAN WE LEARN FROM PRACTITIONERS?

Some Thoughts and Take-Home Messages for Internal Evaluation Units

Marlène Läubli Loud

The various chapters have provided a rich insight into the ways in which those responsible for evaluation inside organizations are attempting to optimize the use and usefulness of evaluation. They are operating in different political and organizational contexts; some units are far better resourced than others; some are providing only one service; others are providing many. For instance, some are expected to conduct evaluations themselves, others not; some are expected to support others' management of evaluation, others not; and some are expected to manage commissioned evaluations, others not. There is also considerable variation between them about how evaluation is set up and managed in their organizations. Yet despite these differences, there is quite some similarity in the challenges they face in attempting to add value to their organizations through evaluation. But the strategies they are using in response are not necessarily the same, have the same emphasis, or even have the same results; they have been shaped to a large degree by features relating to their own specific environments.

In this final chapter, I should therefore like to compare and contrast the experience of our chapter authors and, wherever relevant, add some of my own experience-based reflections. I shall not attempt to cover all the issues raised, as this would likely become repetitive and unnecessarily lengthy! Instead, I shall draw on a selection of those that seem to be of common concern. The discussion starts with considering the more organizational challenges and corresponding strategies before turning to issues that are at the individual, evaluation project level. The question of evaluation managers' competencies then comes under review and completes these reflections. This final chapter ends with some general lessons for those people who are committed to enhancing the use and usefulness of evaluation in their respective organizations and/or policy arena.

THE INDEPENDENCE OF AN INTERNAL EVALUATION UNIT AND ITS STAFF

To best ensure the quality and credibility of an evaluation, the various chapters provide examples of why evaluators and managers need to maintain their independence from line management. Hawkins, for example, is adamant that ensuring evaluators' "independence from operational or program units" is essential if one wants them to be able to "speak truth to power." Keeping them at "arm's length" from the managers responsible for the implementation of the programs or policies being evaluated will also increase the credibility of the evaluation. Citing Robert Picciotto, former director of the World Bank's Independent Evaluation Group, Hawkins notes that indeed the whole process will be treated with some skepticism if the independence of all parties concerned—that is, commissioners, managers, and evaluators—is not guaranteed by delegating the entire project to external entities and specialists. The same concerns apply to evaluating the effectiveness of public actions in any policy field and are therefore not exclusive to development and cooperation initiatives. But while externalizing the whole process may increase an evaluation's credibility, it does not necessarily guarantee total independence either. As de Laat's chapter on "the tricky triangle" suggests, independence and objectivity are not synonymous; bias can be introduced at various points throughout the evaluation process even when the entire project is outsourced. For example, the agency responsible for a policy's effectiveness may well supply the external evaluator with only minimal, and often guarded, information as a way of protecting against criticism. Another possibility is that the evaluation questions are slanted in a particular way to serve the interests of either the authority responsible for the mandate, the commissioner, or the most vocal or influential members of a commissioner's advisory committee, where this exists. Last but not least is the question of transparency, especially the publication of evaluation findings. For example, even though a policy of transparency may be in place to ensure that reports are available in the public domain—often, and at the very least, via the internet—the evaluators, managers, or even commissioning body may not have the power to publish without the agreement of a higher authority. There may be a myriad of reasons, justifiable or otherwise, that may be used to delay such publication.

In short, externalizing the whole evaluation process does not guarantee independence, nor indeed does it guarantee a quality evaluation process or product. "Independence" should not be an end in itself; more to the point is ensuring that a quality evaluation is conducted and delivered in a timely fashion so that it can be useful in relation to its initial purpose and used. There are a number of alternative measures that can be put into place to guard against bias and protect impartiality. For instance, advisory committees made up of internal and external stakeholders can be set up to comment on the terms of reference and follow the evaluation process from start to finish. Another option is to encourage evaluators and/or evaluation managers to report on any pressures or obstructions encountered during the evaluation process that could be affecting their impartiality. Providing there are some rules and procedures in place to deal with this kind of situation, the problem could then be referred to a higher authority.

As such, quality evaluations can be managed and conducted using external, internal, or various configurations of both internal and external entities.

 KEY POINTS

- Whether the evaluation process is totally or partially outsourced or totally managed "in-house," de Laat's chapter shows where and how bias can be introduced. Evaluations do not take place in a vacuum; they develop, expand, and are influenced by factors specific to their environment, such as the political, economic, and technological issues, that are dominant at the time. And hence, they are never completely independent.

- Independence may improve the credibility of a study but does not guarantee quality. It is not, and should not be considered, an end in itself.

- The more knowledgeable and experienced the organization with evaluation practice, the more likely it is that it will have set about institutionalizing a number of rules and procedures to guard against possible bias or misuse. Such procedures are likely to be featured in the organization's evaluation policy, framework, or system.

- Having institutional rules and procedures in place can help reduce bias and improve evaluation's use, but putting them into practice depends on other factors. Those discussed in the following paragraphs concern the organizational location of an internal Evaluation Unit; challenges and responses to engaging the commitment of the executive, senior management, and the organization as a whole; and the quality and credibility of the studies and in-house evaluation staff.

THE LOCATION OF AN INTERNAL EVALUATION UNIT

As part of an organization's evaluation policy, having internal units report directly to the head of the organization is often thought to be a satisfactory solution for safeguarding its ability to "speak truth to power" for two reasons: for guarding against possible divisional or programmatic protectionism and for helping build up an organizational evaluation culture. Such an institutional arrangement is therefore supported by the UN Evaluation Group and is becoming the norm in all UN agencies (e.g., World Health Organization [WHO] and International Labour Organization [ILO]). Many UN agencies have a combination of devolved, decentralized, and centralized evaluation entities to handle the separate needs of corporate, program, or regional issues. Devolved and decentralized evaluations focus more on learning and improvement, leaving the central office to deal with corporate, overarching thematic issues such as effectiveness and impact.

Even so, as indicated in the country chapter, it seems to be more the norm in public administration to have only one Evaluation Unit dealing with both. In each case, the internal unit is located closer to a strategic planning or policy division, reporting directly, or more likely indirectly, to the organization's head or executive.

Compared with other chapter studies, the structural organization of evaluation activities in the European Commission (EC) is somewhat different but closer in nature to that of the WHO; there are different configurations to suit the needs of different policy or thematic areas. Evaluation is decentralized; each directorate-general (DG) is responsible for the evaluation of its own activities within a framework established and coordinated by a central unit situated within the Secretariat-General, being the central DG and highest "political body." In turn, responsibility for the evaluation within some DGs is devolved to the member states, for example, in Structural Funds, which support regional development programs.

Hence, in all our chapter studies, a central Evaluation Unit is structurally located close to the executive. This has helped each of them anchor an evaluation function that serves the organization as a whole; by establishing an evaluation framework or policy that sets out the purposes, expectations, norms, and processes and, more often than not, by also supplying guidelines and tools to support its implementation. But equally, such a choice is not without risk: Locating internal evaluation support next to the executive can nurture both positive—*respect for the strategic role that evaluation can play*—and negative—*an imposition by management, an accountability instrument to be used to reduce or reassign budgets*—reactions from other departments or business units that may ultimately impact on its ability to develop an evaluation culture throughout. There is also the issue of competitiveness, especially over securing executive support for resources. This is particularly acute during the relatively frequent structural reorganizations that take place in the public sector. Different departments and services offer arguments for keeping—or even increasing—their same level of staff and funding—often by suggesting a reduction of others' resources. Inevitably, during such times and despite the existence of an internal evaluation policy, the need for evaluation is called into question. When the internal Evaluation Unit has no direct reporting line to the head of the agency, it must rely on its hierarchical superior to present its arguments. It then very much depends on how such a person assesses the value of evaluation to the organization and what evidence is used to present the case.

 KEY POINT

- While the location of an internal Evaluation Unit within the organization is an important contributing factor for improving evaluation's use, it is only one part of the puzzle; it might indicate top-level commitment, but this can also be little more than passively conforming to external pressures. The *active* engagement of the executive or at least of senior management is also needed to build up and sustain the organization's evaluation policy and, more particularly, to support measures for developing a culture of evaluative thinking and improved use.

ENGAGING THE ORGANIZATION'S EXECUTIVE AND/OR SENIOR MANAGEMENT

Many of our chapter authors suggest that engaging the participation of the executive or, at least, the senior management in some aspect of evaluation is a desirable but significant challenge; without such support, inevitably its need is periodically questioned. For example, assessment methods, such as performance measurement and audit, are frequently proposed as feasible and less costly alternatives, especially in times of austerity and budget cutbacks. In other words, in order to secure the sustainability of an internal evaluation service, it is essential that senior managers understand and believe in the unique benefits of evaluation, especially as a strategic tool. Gaining firsthand experience through, for example, accompanying an individual study is an ideal means. But senior managers are often already overcommitted and burdened with heavy workloads. Their participation can already be difficult to achieve in national organizations, but, as chapters on the European Commission (EC), the World Health Organization (WHO), and the International Labour Organization (ILO) show, the task becomes that much more complex when working with different geographical regions and different countries.

So what are the *various strategies being used* to secure this level of engagement? Below are those most frequently mentioned, either alone or in combination with others, for involving senior management:

- Discussing and agreeing on an overall evaluation policy for the organization
- Agreeing on a multi-annual evaluation plan in line with the organization's legislative period
- Engaging their membership in an evaluation advisory committee as a way of taking an active part in understanding the benefits of evaluation more generally and/or of specific evaluations and their strategic utility

The choice of strategy seems to be very much context dependent; it depends on the history, the development, and overall organization of the evaluation function.

The Benefits of an Evaluation Policy for Engaging Top Management Support

Each of the country agencies, as well as the supra and international agencies presented in this book, has an evaluation policy. In the main, most had the initial "push" from external pressures (e.g., Switzerland, Canada, UN agencies). But how well such policies are implemented depends on the level of internal and organizational support they get. The longer the policy has been in place, the more likely mechanisms are there to ensure that such support can be engaged. For example, in the case of our two UN agencies, there are clear differences in where both are today in terms of engaging executive support.

The UN Evaluation Group provides an overall framework, guidelines, and standards, but each of the agencies is encouraged to develop its own dedicated policy to respond to its specific needs and context. For historical and administrative reasons, the WHO has only recently drawn up its policy and received executive agreement. For a number of years, evaluations were conducted throughout the various WHO regions and countries according to their own rules and processes. Often the drive came from external funders rather than internal needs. Hence, when a corporate Evaluation Unit finally got set up, the choice of its location was fundamental for conveying a certain identity and image. But even though it was situated at directorate level, it was positioned in various offices under the cluster of general management, or later, with the auditors in the Internal Oversight Services so that for many, evaluation became synonymous with audit or performance management and review. This misconception coupled with a history of heterogeneous styles of evaluation management practices acted as more of a hindrance than a help to WHO's corporate Evaluation Unit and its capacity-building efforts. It is only recently, and again to comply with external pressure such as the UN's results-based management policy and the UN Evaluation Group's guidelines, that WHO has secured executive support for a policy that will "pull things together" and try to create a common set of values and practices. It is still too early therefore to see how top management will or can support its implementation.

The ILO, on the other hand, has a longer standing internal evaluation policy. Its corporate, central Evaluation Unit is therefore less focused today on the role and function of evaluation but more on improving its strategic use for both accountability and management and performance. To help with this task, it has the support of an advisory committee that oversees implementation of the policy and, in particular, reports to the executive on evaluation findings and their uptake.

The Role and Utility of Advisory Committees

Involving senior management in an Evaluation Advisory Committee is a seemingly popular strategy that some of our authors have or wish to pursue(d). We can identify two types: (a) a committee to oversee evaluation generally and represent its interests at executive level, and (b) one established ad hoc to oversee the evaluation process of a particular study, discuss the findings, and develop plans for using the information generated. Both are needed but have different explicit objectives. In type (a), members are usually drawn from the senior management of the various divisions or departments to help draw up and present to the executive, for approval, key documents such as an evaluation policy, a multi-annual evaluation plan, and others to ensure that they include the interests of the various internal stakeholders as well as some more transversal themes of common interest to the organization as a whole. Equally, they can provide a central Evaluation Unit with guidance and support, and represent an internal Evaluation Unit and its work in reporting upward.

However, even when such committees have been established, there is always a risk of their being dissolved for a number of reasons such as

- internal competitive pressures—for example, because the arrangement is privileging one service over others;
- work pressures—members cannot sustain their involvement over any length of time, even on a rotating basis, due to increasing tasks and pressures; or
- delegating "downward"—over time, senior managers delegate participation to more junior and therefore less authoritative members of their staff, which, in a way, totally defeats the initial objective.

To some degree, this may depend on how well detailed the organization's evaluation policy is regarding organization, processes, and responsibilities. The more specific, the less likely this situation will occur.

To counteract such risks, type (a) advisory committees have been known to involve both internal (senior managers) and external stakeholders. The aim here is to provide a more sustainable and impartial support to the internal Evaluation Unit and, again, represent its interests in discussions with the executive. Yet while the mixture of internal and external stakeholders can possibly ensure more balanced advice, it does not necessarily overcome the problem of ownership; the contribution of "outsiders" can be undermined by their lack of intimate knowledge of the organization's day-to-day issues and concerns. Moreover, the organization and support of committee meetings present an additional task for the internal Evaluation Unit's staff and therefore warrant a careful review of the costs and benefits involved.

The main aim of a type (b) advisory committee is to oversee an individual evaluation. Members consist of internal and often external stakeholders to ensure that wider interests are taken into account. Such committees comment on the evaluation terms of reference, design, and process and are especially asked to help with disseminating and using the information generated through the study. While such committees are more commonplace these days, engaging senior managers' participation, particularly their sustained participation, is proving somewhat difficult, for example, as shown in the EC's chapter. Similar to type (a), there is always the risk that the task maybe delegated downward, resulting in an operational rather than a strategic focus for the evaluation; the chance for engaging senior management in the more overarching, strategic issues can be lost. In other words, the answers one gets are going to be only as good as the questions asked.

KEY POINT

- Involving the executive and/or senior management in evaluation is strategically desirable but difficult to achieve. Improving evaluation's utility and use is therefore more likely to need the support and interest of the "whole" organization rather than from isolated areas.

ENGAGING ORGANIZATION-WIDE COMMITMENT FOR IMPROVING USE

To create a favorable climate for getting the best out of evaluation, it has been argued here (e.g., in the Porteous and Montague, Neubecker et al., and Läubli chapters in this book) that we need to foster an understanding and appreciation of evaluation's unique contribution to management throughout the whole of the organization. Moving evaluative thinking from pockets of individuals and departments to the entire organization is preferable for sustainable, organizational learning and commitment to the principles and ideals of evaluation. In short, the focus is on building up and managing the structures and processes needed to integrate evaluation into an organization-wide learning and improvement-oriented framework, for example, results-based management. Contributors' examples of taking a much more holistic, organizational approach are certainly innovative but somewhat demanding.

For Porteous and Montague, with the experience of a decentralized evaluation organization behind them, in the current centralized model, the idea is to bring together the best of both worlds. With executive support already secured, the challenge now facing the newly formed corporate Evaluation Unit is engaging the whole of the organization in learning to think and act "evaluatively." The authors describe the four strategies they are using toward this end. Compared to those described in other chapters, two are unique to Canada: putting in place *systematic measures* for keeping abreast with priorities, planning, and new developments across the whole organization (to help design relevant and useful evaluations as well as demonstrate a partner relationship) and creating an organizational-level logic model to incite a results focus for the agency and to show how the different parts of the puzzle (work of the various departments) fit together to make a whole. All chapter authors suggest that there is a need to keep abreast of what's happening across the whole organization, but Canada is exceptional in setting up systematic measures for doing this and allocating staff time to ensure follow-through. The organizational-level logic model is again a most laudable strategy for helping improve staff understanding of the whole (and thus where evaluation can help). Both are most impressive, but time-consuming (included in the 30% staff time not assigned to the conduct of individual evaluations) and demanding tasks that could not be easily achieved without a large staff (20 in Canada's case). Moreover, they are strategies that require a mature understanding of the place and value of evaluation, which Canada has gained over several decades. Canada's political context shows a long-standing commitment to use evaluation as a means of gaining knowledge about public sector performance, results, and effectiveness. Indeed this is a reflection of Canada's evaluation policy, one which is driven by the Treasury Board and places great emphasis on investment in public actions that can show "value (effective actions) for money (public expenditure)."

The need to demonstrate the unique contribution that evaluation can bring to the organization is an underlying factor in these and others' strategies. Most of the authors have referred in some way or another to their attempts toward such ends. For instance, the ILO's focus on improving knowledge management is a strategic measure for securing evaluation's integration into "whole system" learning processes through demonstrating its utility. As a consequence, it has put a range of activities in place to stimulate engagement in knowledge use; engaging in platforms and other types of ILO "learning events" to inform the discussion with evaluation evidence are some examples.

More recently, in order to provide a broader picture than is possible with individual evaluations, ILO's Evaluation Unit is now also attempting to report on a synthesis of conclusions and recommendations that stretch across several evaluations. They feel that moving from the particular to the general, linking evaluative knowledge into the wider, strategic picture should prove more useful for providing a quick response to management's strategic information needs.

The shift toward synthesizing the findings of several evaluations has also been taken on board by Scotland's Public Health Agency as an integral part of its knowledge-to-action strategy, especially to support "evidence-based" policy. However, what makes Scotland's experience quite innovative is that it is using its brokerage role to (a) gather and synthesize information from a range of sources, including evaluations, and (b) then reaching out to include external partners in the analysis of such information, as part of its policy review process.

Seeking ways to reach out to the whole of the organization is almost certainly a preoccupation of all internal Evaluation Units. But finding the appropriate route and the right time to deal with this is context bound. For example, the ILO's current efforts on improving knowledge management and demonstrating utility are partially in reaction to external pressures from the UN Evaluation Group, which criticized UN agencies for their underuse of evaluation. Similarly, Scotland is in part reacting to the call for "evidence-based policy" as introduced under the Tony Blair government in the 1990s.

 KEY POINT

- What we learn from our authors is that in order to optimize evaluation's use, a sound knowledge is needed of what the organization as a whole is expected to achieve in relation to political and social expectations. Engaging organization-wide commitment is essential for gaining such understanding for improving evaluation's use and usefulness as well as strengthening its place and role across the whole of the organization.

QUALITY EVALUATIONS

So far, the discussion has primarily centered on some of the challenges our authors have faced in trying to optimize evaluation's use. As such, building up and implementing a framework for managing an organization's evaluation capacity is common practice for some of our authors; it is the means toward this desired end. But ensuring the quality of individual evaluation studies and, thus, the credibility of evaluation's benefits is usually the initial and ongoing preoccupation. This is, in fact, the main feature of the chapter on the European Commission's experience with evaluation, but it is also a subtheme in others' chapters, for example, those on WHO, Switzerland, and the ILO. Many suggestions about the measures that managers should take to ensure quality evaluations have been forthcoming. But authors' experience with the terms of reference for contracting an evaluation and the benefits of having an evaluation advisory committee accompany the study are the two features that deserve particular attention here.

Terms of Reference

Without a doubt, the evaluation's Terms of Reference is the critical document for setting out the rules and procedures to support quality evaluations. Determining what should be included is usually an iterative process between the various parties concerned with the mandate, such as the evaluation managers and/or commissioners and/or clients. The EC's chapter in particular goes into some detail about this issue, particularly about the consequences of any information "gaps."

One of the major problems concerns the *timeliness of delivering the evaluation's findings*. A first important lesson for any newcomers to policy or policy-related evaluation therefore is the need to understand at what stage in the decisional process the results should be made available, to be useful. For example, Switzerland works on a four-year legislative cycle at the federal level; the EC's is seven years. But in preparing for the next cycle, the documents are usually required some 12 to 18 months beforehand; evaluations therefore have to produce the required information well before the start of the next cycle.

Another is recognizing the importance of *clarifying the roles and responsibilities of the various parties involved*, the evaluation client, the evaluation manager, the evaluator, and possibly the evaluation project's advisory committee. For example, while the evaluation client usually determines his or her information needs, by when and toward what end, refining the questions and advising on an appropriate evaluation approach and methods are usually the domain of the evaluation manager and evaluator. Even when distinguishing between these different roles seems clear, in practice, there can be some critical moments. For example, in contracting out, when an internal client's choice of a certain evaluation team conflicts with that of the internal evaluation manager because of the latter's methodological quality, ideally, one should renounce both and call for new proposals. However, oftentimes, pressures do not allow for such a response. Instead, some compromise is made, which can prove unsatisfactory to all parties concerned.

Appropriate Budget and Study Period Relative to Methodological Expectations

This issue is raised in both the EC and a little more emphatically in the WHO chapters. Each refers to the dilemma of trying to ensure "gold standard" evaluations with the least expenditure and executed in the least possible time. Many policy areas are growing in complexity. For evaluations to address complex issues, they require more sophisticated evaluation approaches that are sufficiently resourced with appropriate funds, expertise, and time.

For example, public health targets, similar to other policy areas, now go well beyond the barriers of traditional disease prevention; modern-day challenges such as violence, sexuality, stress, threats of bioterrorism, and the economic and social contexts that influence health disparities are now high on the health agenda. In turn, health actions and interventions have become more complex, making cause-effect relationships in particular more difficult to analyze. Traditional partnerships and approaches have also been and are still being fundamentally reworked. Today, public health interventions are characterized by an interdisciplinary approach and are conducted increasingly in partnership with a range of actors and institutions from the public, nonprofit, and private sectors. As health targets have become more complex, so too has the task of analyzing the effectiveness of public health actions. For international development and cooperation themes, the task is even more challenging. A combination of different methods are often needed to provide a comprehensive picture of what is working, for whom, under what conditions, and at what cost. For international work, local evaluation expertise is also desirable to help with language and contextual analysis. Hence, such analysis will be severely impaired if the budget, time, and evaluator expertise is inadequate. Rather, managers would be better advised to plan for fewer evaluations but of better quality in terms of their design and execution—and so requiring adequate time and finance—or more evaluations but for less demanding studies.

Advisory Committees to Accompany the Evaluation Process

The greatest advantage for policy and strategic decisions is said to be that "others'" engagement helps contextualize the information and improve both internal and external ownership of the findings and "take-away" messages. Setting up an advisory committee to accompany discrete evaluations is therefore growing in popularity; but often, expectations about members' purpose and responsibilities are not adequately thought through. For example, while it is clear from the title that members are expected to "advise" or give an opinion, it is not apparent how significant differences between the stakeholders or between the stakeholders and the commissioners might be resolved. Similarly, the choice of members is not always adequately questioned. Should the membership be limited to internal stakeholders or be extended to bring in external representation too? Consider, for example, the idea to engage political or strategic commitment for turning a demonstration project into one that can be launched at the national level. Certainly, political as well as administrative representation will be important in such cases.

KEY POINTS

- Quality issues are a very topical and well-researched area. Our authors have identified and discussed many of these. They have recognized and devised their own ways of dealing with them, albeit often through trial and error. There are many publications, guidelines, and other resources to help conduct and manage a quality evaluation. However, one message is clear; they have to be adapted to the peculiarities of the organization's context and situation.

- In drawing up the terms of reference for an evaluation, managers need to be sensitive to the scope, expertise, and time expectations so that adequate funds are made available to meet such needs.

- Involving stakeholders in the evaluation process is desirable. Inviting their membership on advisory committees is growing in popularity. But careful thought is needed in deciding whom to involve and why; in turn, being transparent about the organization's expectations is also needed.

STAFFING ISSUES: COMPETENCIES AND SHARING THE TASKS

The previous sections have reflected on some of the authors' ideas for improving evaluation's use within their organizations. Inevitably, this leads us to the issue of competencies; what skills do evaluation commissioners and managers need to commission, manage, or undertake quality evaluations in-house and, at the same time, promote and manage activities aimed at institutionalizing evaluation and implanting an evaluation culture?

Even though evaluation demand appears to be growing in the agencies and organizations discussed in this book, the budgets are not necessarily keeping pace with such demand. Managers therefore have to continually reflect on what tasks can be done with how many staff, what skills do members need to best do their work, and what skills might they need in the future.

Allocating Time to Managing Studies and Capacity-Building Efforts: Finding the Right Balance

From our chapters, it seems that *the first challenge or dilemma* managers are facing is working out a feasible balance between meeting organizational priorities, which most often concern the management and delivery of quality evaluation studies, and, at the same time, developing and putting into practice an overall framework aimed at improving evaluation's use and value to the organization. Capacity-building measures, as explained above, are critical for developing a supportive climate in which to conduct evaluations. But, particularly in a context of austerity and budget restrictions, senior management often considers that time spent on such tasks is superfluous. In this situation, Evaluation Unit managers can be faced with a real dilemma about how best to accommodate both. Obviously, the number of staff allocated to the evaluation function plays a critical role, but even with a minimal number, encouraging staff to engage in both types of activity is more likely to sustain their job interest and satisfaction. Canada's chapter is exemplary in showing sensitivity to this issue.

The "Right" Person for the "Right" Tasks

The second challenge is engaging the "right" staff for the "right" tasks. If the staff need evaluation skills to be employed in an internal Evaluation Unit, then those skills need to be kept actively employed, through conducting internal evaluations, and/or being kept "up-to-date" through regular professional development events. A combination of conducting and managing external evaluations can be a more satisfactory solution than doing only one or the other. But when managing external contractors for all or part of an evaluation, then staff's skills need also to be updated with some more management-related skills. But which skills are these?

So much for the issue of skill needs in relation to managing quality evaluations. But for developing and supporting strategies for engaging an organization's interest and commitment to evaluation, there is the strong likelihood of needing additional skills. Thus, for all three—doing, managing, and promoting evaluation— some core skills are needed, but they will require different levels of expertise for each.

We have seen from our chapters that nothing is static and change is inevitable. Managers need to keep one step ahead in *assessing* staff competency needs in an evolving organizational context. For example, as previously said, with each structural reorganization, the expectations for an organization's service units, such as internal evaluation, may change. Wimbush's chapter hints at her agency's growing need for information based on knowledge synthesized from different sources. Neubecker et al. and Porteous and Montague suggest there is a similar need in their organizations. Embracing such an additional task requires additional skills, those of research and synthesis.

In the current, unstable economic climate, there could well be budgetary cutbacks, resulting in reductions to current and possibly future staffing levels. As Porteous emphasizes, there is a strong need for Evaluation Unit managers to keep abreast of developments and future planning within one's organization (for planning useful evaluations); but assessing and planning staff competencies in relation to change is also part and parcel of this process.

→ KEY POINTS

- In-house evaluation managers need to prepare for evolving contexts and the consequent structural changes by permanently assessing what can be done now with current staff and what different skills sets may well be needed to meet upcoming challenges.

- Over the past decade, there have been efforts to determine evaluators' skill needs, but so far, less attention has been paid to the staff inside organizations whose responsibilities extend beyond conducting discrete evaluation studies. This is a neglected area that is just beginning to be addressed.

FINAL THOUGHTS

This final chapter does not offer conclusions; rather, it offers some reflections on what the contributing authors have tried to do to enhance an in-house appreciation of evaluation so that it can be used by their organizations to better and better effect. In reading through the individual chapters, one gets a sense of the author's dedication and eagerness to find the right path to achieve this ultimate goal. The chapters written by evaluation managers in particular provide interesting lessons. These authors were asked to share with us the challenges they had had or were facing to enhance the value of evaluation within their organizations and their experience in handling such situations. They were asked to do this in their own way, without keeping to a specific format. Each tells his or her own story, in his or her own way, providing some background details about the context and development of the individual's agency and evaluation within it. There is much to be learned from sharing this knowledge; the conclusions and lessons they draw from the experience are written up in each chapter. Below, I have therefore set out some more general lessons for improving the utility of evaluation by and for organizations.

SOME "TAKE-HOME" MESSAGES FOR INTERNAL EVALUATION UNITS

 KEY POINTS

- **Establish an organization-wide evaluation policy** that specifies the rules, responsibilities, processes, and procedures to support the evaluation activities that are intended to add value to the work of the organization. But in itself, this is not enough to counteract bias or misuse or ensure an organization's commitment to evaluation. A number of capacity-building activities have been suggested for reinforcing the engagement and improved use of evaluation, and there are many more. The policy, however, should reflect the particularities and needs of its organizational context. We have seen from all of our chapters that nothing is static; organizations are systematically evolving to respond to new situations, new needs. Hence, a periodical review and possibly revision of the organization's evaluation policy should be done to keep abreast of these new situations and needs.

- **Recognize that there is a difference** between managing quality evaluations and planning and managing activities aimed at developing an appreciation of evaluation's value to the organization. Both are necessary if an evaluation culture is to be developed and sustained over time and throughout the whole of the organization. One should therefore plan for resources to ensure that both needs can be met now and in the future while keeping a workable balance between the two.

- **To improve the use of evaluation, managers should devise strategic solutions** that reflect the peculiarities and needs of their organization. While there are definite sets of "good practice" for managing evaluation studies, activities, and its overall function within an organization, managers ought to "pick and choose" those that are appropriate to their situational needs. There is much to be gained from learning from others' experience, and indeed reinventing the wheel would be a waste of precious time; but good practices must be adapted to meet contextual needs. How advanced is the institutionalization of evaluation, in which areas, and what has been the experience so far? These are just some of

(Continued)

(Continued)

the questions that should be answered in the quest for determining how evaluation can best be used today and what improvements could be made to enhance its use tomorrow.

- **Strive to develop partner relationships with senior, middle, and junior management across the whole of the organization** to keep abreast of priorities, planning, and new developments. This will help design relevant and useful evaluations as well as provide opportunities for capacity building and reinforcing the value of an internal evaluation function.

- **Always keep an eye out for organizational and political "windows of opportunity"** to steer the evaluation function toward enhanced usefulness and use. This means keeping abreast with what's happening outside as well as inside the organization in relation to its mission and what's planned for the future. There are numerous opportunities that can be missed if one is not sensitive to this issue.

- **Assess staff skill needs to ensure relevance to an evolving situation**—what skills are needed over time to meet new challenges—managers should not only deal with today's needs but also have an eye on the future and develop existing staff skills or hire in new staff with the necessary skills accordingly.

- **Allocate time to the regular monitoring and reviewing of evaluation's use and usefulness to the organization**. This is particularly needed for three reasons: (a) so that capacity-building strategies can be adjusted wherever necessary to ensure that such information is available; (b) to always have evidence readily available on what is working, for whom, why and why not, and under what conditions in order to contribute to planning and decision making; and (c) to provide examples of how knowledge from evaluation has been used in different ways and toward different ends by internal and external partners.

INDEX

About the Editors

Marlène Läubli Loud (DPhil) is currently an independent consultant and trainer in public sector evaluation. She has worked with a range of organizations, small and large, including the European Commission, the World Health Organization, the UN Evaluation Group, the U.K. Department of Employment, U.K. Health Promotion Agency (now merged and known as the National Institute for Health and Clinical Excellence [NICE]), and the English National Board for Nursing, Midwifery and Health Visiting. She was head of the Research and Evaluation Unit at the Swiss Federal Office of Public Health (FOPH) for nearly 20 years where she gained much experience in evaluation management, and especially in the ways and means for improving the use and utility of evaluation in organizations. She continues to have a keen theoretical and practical interest in this area and is now leading a working group for the Swiss Evaluation Society (SEVAL) on competencies for evaluation managers. Prior to her work with the FOPH, she was an independent evaluator in the United Kingdom, specializing in the evaluation of developmental programs in health and general education. She was also a research fellow at the Department of Education, University of Surrey, and in the Social Science Faculty, University of Oxford, United Kingdom.

Marlène has facilitated several workshops on public sector evaluation for a range of health and other practitioners and has also contributed to several university courses. She was a session lecturer in the University of Fribourg's sociology and social policy master's program for more than 10 years and a guest lecturer at several other Swiss universities. She is a member of the European Evaluation Society and the SEVAL. She served on the SEVAL Executive Committee for more than 10 years with special responsibility for professional development.

Marlène has many years of international experience too. She has worked in several countries, including Algeria, Switzerland, the United Kingdom, and Italy. She was also part-time director of the European Office of International Physicians for the Prevention of Nuclear War—winner of the 1985 Nobel Peace Prize.

John Mayne (PhD) is an independent advisor on public sector performance. He has been working with a number of organizations and jurisdictions around the world, including several agencies of the United Nations and development banks, a number of governments and international nongovernmental organizations (NGOs), the European Union, the Organisation for Economic Co-operation and Development (OECD), and several Canadian federal departments on results management, evaluation, and accountability issues. Until 2004, he was at the Office of the Auditor General where he led efforts on developing practices for effective managing for results and performance reporting in the government of Canada, as well as leading the office's audit efforts in accountability and governance. Prior to 1995, John was with the Canadian Treasury Board Secretariat and Office of the Comptroller General. He has authored numerous articles and reports on results management, evaluation, and evaluation methodologies and edited five books in the areas of evaluation, public administration, and performance monitoring. In 1989 and in 1995, he was awarded the Canadian Evaluation Society Award for Contribution to Evaluation in Canada. In 2006, he became a Canadian Evaluation Society Fellow.

ABOUT THE CONTRIBUTORS

Penny Hawkins is an experienced evaluation specialist and currently senior evaluation officer at The Rockefeller Foundation in New York. She was previously head of Evaluation for the New Zealand Aid Program at the Ministry of Foreign Affairs and Trade and vice-chair of the OECD-Development Assistance Committee (DAC), Network on Development Evaluation. Penny is the coeditor, with Jean-Claude Barbier, of the book *Evaluation Cultures: Sense-Making in Complex Times*. She is also the author of journal articles and other publications on evaluation. She has served as the president of the Australasian Evaluation Society, a founding board member of the International Organization for Cooperation in Evaluation (IOCE), and a member of the International Research Group on Policy and Program Evaluation (INTEVAL). In 2007, she received the Australasian Evaluation Society Award for her Outstanding Contribution to Evaluation and in 2009 was made a fellow of the society. Penny has facilitated workshops and seminars and given lectures in Africa, Asia, the Pacific, Europe, North America, Australia, and New Zealand. For the past 10 years, she has been a faculty member of the International Program for Development Evaluation Training at Carleton University in Ottawa, Canada.

Maria J. Santamaria Hergueta (PhD) is the evaluation lead at the Office of Internal Oversight Services of the World Health Organization. She is a medical doctor and field epidemiologist, with an MD from Madrid University, Spain, and a PhD in environmental epidemiology from Tsukuba University in Japan. After a 22-year professional career at the Ministry of Health in Spain and at the World Health Organization in the field of infectious diseases and epidemic management, she pursued further academic studies. She received an MSc in health planning, policy and financing from the London School of Economics, and later a DrPH in organizational management from the London School of Hygiene and Tropical Medicine. Her professional interests focus on assessment approaches and their contribution to institutional development. She has researched the relations between functional and structural settings and organizational performance and the challenges of assessing the performance of multilateral development agencies in—often complex—country settings. Taking a systems perspective, her research uses theory-based evaluations and realistic assumptions to contextualize institutional change. Since 2004, she has been working at the WHO's Office of Internal Oversight Services, where she is involved in designing and conducting evaluations, as well as improving the methodology to assess performance of WHO at the country level. She has contributed to the development of the WHO evaluation policy and is currently involved in its implementation.

Bastiaan de Laat (PhD) is evaluation expert and team leader at the European Investment Bank (EIB). He has a long-standing experience in evaluation as well as in foresight. As founder-director of the French subsidiary of the Technopolis Group (1998–2006), he led many evaluations for, and provided policy advice to, a great variety of local, national, and international public bodies. He also trained several hundreds of European Commission staff and national government officials in evaluation and designed monitoring and evaluation systems for various public organizations. Before joining the EIB, he worked as evaluator at the Council of Europe Development Bank. He has developed tools and performed program, policy, and regulatory evaluations, both ex ante and ex post, in a variety of fields such as research and development (R & D) and innovation policy, small to medium-sized enterprises (SME) support, EU regional development, urban renewal and social housing, development aid, and natural disaster management. He has been Secretary General of the European Evaluation Society since 2011.

Steve Montague is a management consultant, partner, and cofounder of Performance Management Network Inc. and adjunct professor at the School of Public Policy and Administration, Carleton University. He has three decades of experience in performance planning and measurement, program evaluation, market research, review, and audit projects as a management consultant and as an evaluation manager in a major Canadian federal government department. Steve is the author of *The Three R's of Performance Management* and has published articles in *Research Evaluation, Evaluation, The Canadian Journal of Program Evaluation,* and *Evaluation and Program Planning.* Steve has managed major projects, analyzing a wide variety of programs for Canadian federal, provincial; United States; and Australian governments, as well as conducting work for the OECD, the Scottish Government, and the World Bank. He was made a fellow of the Canadian Evaluation Society in May 2011.

Janet Neubecker has worked at the International Labour Office (ILO) in Geneva, Switzerland, for more than 28 years, with the last 12 years working as a knowledge management officer in evaluation. Her expertise has been focused on developing knowledge strategies that improve utilization of evaluation findings and enhance organizational performance. She has modeled databases for the capture of data on lessons learned and recommendations and worked extensively with guidance and internal mechanisms to improve the quality of evaluation reporting and utilization of evaluation findings. She is working with the ILO evaluation team on designing and establishing a process for the identification and validation of good practices, derived from independent evaluations of its projects and programs. This effort includes the use of a range of knowledge platforms including web-based databases, communities of practice, working papers, and other media for knowledge sharing and dissemination. A member of the European Evaluation Society, Janet holds a BSc in international relations and a MSc in development studies with a concentration in sustainable development and evaluation from Imperial College, London.

Nancy L. Porteous has worked in government and as a consultant in program planning, monitoring, and evaluation for over 20 years. She is currently executive director of Evaluation at the Public Health Agency of Canada. Nancy has been an active member of evaluation-related organizations: Canadian Evaluation Society (CES), National Capital Chapter president; president of CES National Council; founding board of the International Organization for Cooperation in Evaluation (IOCE); and chair of the CES Educational Fund. Nancy was awarded the Contribution to Evaluation in Canada Award by CES National Council and the Karl Boudreault Award for Leadership in Evaluation by the National Capital Chapter of CES. She holds the Credentialed Evaluator designation and currently serves on the CES Credentialing Board. Nancy was recently made a Fellow of the Canadian Evaluation Society. She is a faculty member of the International Program for Development Evaluation Training (IPDET) and is currently a session lecturer for Carleton University's master's program in evaluation. Nancy is passionate about evaluation and is grateful to the many colleagues, team members, students, clients, and mentors who have taught her so much over the years.

Matthew Ripley has worked in evaluation and program management for the United Nations in Geneva, Vienna, New York, and Jakarta. His expertise is in the use of impact assessment and results measurement systems to improve management and organizational decision making. At the ILO, he helped establish and then run an appraisal mechanism for new projects in Asia-Pacific and Arab States regions. At United Nations Children's Fund (UNICEF), he led on developing program guidance for performance monitoring. He has participated in and managed numerous country-based, thematic-, and policy-level evaluations and was a regular contributor to project management courses at the International Training Centre in Turin. He is currently managing the monitoring and evaluation system for a market development program in Nepal, funded by the U.K. Department for International Development (DFID). He graduated from University College London and completed postgraduate studies in the political economy of development at King's College, London.

Craig Russon (PhD) has been involved in program evaluation for over 30 years. He is currently a senior evaluation officer with the ILO in Geneva, Switzerland, with previous experience as an evaluation manager with the W. K. Kellogg Foundation and senior principal research associate at the Western Michigan University, Evaluation Center. He has served on the Board of Directors of the American Evaluation Association (AEA) and the Michigan Association for Evaluation and is currently board chair of the Evaluation Capacity Development Group. He is the nominal owner of XCeval, a listserv for international evaluators. Craig also participated in the effort to develop a coalition of regional and national evaluation organizations that led to the creation of the International Organization for Cooperation in Evaluation (IOCE), for which he received AEA's Robert Ingle Service Award. He is the author of numerous books and articles on evaluation, and his professional interests include the application of systems principles to evaluation. Craig holds a master's degree in educational psychology and a PhD from the University of Illinois at Urbana-Champaign in the evaluation of agricultural education programs. He also holds an MBA from St. Ambrose University in Davenport, Iowa.

Alan Schnur worked with the World Health Organization for more than 30 years at country, regional, and headquarters levels. He retired in March 2010, after working for 6 years as senior evaluation officer with the Office of Internal Oversight Services. During this period, he led or participated in programmatic and thematic evaluations and assessed WHO performance at country, regional, and headquarters levels, using different approaches. His previous experience includes leading or participating in national immunization program reviews and coverage surveys at country level while working at the WHO regional offices for Southeast Asia and the Western Pacific from 1981 until 1994. He was a member of the Polio Eradication Task Force at the Regional Office for the Western Pacific, participating in concurrent and retrospective reviews of polio immunization and surveillance activities. He had senior technical and managerial responsibilities and was involved with a broad range of WHO programs at the WHO country office in China from 1994 to 2003. He has authored or coauthored 13 book chapters and journal articles on smallpox eradication, immunization programs, polio eradication, and severe acute respiratory syndrome (SARS), the most recent being a book chapter on innovation and evaluation in the smallpox eradication program.

Deepak Thapa qualified as a chartered accountant from the United Kingdom. He was the chief executive officer of the Nepal Oil Corporation for three years. For the last 20 years, he has been involved in various internal oversight functions at the WHO and is currently deputy director of the Office of Internal Oversight Services and heads its evaluation function. He also represents WHO at the United Nations Evaluation Group.

Kevin Williams is head of evaluation at the Organisation for Economic Co-operation and Development (OECD). He has extensive experience of building evaluation capacity and of embedding evaluation practice within organizations, particularly at international and supranational levels. He has set up evaluation functions in both the OECD and the European Commission and has contributed to the development of practical evaluation guidance and training initiatives in a range of areas including EU regional development programs, economic policy, and the Common Agricultural Policy. He has also contributed toward the development of frameworks to adapt evaluation practice to a range of nonprogrammatic evaluand, including intergovernmental committees and legislative initiatives in both ex ante and ex post contexts. He graduated in European economics, via the Erasmus programme, from the universities of Nantes (France) and Middlesex (United Kingdom) and holds a master's degree in industrial economics from Université Lumière, Lyon 2 (France).

Erica Wimbush (PhD) is currently head of Evaluation at NHS Health Scotland, the national agency for public health in Scotland, and a member of the Faculty of Public Health. Erica began her career in public health in 1992 with a first degree in sociology and social anthropology and a doctorate in community education. She has 20 years experience of working in public health as a commissioner and manager of research and evaluation to inform decision making. Prior to this she worked in university and consultancy contexts, carrying out social research commissioned by public sector agencies. Since 2004, she has been leading a team focused on policy and program evaluation, evaluation capacity-building, and embedding an outcomes-focused performance culture within her own organization. In the 2009 to 2010 award season, Erica was awarded an Economic and Social Research Council (ESRC) Fellowship with the University of Edinburgh Business School to develop work on adapting contribution analysis to the Scottish context of public management and partnership accountability. She has published in the fields of health promotion, evaluation, and knowledge utilization and continues an active role in teaching and training on evaluation in the public health field, including an annual Evaluation Summer School.

⑤SAGE research**methods**

The essential online tool for researchers from the world's leading methods publisher

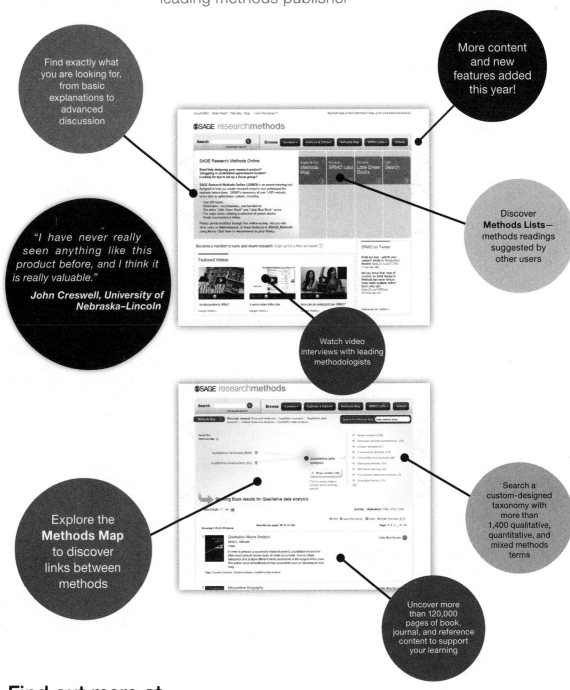

Find exactly what you are looking for, from basic explanations to advanced discussion

More content and new features added this year!

"I have never really seen anything like this product before, and I think it is really valuable."

John Creswell, University of Nebraska–Lincoln

Discover **Methods Lists**— methods readings suggested by other users

Watch video interviews with leading methodologists

Explore the **Methods Map** to discover links between methods

Search a custom-designed taxonomy with more than 1,400 qualitative, quantitative, and mixed methods terms

Uncover more than 120,000 pages of book, journal, and reference content to support your learning

Find out more at
www.sageresearchmethods.com